DATE DUE			
SEP 2 0 1995			

The Female Intruder
in the Novels of Edith Wharton

The Female Intruder
in the Novels
of Edith Wharton

Carol Wershoven

Rutherford • Madison • Teaneck
Fairleigh Dickinson University Press
London and Toronto: Associated University Presses

Associated University Presses, Inc.
4 Cornwall Drive
East Brunswick, N.J. 08816

Associated University Presses Ltd
27 Chancery Lane
London WC2A 1NF, England

Associated University Presses
Toronto M5E 1A7, Canada

Library of Congress Cataloging in Publication Data

Wershoven, Carol.
The female intruder in the novels of Edith Wharton.

Bibliography: p.
Includes index.
1. Wharton, Edith, 1862-1937—Criticism and interpretation.
2. Women in literature.
3. Outsiders in literature. 4. Social status in literature. I. Title.
PS3545.H16Z92   813'.52   81-68349
ISBN 0-8386-3126-6   AACR2

PRINTED IN THE UNITED STATES OF AMERICA

for *William Wershoven* and *Rosa De Raedemaeker Wershoven*

Contents

Acknowledgments

I would like to thank Dr. Motley Deakin, whose encouragement, support, and critical insight helped me complete this study, and Dr. Howard Pearce, who taught me the basics of literary research.

Also, I wish to thank the following for permission to quote from published works:

Used with the permission of Charles Scribner's Sons:
Edith Wharton, *The Age of Innocence*. Copyright 1920 by D. Appleton and Company; copyright renewed. (New York: Charles Scribner's Sons, 1970 [with Introduction by R. W. B. Lewis]).
Edith Wharton, *The Custom of the Country*. Copyright 1913 by Charles Scribner's Sons. Copyright renewed (New York: Charles Scribner's Sons, 1941).
Edith Wharton, *The Valley of Decision*. Copyright 1902 by Charles Scribner's Sons; copyright renewed (New York: Charles Scribner's Sons, 1902).
Edith Wharton, *The House of Mirth*. Copyright 1905 by Charles Scribner's Sons; copyright renewed (New York: Charles Scribner's Sons, 1933).
Edith Wharton, "The Valley of Childish Things and Other Emblems." In *The Collected Short Stories of Edith Wharton*. Edited and Introduction by R. W. B. Lewis. Copyright © 1968 by William R. Tyler. (New York: Charles Scribner's Sons, 1968).
Edith Wharton, *A Backward Glance*. Copyright 1933, 1934 by William R. Tyler; copyright renewed. (New York: D. Appleton-Century Company, 1934; New York: Charles Scribner's Sons, 1964).
Edith Wharton, *The Children*. Copyright 1928 by William R. Tyler; copyright renewed (New York: D. Appleton and Company, 1928; New York: Charles Scribner's Sons, 1969).
Edith Wharton, *The Gods Arrive*. Copyright 1932 by D. Appleton and Company; copyright renewed (New York: D. Appleton and Company, 1932; New York: Charles Scribner's Sons, 1969).
Edith Wharton, *Hudson River Bracketed*. Copyright 1929 by D. Appleton and Company; copyright renewed (New York: D. Appleton and

Introduction

For many years Edith Wharton was forced by her readers and critics into the stereotype of an aristocratic "lady" who wrote novels about the upper classes of old New York while the major social problems and changes of the world around her passed her by. Even while she was alive her literary reputation declined; in her later years her novels came to be seen as nostalgic evocations of a lost past, a past somewhat irrelevant to the mainstream of American life. An extreme form of the criticism directed at her is Vernon Parrington's comment, in 1921, that

> she is too well bred to be a snob, but she escapes it only by sheer intelligence. The background of her mind, the furniture of her habits, are packed with a potential snobbery, and it is only by scrupulous care that it is held in leash. She is unconsciously shut in behind plate glass, where butlers serve formal dinners, and white shoulders go up at the mere suggestion of everyday gingham.[1]

Even while many critics were willing to grant the technical brilliance of Wharton's social observation and to concede that she could, at times, be critical of certain aspects of the aristocratic world, the consensus was that Wharton primarily opted for the tradition and convention of the New York of her youth as the only alternative to the chaos and emptiness of absolute individual freedom.

This oversimplified categorization cast Wharton into a kind of critical oblivion, for how much could be said of a voice "whispering the last enchantments of the Victorian age"?[2] However, more recent criticism has reexamined Wharton's work. Blake Nevius's full-length study of her work in 1953, with its emphasis on the "trapped sensibility" in the fiction, was the beginning of critical attention. Recent books of criticism include *Edith Wharton: Convention and Morality in the Work of a Novelist*, by Marilyn Jones Lyde (1959); *Edith Wharton*, by Louis Auchincloss (1961); *Edith Wharton: A Critical Interpretation*, by Geoffrey Walton (1970); *Edith Wharton and the Novel of Manners*, by Gary Lindberg (1975); and critical studies of Wharton, *Edith Wharton*, by Margaret McDowell (1976), and *Edith Wharton* by Richard H. Lawson (1977).

In addition, Grace Kellogg's biography, *The Two Lives of Edith Wharton: The Woman and Her Work*, appeared in 1965, to be followed by R. W. B. Lewis's biography, *Edith Wharton*, ten years later. The Lewis biography, utilizing previously unavailable letters and diaries, shattered the image of the repressed, arrogant grande dame that had done so much to damage Wharton's literary reputation. Cynthia Griffin Wolff's book, *A Feast of Words: The Triumph of Edith Wharton* (1977), is a fascinating attempt to connect this new picture of Wharton to her work.

Despite the growth of Wharton criticism, reappraisal of the writer remained full of reservations. Many of the earlier critical attitudes lingered on. The label of social historian or novelist of manners seemed to minimize Wharton's achievement. Many agreed with John Harvey's assessment that "Mrs. Wharton's major achievement is the satiric revelation of a collapsing society,"[3] but this very strength was, in a sense, held against Wharton. She was perceived as "the memorialist of a dying aristocracy,"[4] a woman "never able altogether to escape the New York and Newport of her youth."[5] As such, she seemed historically interesting, perhaps, but basically limited by what Grace Kellogg calls "The Cage" of her time and her class.[6]

Even those who admired Wharton's earlier work, such as *The House of Mirth* and *The Custom of the Country*, and recognized more in it than satire about the *nouveaux riches* and the weakened "old money," tended to view Wharton's later work as the rigid conservatism of a woman whom life had passed by. The conclusion generally arrived at was that while Wharton saw many flaws in the traditions and conventions of old New York society, she eventually chose it, in horrified reaction to the destruction and disorder she witnessed in World War I. Alienated and bitter, Wharton supposedly sought refuge in nostalgia or indulged in shrill attacks upon the modern world.[7] Typical of such criticism is Irving Howe's comment that "in the novels written during the last fifteen years of her life, Mrs. Wharton's intellectual conservatism hardened into an embittered and querulous disdain for modern life; she no longer really knew what was happening in America; and she lost what had once been her main gift: the location of the target she wished to destroy."[8]

One of the most pervasive reservations about Wharton's work is the accusation that it lacks moral positives. The often brilliant satirist, it is said, offers the reader no moral alternatives, no values that run counter to the false values she attacks. Q. D. Leavis says that beyond "the simple goodness of the decent poor" of *The Bunner Sisters* or *Summer*, "Mrs. Wharton has only negatives, her values emerging ... as something other than what she exposes as worthless. ... It seems to be the fault of the disintegrating and spiritually impoverished society she analyzes."[9]

Similarly, Gary Lindberg comments on the lack of such figures as "Hester Prynne, Ishmael, the 'I' of Walden, Leatherstocking, Huck Finn, Isabel Archer" in Wharton, traditional American figures who are "not so much rebelling against the complex imperatives of social experience as freed from them, grasping their way tentatively, experimentally, often unwillingly, through their feelings and intuitions toward other imperatives."[10] Nor, continues Lindberg, do we find "images of the human spirit asserting itself in implacable, even if futile, resistance." Instead, we are "affirmed in our weakness, shown that our limitations are inevitable, that genuine resistance to them only denies the roots of our personality."[11] Not only is Wharton perceived as herself limited to her world and its conventions, but her characters are perceived as sharing the same limitations.

It is not difficult to contrast the stereotype of Edith Wharton as the prisoner of convention with the real woman who violated her own traditions in her personal life by her choice of a career, by her adulterous affair, and by her divorce, and to challenge Wharton's supposed literary conservatism with her own words. In her autobiography Wharton expresses her awareness that "we who fought the good fight are now being jeered at as . . . prigs and prudes,"[12] and attempts to defend herself by placing her own literary beginnings into the context of a time when

> a well-known New York editor, offering me a large sum for the serial rights of a projected novel, stipulated only that no reference to "an unlawful attachment" should figure in it; when Theodore Roosevelt gently rebuked me for not having caused the reigning Duke of Pianura (in "The Valley of Decision") to make an honest woman of the humble bookseller's daughter who loved him; and when the translator of Dante, my beloved friend, Professor Charles Eliot Norton, hearing . . . that I was preparing another "society" novel, wrote in alarm imploring me to remember that "no great work of the imagination has ever been based on illicit passion!"[13]

It is hard to reconcile the picture of the prudish aristocrat with the writer who fought such attitudes and who sympathized with and defended George Eliot and who made pilgrimages to the home of George Sand.[14] And, for a person who supposedly clung to her own class, Wharton uses a surprisingly large number of heroines from outside that class, as well as a number of settings far from old New York.

To the charge that much of Wharton's late work is reactionary, one might answer that reexamination reveals it to be remarkably consistent with her earlier work in its objects of scorn. Granted, the satire often becomes less subtle, but then the new world was more exaggerated than the old; it was a broader target.

All the widely held critical assumptions, however, including the charge of the absence of moral positives in her work, may be challenged more fully if one approaches Wharton's novels from a new perspective. One of the reasons why Wharton may be so readily identified with the conventional is connected to her novelistic practice of using a character who is closely linked to a conventional society as the center of consciousness. Such characters are George Darrow and Anna Leath in *The Reef* and Newland Archer in *The Age of Innocence*. It is easy to assume that such characters speak for the author, but this may not be the case. Wharton often distances herself from these characters through the use of irony and authorial comment. If one examines the novels from another perspective and considers a type of character and a pattern that are present from Wharton's first novel, *The Valley of Decision*, to her last, unfinished one, *The Buccaneers*, one perceives Wharton's social criticism quite differently. Such an analysis reveals this criticism as constant and consistent, aimed at all the worlds Wharton writes of, including conservative New York, and balanced by positive values that permeate the work.

This pattern, which emerges in too many of the novels to be casual or accidental, always contains one type of character, which I will call the female intruder. This intruder may be defined as the woman who is in some way outside of her society; she is different from other women, whether because of her background or lack of social status or because she has violated some social taboo. She is Lily Bart in *The House of Mirth*, Ellen Olenska in *The Age of Innocence*, Judith Wheater in *The Children*, Sophy Viner in *The Reef*. Her presence in the novel is central to both the social criticism that the book contains and the values it advocates. Depending upon the novel, the intruder functions in all or several of the following ways:

1. Her presence forces a representative member of society, usually a male, to reexamine his world, which often results in shattering his complacency.[15]

2. Placed in contrast to the other women in the novel, the intruder's way of life often shows how trapped and suffocated other women in society are. And since the male protagonist cannot easily place the intruder into a stereotype, he may begin to reexamine the stereotyped roles themselves.

3. Having caused the protagonist to become less pleased with his own world or way of thinking, the intruder often teaches him about alternative ways to live, exposing him to options and attitudes that may puzzle or attract him, and that he may reject because he, too, is trapped and afraid to change.[16]

4. By her very existence, and by her desire, like that of Kate Chopin's heroine in *The Awakening*, to be the "bird that would soar above the level plain of tradition and prejudice,"[17] the intruder is a kind of reproach

to the false values of society; the awareness of these false values may come more fully to the reader than to the protagonist, but the awareness for both is there by the end of the novel.

5. The experience of the intruder forces the reader to judge society in terms of the intruder. For example, when Lily Bart dies, what does her death say about the world she lived in? When Undine Spragg slashes her way to status and success, what kind of society accepts her?

6. Finally, and perhaps most important, the intruder embodies or develops values that Wharton approves of, values that are not associated with any time period but that are lacking in the particular society of the novel. Often, as the male protagonist's world widens because of the action of the intruder, so too the intruder herself develops and grows over the course of a novel, her experience, her decisions, and her actions changing and forming her. This development of the intruder may best be observed in the characters of Lily Bart and Sophy Viner, although others, like Ellen Olenska and Halo Tarrant, change also.

An intruder cannot be found in every novel by Wharton, and every intruder does not function in precisely the same way, but the character and the pattern are sufficiently prevalent to warrant analysis. The pattern indicates certain significant elements in Wharton's fiction that have been ignored.

The question "Why a female intruder?" must be dealt with. There are, in the novella *Madame de Treymes* and in the novel *Summer*, males who function as intruders,[18] but a female seems more appropriate. One of the intruder's basic functions is to act as a vehicle for Wharton's social criticism, and as such, it is logical that a woman character should be used. It was far easier for a woman to become an outsider in the world of Wharton's novels, and it was far more likely that a woman would judge the world harshly.

The societies that Wharton writes about are ones in which money is the supreme good, and thus the source of power. Women in these worlds can achieve access to great wealth only through association with a male — a father, a lover, a husband — hence they have no direct power. While their functions might include the formation and upholding of certain superficial and unimportant customs and traditions, no conventional woman in Wharton's novels makes any important rules for her world; she is merely expected to live by them. Even the supposedly omnipotent matriarch of *The Age of Innocence*, Mrs. Manson Mingott, has attained her power through marriage to a wealthy man and through subsequent widowhood, and even Mrs. Mingott never dares to violate any of the real taboos. Essentially, the woman who lives within society remains dependent upon a male as protector and provider, her dependence being rewarded by a certain material security, societal approval, and an extremely limited life.

The woman in society is thus trapped — by rules (such as the double standard) not of her own devising, by a materialism that makes her only the chief ornament in her husband's establishment, and by a society that encourages her to remain a child, "innocent" of reality and protected from life, while her man lives it elsewhere, in Wall Street, or the law office, or with another woman. Some of Wharton's characters manage to find a certain satisfaction within the trap. May Welland, for example, makes the socially approved match and retains her valued innocence. Bertha Dorset and Judy Trenor thrive on their husbands' money and devote a lifetime to being fashionable and to seeking appropriate settings for their beauty.

But it is very easy for a woman to cross the boundaries into the bleak world of social disapproval or even ostracism. Some women, such as Ellen Olenska or Nan St. George, do so deliberately, unable to endure the suffocation of an unhappy marriage and desperate for freedom. Others do not, at first, deliberately violate or challenge society's dictates, but instead simply fail to become the standard marriageable product. Such women are Lily Bart, whose lack of a dowry and of respect for the marriage game itself spoils her chances, and Mattie Silver, whose extreme poverty makes it difficult for her to find a man who will take her. Others — Fulvia Vivaldi, Justine Brent, Margaret Aubyn — are too bright, too "masculine" in their interests and abilities, to fit into the female role.

The women, then, become outsiders, and an outsider has a view of the world different from one who functions happily and successfully within it. She becomes an observer, often a critical observer, likely to ask "the reason of things that have nothing to do with reasons,"[19] as one agitated conformist in a Wharton novel, disturbed by an intruder, complains. Often the woman cast outside begins to form her own, new values, and to act and to grow independently. She also, inevitably, is a symbol of what her society cannot accept, and a danger to those within it.

The pattern of the intruder and her dual function as bearer of values and catalyst for social criticism is one that contradicts the old stereotype of Wharton as spokesman for a dying world. Wharton, in her use of this pattern, is critical of many historical periods, especially of old New York. And the qualities that are the focus of her criticism are constant, whatever the time: materialism, repression, intolerance, and the refusal to face unpleasant reality or pain. Similarly, the values she believes in, often embodied in the outsiders, include compassion, the open and spontaneous expression of emotion, the courage to face reality, a receptivity to whatever life offers, and a sense of self that is not solely defined by the social milieu. Certain of these positive values, such as the compassion and emotional openness that characterize the intruders, would seem to be traditional feminine qualities, but the emotions that these female characters feel free to express often include such "unfeminine" ones as anger or defiance. In her fearless stance before a hostile world, her assumption of an active rather than passive role in life, and, most important, in her courage in becoming more and more "herself" and less a type, the intruder is hardly a model of the feminine ideal. She is not a type from the past; she is, rather, an embodiment of what Edith Wharton valued in life and a vehicle to criticize those qualities which, she felt, make life empty.

The presence of the intruder in Wharton's novels, serving as both critic of society and carrier of positive values, takes Wharton out of the category of literary anachronism and places her in the mainstream of American literature. For if, as R. W. B. Lewis says, the central theme of American literature is the theme of loneliness, "the story of the hero in space,"[20] and the American hero begins "outside the world, remote or on the verges"; and "its power, its fashions, and its history are precisely the forces he must learn, must master, or be mastered by,"[21] then Wharton's novels with their intruder heroines are a variation on the American theme. These characters, rebelling and struggling against the limits of convention and toward their own autonomy, are the sisters of Hester Prynne or Isabel Archer; they are "heroines in space" confronting a hostile world.

The intruders bear a close relationship to their creator as well, for their endless struggle to maintain some sense of self that threatens an intolerant society is a struggle that Edith Wharton, from her own experience, understood well. The pattern of Wharton's life parallels the conflicts she wrote of so frequently in her novels, and the pain, rejection, and isolation with which Edith Wharton lived most of her life provided her with a special identification with those female characters who suffer and grow as she did.

The sense of suffocation that so many Wharton characters endure was Wharton's birthright, for her childhood in rich, aristocratic old New York of the 1860s provided her not with the money to buy new and varied experiences, but with the limiting shelter of privilege. Money and rank meant only imprisonment in an exclusive cage where the main topics of conversation were food, fashion, and good form, and where one's day was filled with visiting, dining, and gossip about the select few in one's set. Even as New York society changed around them, Edith Newbold Jones's family remained isolated and aloof. As R. W. B. Lewis points out,

The Joneses and their kin ... belonged to the narrowest and stablest portion of society: an enclave of sorts within — in their view, *above* — the broader, looser and much more conspicuous element. The latter was made up of exceedingly wealthy and often recently arrived commercial folk, with homes on Fifth Avenue, and it was their children, in a phrase of the 1880s, who filled the ranks of ''the ultra-fashionable dancing people,'' and who constituted society for the outsider or the visitor.[22]

Cut off from the more exciting world of the *arrivistes* and bored by the stifling existence led by her family, the sensitive child found a refuge in books, in stories, in ''making up.'' ''What the family home offered Edith was not an opening into contemporary history,'' Lewis explains; ''it was rather an escape from it, with her father's mild and crucial encouragement, into his library.''[23]

The escape into words, into the world of ideas, was to isolate Wharton not only from the larger world outside old New York, but from her own family and friends as well. As Wharton herself explained later, her parents' society was one in which ''art and music and literature were rather timorously avoided,''[24] and ''in the eyes of our provincial society authorship was still regarded as something between a black art and a form of manual labour.''[25] The girl who at the age of fifteen attempted her first novel found no one with whom she could share her love of ideas: ''All the people I have known who have cared for *les choses de l'esprit* have found some degree of sympathy and companionship either in their families or among their youthful friends,'' Wharton wrote. ''But I never exchanged a word with a really intelligent human being until I was over twenty.''[26]

The consequences of her intellectual interests were brought home to Wharton in the fate of her own father, the prototype of the Wharton fictional hero, a sensitive, weak man destroyed by society. For the imaginative and creative side of her father, Wharton perceived, was destroyed by the disapproving attitude of her mother, who was old New York to her core, scornful of the life of the mind:

> I imagine there was a time when his [her father's] rather rudimentary love of verse might have been developed had he had anyone with whom to share it. But my mother's matter-of-factness must have shrivelled up any such buds of fancy ... I have wondered since what stifled cravings had once germinated in him, and what manner of man he was really meant to be. That he was a lonely one, haunted by something always unexpressed and unattained, I am sure.[27]

George Jones, too timid to satisfy his own need for something more than dinner parties and fashion, left his daughter to herself, to become an outsider in her own family, with ''a childhood and youth of complete intellectual isolation — so complete that it accustomed me never to be lonely except in company.''[28] Her intelligence and creativity made Wharton an outcast, who, she explains, ''had to fight [her] way to expression through a thick fog of indifference, if not of tacit disapproval.''[29]

Adulthood and a fashionable marriage to Bostonian aristocrat Edward Wharton only made the young woman an intruder in two worlds. ''I was a failure in Boston . . . because they thought I was too fashionable to be intellectual, and a failure in New York because they were afraid I was too intelligent to be fashionable.''[30] Married to a man who, easygoing and genial as he might be, was utterly incapable of becoming Edith Wharton's intellectual companion, Wharton was more alone than ever. Again the escape was into books, this time as a writer herself. But literary success only ''puzzled and embarrassed my old friends, far more than it impressed them,'' and in Wharton's own family the subject of her books ''was avoided as though it were a kind of family disgrace, which might be condoned but could not be forgotten.''[31] It is little wonder that after twelve years of marriage Wharton still had not satisfied her ''longing to break away from the world of fashion and be with my own spiritual kin,''[32] and that in 1903, the eighteenth year of her marriage, Wharton's commonplace book contained the following lines from *Madame Bovary*, underlined: ''Her life was as cold as a garret whose windows face north, and boredom like a spider spun its web in the shadows, to all the corners of her heart.''[33]

Like so many of her intruder characters, Wharton learned that deliverance from the prison of convention can come only through open rebellion, through violation of society's taboos. Having failed in all her attempts to conform to society's standards, having failed to gain social approval or secure social status, Wharton, already a rebel in her insistence on an intellectual life, rebelled even further in her love affair with journalist Morton Fullerton. At forty-five Wharton confided to her diary that she was ''like a new creature opening dazzled eyes on a new world'';[34] ''I have drunk the wine of life at last,'' she exulted, ''I have known the thing best worth knowing, I have been warmed through and through, never to grow quite cold again till the end.''[35] The woman who for so long had tried to appease an intolerant society finally made an open break with her past by divorcing Edward Wharton in 1913, after twenty-eight years of marriage. Rather than seclude herself in shame, Wharton's defiance of social sanctions continued; she spent the summer after her divorce traveling with her beloved friend Walter Berry, even being admonished by the management of an Italian hotel for allowing Berry to visit her room.[36]

As she grew older Wharton remained a figure difficult to stereotype. During World War I the former socialite, who as a child had declared that her one ambition was to be ''the best-dressed woman in New York,''[37] became director of two of the largest European relief agencies —

American Hostels for Refugees and The Children of Flanders Rescue Committee — and revealed what R. W. B. Lewis calls "something amounting to organizational genius."[38] Her frequent visits to the front lines of France and Belgium provided Wharton with another new role, that of journalist, reporting on the battle areas for *Scribners* magazine and the New York newspapers.

And after the war, as she watched the world she knew change dramatically, Wharton did not retreat into the past but continued to explore the promise of the present and to risk its pain. "I wish I knew what people meant when they say they find 'emptiness' in this wonderful adventure of living," she wrote a friend at age seventy-five; life, she continued, "seems to me to pile up its glories like an horizon-wide sunset as the light declines. I'm afraid I'm an incorrigible life-lover, life-wonderer, and adventurer."[39]

The life-wonderers, the adventurers of Wharton's novels, are the female intruders. Like Wharton, they are outsiders, outcasts faced with hostility and intolerance and repressiveness. Like Wharton they rebel, often only to be punished for their rebellion, but sometimes to find freedom and joy. Only the intruders in Wharton's fiction can live up to her own criterion for survival: "In spite of illness, in spite even of the arch-enemy sorrow, one *can* remain alive . . . if one is unafraid of change, insatiable in intellectual curiosity, interested in big things, and happy in small ways."[40] Their vitality, their spontaneity, their very *aliveness* in the midst of a world designed to stifle that spirit, make the intruders Wharton's spiritual kin, reflectors of the conflicts and triumphs of her own life.

Wharton the aristocratic New Yorker is a sister not only to the intruders of her own class, like Ellen Olenska, or to people of her own profession, like the writer Margaret Aubyn, but to the heroines of all types and classes who fill her novels. In fact, the heroine of the novel that presents the pattern of the intruder in its simplest, barest form is about as far removed from Edith Wharton in class as she can be. This intruder is Mattie Silver, the farm drudge of *Ethan Frome*, a woman who, superficially, is different from Wharton herself and from other more intelligent, more socially polished intruders.

And yet Mattie's story, and *Ethan Frome*, present the struggle of the intruder in society in almost parable form.[41] There is the typical setting of the prison world — here Starkfield, a place of desolation, of living death. It is a town of eternal winter,[42] for in it nothing changes, nothing develops or grows. Images of death and stasis crowd this novel; in the countryside the occasional farmhouse stands isolated, "mute and cold as a gravestone,"[43] and the very tombstones seem to call out mockingly to the passerby: "We never got away — how should you?" (p. 50). Starkfield's chief prisoner is

Ethan Frome, the typical Wharton male, a man of greater perception and sensitivity than those around him, trapped by his weakness and by marriage to Zeena, a living symbol of Starkfield and its paralysis.

When Mattie Silver enters this world she disrupts it, changing the lives of Ethan and Zeena forever. She is at once contrasted with the conventional Zeena, her vitality and gaiety introduced in the first description of her, dancing, flushed by a warm fire, her red "fascinator" streaming behind her as Ethan watches her outside, in darkness and snow.[44] Juxtaposed with this scene is the reader's first glimpse of Zeena, a grim specter at the threshold of her home,

> tall and angular, one hand drawing a quilted counterpane to her flat breast, while the other held a lamp. The light ... drew out of the darkness her puckered throat and the projecting wrist of the hand that clutched the quilt, and deepened fantastically the hollows and prominence of her high-boned face under its ring of crimping pins. (p. 52)

Mattie brings Ethan back to life, and soon "all his life was lived in the sight and sound of Mattie Silver, and he could no longer conceive of its being otherwise" (p. 39). Her presence is like "the lighting of a fire on a cold hearth" (p. 33), and her energy revitalizes the despairing Ethan: "from the first," Mattie, "the quicker, finer, more expressive, instead of crushing him by the contrast, had given him something of her own ease and freedom" (p. 41).

When society, in the form of the silent and vicious Zeena, expels the intruder, Ethan is offered a chance to escape from Starkfield himself. But, again like the typical Wharton male, Ethan cannot free himself, for he has never left his winter world except in fantasy. Ethan has never acted or planned to make his fantasies real, but instead has only imagined "we'll always go on living here together. . . . He was never so happy with her as when he abandoned himself to these dreams" (p. 50). In the real world Ethan remains a prisoner of society.

It is Mattie who must take the initiative, who must make one last attempt to keep Ethan and to free him in the only way she can think of — in death. Mattie suggests the attempt, willing her lover down the hill, encouraging, pushing, forcing him to take the only way out. But the escape through death is denied the pair, for as Ethan is about to hit the fatal tree, the real world intrudes: "his wife's face, with twisted monstrous lineaments, thrust itself between him and his goal" (p. 170). Starkfield has won. It has gained a new prisoner for its frozen world. The novel ends as it began, with paralysis; not only Mattie's physical paralysis, but the living death that results when one cannot change, cannot act. Mattie's fate is the worst of all the Wharton intruders, for although others die in their attempts to widen their worlds, Mattie, more horribly, lives. Crippled, querulous, damned, she is transformed into the proper inhabitant of Starkfield.

Ethan Frome is the bleakest and perhaps the cruelest of Wharton's novels. It contains no prettiness of scene nor polish of manners to soften the impact and consequences of the intrusion of its heroine into the nightmare world of Starkfield. Its intruder herself, Mattie, lacks the wit and critical intelligence of many other Wharton intruders. And yet the book is the archetypal Wharton novel; the story, however remote from New York and disguised by its bareness, is the archetypal Wharton conflict.

It is the essential conflict, the recurring motif, of the woman who is at once more vital, braver, and more receptive to all of life than the society she must confront and challenge. In certain ways Mattie is not like other, more refined intruders, Lily Bart, or Halo Tarrant, or Justine Brent. But in the essential qualities of courage and energy, in her role as disrupter and as living alternative to the suffocation around her, Mattie is an intruder. Perhaps Mattie and Starkfield are deliberately different from other Wharton heroines and other Wharton settings, are disguised and remote from Wharton's own milieu,[44] because what happens to Mattie represents Wharton's hidden fear: the fear that there is no escape from stifling convention, that the brave life-wonderer will only be destroyed.

If this is so, if the ultimate destruction of the intruder at the hands of society was a fearful possibility to Wharton, it was not a possibility that haunted her. For every intruder in Wharton's fiction who dies or is otherwise shattered by a repressive world, there are other intruders who remain free, happy, alive. The image of the questioning woman confronting a hostile world permeates Wharton's novels, and the victor in such confrontations is not always society. Similarly, the character of the intruder herself is never the same; the pattern varies, from Wharton's first full-length novel, *The Valley of Decision* (1902), a novel that is set in the eighteenth century but that may be read as a parable of old New York, to her last, unfinished work, *The Buccaneers* (published posthumously in 1938). There are intruders in the novels of social climbs (and falls), *The House of Mirth* (1905), and *The Custom of the Country* (1913). In other novels, *The Age of Innocence* (1920), *The Reef* (1912), and *The Children* (1928), the intruder is part of a triangle involving one male caught between her and a conventional woman filled with the "innocence" Wharton despised, the innocence that hides from life.

There are novels with double intruders — *The Fruit of the Tree* (1907) and *Twilight Sleep* (1927). In *Hudson River Bracketed* (1929) and its sequel, *The Gods Arrive* (1932), the intruder functions primarily as teacher. Even in the novellas, *The Touchstone* (1900) and *New Year's Day* (1924), the intruder can be found.

Her character and conflicts may vary, her setting may be old New York or the decadent Europe of the 1920s. Whatever the variations, the intruder is a significant feature of Wharton's fiction, a recurring type whose presence and functions should be examined in order to understand Edith Wharton's work. It is that examination which is the focus of this study.

NOTES

1. "Our Literary Aristocrat," *The Pacific Review* (June 1921), rpt. in Irving Howe, ed., *Edith Wharton: A Collection of Critical Essays* (Englewood Cliffs, N.J.: Prentice-Hall, 1962), p. 153. For similar comments, see Percy Boynton, "Edith Wharton," *Some Contemporary Americans* (Chicago: Univ. of Chicago Press, 1924), pp. 89-107, and Alfred Kazin, "Two Educations: Edith Wharton and Theodore Dreiser," *On Native Grounds: An Interpretation of Modern American Prose Literature* (New York: Reynal and Hitchcock, 1942), pp. 73-90. E. K. Brown ("Edith Wharton," *Etudes Anglaises*, 2, no. 2, [1938]: 16-26) stresses Wharton's growing nostalgia for her past but also concedes her angry criticism of the puritanical morality and conventionalism of old New York.

2. Robert Morss Lovett, *Edith Wharton* (New York: Robert M. McBride and Co., 1925), p. 87.

3. "Contrasting Worlds: A Study in the Novels of Edith Wharton," *Etudes Anglaises* 7 (1954): p. 192.

4. Henry Seidel Canby, "Fiction Sums Up a Century," *Literary History of the United States*, ed. Robert Spiller et al. (New York: Macmillan Co., 1963), p. 1211.

5. Louis Auchincloss, *Edith Wharton: A Woman in Her Time* (New York: Viking Press, 1971), p. 13.

6. *The Two Lives of Edith Wharton: The Woman and Her Work* (New York: Appleton-Century, 1965), p. xiii. Richard H. Lawson in *Edith Wharton* (New York: Frederick Ungar Publishing Co., 1977) goes as far as to say that Wharton "continued to believe that the mores of her own class and era were inherently — owing to social prerogative if not divine right — superior to all other mores" (p. 15).

7. For an interesting discussion of how various critics resolve all the contradictions this attitude can lead to when examining specific works by Wharton, see Marilyn Jones Lyde's first chapter, "Apparent Contradictions in Thought," pp. 3-24, in *Edith Wharton: Convention and Morality in the Work of a Novelist* (Norman: Univ. of Oklahoma Press, 1959).

8. "Introduction: The Achievement of Edith Wharton," *Edith Wharton: A Collection of Critical Essays*, ed. Irving Howe, pp. 5-6. For similar viewpoints, see Marilyn Jones Lyde, *Edith Wharton: Convention and Morality*, pp. 168-69; Blake Nevius, *Edith Wharton: A Study of Her Fiction* (Berkeley: Univ. of California Press, 1953), p. 251; and Cynthia Griffin Wolff, *A Feast of Words: The Triumph of Edith Wharton* (New York: Oxford Univ. Press, 1977), p. 374. Exceptions to the prevailing attitude that Wharton turned ranting conservative and lost her literary powers after World War I are Geoffrey Walton, *Edith Wharton: A Critical Interpretation* (Rutherford, N.J.: Fairleigh Dickinson Univ. Press, 1970), who concludes that Wharton "stands for cultural and social continuity and the maintenance, but also the constant readaptation of traditions," p. 204; and Margaret McDowell, whose excellent article "Viewing the Custom of Her

Country: Edith Wharton's Feminism'' (*Contemporary Literature* 15 [Autumn 1974]: 521-38) and book *Edith Wharton* (Boston: Twayne Publishers, 1976) deal mainly with Wharton as a feminist. And, while Elizabeth Ammons's dissertation, *Edith Wharton's Heroines: Studies in Aspiration and Compliance* (Univ. of Illinois at Urbana-Champaign, 1974) also deals with Wharton's criticism of preconceived American notions of femininity, she concludes that Wharton's work deteriorated after World War I because of her crusade against postwar society.

9. "Henry James's Heiress: The Importance of Edith Wharton,'' *Scrutiny* (Dec. 1938), rpt. in *Edith Wharton: A Collection of Critical Essays*, p. 86.

10. *Edith Wharton and the Novel of Manners* (Charlottesville: Univ. Press of Virginia, 1975), p. 174.

11. Lindberg, *Edith Wharton and the Novel of Manners*, p. 175. Similarly, Irving Howe ("Introduction: The Achievement of Edith Wharton,'' in *Edith Wharton: A Collection of Critical Essays*, pp. 17-18) says that Edith Wharton failed in "giving imaginative embodiment to the human will seeking to resist defeat or move beyond it.''

12. *A Backward Glance* (1934; reprint ed. New York: Appleton-Century, 1936), p. 127.

13. Ibid., pp. 126-27.

14. Early in her career Wharton published an article defending George Eliot's interest in nonliterary fields of knowledge, suggesting that perhaps it was because she was a woman that such interest was attacked, and expressing a generous understanding of Eliot's private life (in R. W. B. Lewis, *Edith Wharton* [New York: Harper and Row, 1975], pp. 108-9). And Wharton made at least two visits to Nohant, George Sand's home, one with Henry James (Lewis, *Edith Wharton*, pp. 169-70, 177). In fact, the role of the female intruder as teacher, which is common in Wharton's fiction, is the focus of George Sand's novel *Mauprat* (1836), in which a good but revolutionary woman rehabilitates and educates her lover.

15. Constance Hedin Carlson (*Heroines in Certain American Novels*, Dissertation, Brown Univ., 1971), in her chapter on Wharton, says that "Edith Wharton has her heroines awaken the heroes to a quality of life that can be finer than that required of them by society'' (p. 48), and that the heroine "awakens the conscience of the hero which has remained latent or in the proper compartments approved by society'' (p. 80). She deals briefly with four novels: *The House of Mirth, The Reef, The Custom of the Country*, and *The Age of Innocence*; however, she identifies Anna Leath as an "awakener,'' with which I disagree, and she does not develop the above statements very extensively.

16. Gary Lindberg discusses what he calls the "buried fable'' of "inward rescue'' in Wharton's fiction. It involves "the release of the protagonist from class dominated ways of seeing,'' and Lindberg identifies three "rescuers'' in Wharton's fiction: Ellen Olenska, who widens the perceptions of Newland Archer; Selden, who sees himself as "rescuer'' of Lily Bart; and Ralph Marvell, who fails to "rescue'' Undine Spragg. *Edith Wharton and the Novel of Manners*, pp. 45 and 58. This theme of moral or perceptual awakening is an important aspect of Wharton's work, but one that I perceive as primarily a function of the female intruder.

17. *The Awakening*, ed. Margaret Culley, Norton Critical Edition (1899; reprint ed. New York: W. W. Norton, 1976), p. 82.

18. In *Madame de Treymes* the intruder is John Durham, an American thrust into a hostile French society, who influences Christiane de Treymes, a member of society, to develop a new moral posture that betrays her own group. In *Summer* it is Lawyer Royall, a man who failed in the outside world and who is trapped in the narrow society of North Dormer. It is Lawyer Royall who is at once superior to his little world and yet scorned by it, and who teaches his ward, Charity, how to deal with conflict and intolerance.

19. *The Buccaneers*, Essay appended by Gaillard Lapsley (New York: D. Appleton-Century Company, 1938), p. 248.

20. *The American Adam: Innocence, Tragedy and Tradition in the Nineteenth Century* (Chicago: Univ. of Chicago Press, 1955), p. 49.

21. Ibid., p. 129.

22. *Edith Wharton*, p. 34.

23. Ibid., p. 28.

24. *A Backward Glance*, p. 61.

25. Ibid., pp. 68-9.

26. "Life and I," pp. 23-4. Wharton Archives, Beinecke Library, Yale University, New Haven, Conn. As quoted in Cynthia Griffin Wolff, *A Feast of Words*, p. 44. Wolff describes "Life and I" as a long autobiographical manuscript written as early as 1920 or 1922.

27. *A Backward Glance*, p. 39.

28. Ibid., p. 169.

29. Ibid., p. 122.

30. Ibid., p.119.

31. Ibid., pp. 143-44.

32. Ibid., p. 123.

33. R. W. B. Lewis, *Edith Wharton*, p. 65.

34. Ibid., p. 222.

35. Ibid., p. 226.

36. At a hotel in Trapani, a message was slipped under Wharton's door: "Ladies are requested to receive visits from gentlemen in the public salon, out of consideration for the severe customs of the region." Ibid., p. 343.

37. *A Backward Glance*, p. 20.

38. *Edith Wharton*, p. 370.

39. R. W. B. Lewis, *Edith Wharton*, p. 514.

40. *A Backward Glance*, p. 372.

41. Blake Nevius comments that the recurring theme of the "trapped sensibility" in Wharton's fiction is presented in *Ethan Frome* in its barest and least complex form, because here Ethan, the larger, more generous nature, is a prisoner of Zeena, the narrower character. *Edith Wharton: A Study of Her Fiction*, p. 121.

42. R. W. B. Lewis (*Edith Wharton*, p. 309) comments on the "inner wintriness" of *Ethan Frome*.

43. *Ethan Frome* (1911; reprint ed. New York: Charles Scribner's Sons, 1970), p. 49. Citations in the text are to this edition.

44. It is interesting that *Ethan Frome* is the only novel that Wharton first attempted to write in French, perhaps as another disguise.

The Female Intruder
in the Novels of Edith Wharton

1

The Pattern Begins: *The Valley of Decision*

"I should like to see whatever you will show me."[1]

Odo to Fulvia, *The Valley of Decision*

The Valley of Decision was Edith Wharton's first full-length novel and the one in which the pattern of the intruder fully emerges.[2] Because it is a historical romance set in eighteenth-century Italy, *The Valley of Decision* has not been closely linked to Wharton's other works; in fact, there is little critical discussion of it at all.

The novel is the story of Odo Valsecca, an Italian nobleman who eventually becomes the Duke of Pianura. Before Odo attains the throne he has a varied and adventurous life, experiencing both the corruption of the ruling class of Pianura and the poverty of the peasants who support that class. He is also exposed to the freethinkers who espouse the radical ideas circulating throughout Europe before the French Revolution. Odo, a sensitive, compassionate man, finally assumes the leadership of his country with the intention of reforming the court and of bettering the situation of the poor. What Odo discovers once he is in power, however, is that change is not easily effected and that the common man is wary of any innovation that might threaten what little he already has. Discouraged, defeated by an alliance of the nobility and the Church, which manipulates the peasants, Odo ends as a repressive, reactionary leader who is deposed as the impact of the French Revolution spreads to Pianura.

Several studies have seen the setting and conflict of the novel as analogous to New York in the age of reform, and some have even commented that perhaps Odo's final choice of the restrictive past over the radical present reflects Edith Wharton's own attitudes about change and the dangers of too much freedom. Blake Nevius says of Wharton's choice of subject matter that "for one for whom the past was so much a living part of the present, the resemblances between the social order of Italy before the Risorgimento and that of her own late nineteenth-century New York would have been inescapable,"[3] and, he asks,

Was it simply by accident that during the heyday of progressivism in this country Mrs. Wharton chose to write a novel so contrary in spirit to that vast movement of philanthropy and reform sponsored by scientists, social workers, and even politicians, and somewhat later by journalists and novelists — a novel so devoid of optimism and so skeptical of panaceas? In the light of her background and conventions, I think not.[4]

This interpretation of *The Valley of Decision* presumes that Odo's turn to the right and his final rejection of revolution are Wharton's own, and that, in effect, Odo is essentially Edith Wharton. A closer analysis of the character of Odo Valesecca as it develops in the novel indicates that, while Wharton may have created a sympathetic character in Odo, he is far from being her ideal model of conduct, and that *The Valley of Decision* does not end on a reactionary note. What is characteristic of Odo Valsecca, and what eventually leads to his downfall, is an ever-present dichotomy in his attitudes and beliefs, in his personal relationships, and in his very nature, which can most easily be seen in his connection to his mistress, Fulvia Vivaldi.

Fulvia functions as the female intruder in the novel and Odo himself feels that she is "the symbol of his best aims and deepest failure" (1:303). Odo's connection to Fulvia is characterized by his fatal duality; the relation involves both love and political philosophy, and Odo is faithful to neither. As the conflicts and contacts between Odo and Fulvia progress, the reader discovers that it is Odo's own weakness and ambivalence that destroy his good intentions and make him a reactionary, and not any evil inherent in reform and change.

The *Valley of Decision* is a long, panoramic, historical novel into which Wharton crammed much of her study of eighteenth-century Italy. Often the detail and the multiplicity of scene and character obscure the underlying pattern, but the pattern of the intruder is the focus of the novel. Part of the function of Fulvia Vivaldi in *The Valley of Decision* is to widen the perception of Odo, as Ellen Olenska does for Newland Archer. In fact, *The Valley of Decision* in many ways anticipates the themes and structure of *The Age of Innocence*, with Odo as a kind of eighteenth-century Archer in love with a Fulvia very much like Ellen Olenska. However, in order to see the similarities and to understand how the role of the intruder influences an interpretation of *The Valley of Decision*, one must examine the plot of the novel itself.

Odo Valsecca's childhood is already filled with the duality that will characterize his later life. Although an aristocrat by birth, Odo spends his childhood in the care of a peasant couple while his parents remain at court. These early years familiarize Odo with the life of poverty; in fact, the first description of Odo places him alone in a ruined chapel, transfixed by a battered statue of St. Francis of Assisi, where the "sunken ravaged countenance" of the saint seemed to reflect "the mute pain of all poor downtrodden folk on earth" (1:3). Odo also sees the effect of poverty on a foundling girl, Momola, a drudge at the farm.

Suddenly, when Odo is nine years old, his father dies, and Odo is brought to court by his mother, a self-centered, extravagant, and amoral woman. The imaginative child is exposed to two worlds at once: the splendor of the court, and the misery described to him by the hunchbacked boy, Carlo Gamba, who acts as his companion. As Odo wanders entranced through the magnificent court gardens, Gamba, another foundling, bitterly tells him of another "garden," the "garden" of the Innocenti — of the orphans, the cemetery where lie "the bodies of my brothers and sisters, the Innocents who die like flies every year of the cholera and the measles and the putrid fever" (1:24). The vision of such pain spoils Odo's pleasure in the court gardens. "At every step some fresh surprise arrested Odo, but the terrible vision of that other garden planted with the dead bodies of the Innocents robbed the spectacle of its brightness" (1:25).

Odo's education in such dualism continues. He visits his grandfather, a fierce but upright feudal ruler who lives in a turreted border castle. From his grandfather he hears tales of adventure and chivalry. From his grandfather's chaplain he receives religious instruction that urges him toward a contemplative life. Odo is attracted to both a life of action and a life of reflection. The key to his personality may be seen in the following description of his goals:

> The longing to found a hermitage like the Portiuncula among the savage rocks of Donnaz, and live there in gentle communion with plants and animals, alternated in him with the martial ambition to ride forth against the Church's enemies, as his ancestors had ridden against the bloody and pestilent Waldenses; but whether his piety took the passive or aggressive form it always shrank from the subtleties of doctrine. To live like the saints, rather than to reason like the fathers, was his ideal of Christian conduct; if indeed a vague pity for suffering creatures and animals was not the source of his monastic yearnings, and a desire to see strange countries the secret of his zeal against the infidel. (1:44)

This picture of Odo at age nine characterizes him throughout his life. He would like both to withdraw from the world and to actively attack its injustices, but neither option is thought through clearly. Odo's commitments are "vague," more connected to his emotions than to his reason. Odo will perpetually vacillate between choices, instead of dedicating himself fully to one ideal.

His actions (or his attempted actions) reveal much the same duality.

Now that he lives in comparative luxury, he often thinks of Momola, the orphan at the farm, and once he has a "sudden vision of her bare feet, pinched with cold and cut with the pebbles of the yard" (1:33). One day he has almost decided to speak of the foundling to his mother, but "his attention was unexpectedly distracted by a troop of Egyptians, who came along the road leading a dancing bear; and hardly had these passed when the chariot of an itinerant dentist engaged him" (1:33). Nothing stays too long in Odo's mind or on Odo's conscience.

His youth continues in this manner. Odo has a vague, amorphous sense that something is wrong with his society, that something should be done for "suffering creatures and animals," but he is raised in an atmosphere of luxury and corruption, and while he may disapprove of the corruption, he loves the luxury. A series of deaths in the ruling family brings Odo closer to the throne, and he is flattered and indulged. Educated at the royal academy, he leads a "life of dissipation barely interrupted by a few hours of attendance at the academic classes" (1:94-95). He forms a socially acceptable attachment to a pretty married countess,[7] and becomes a traditional gallant, acting out an expected role.

Yet, underneath, the ambivalence remains. A friend at the academy gives him Voltaire and Rousseau to read, and Odo and his friend share "the stirring of unborn ideals, the pressure of that tide of revolution that was to sweep them, on widely-sundered currents, to the same uncharted deep" (1:103). While his conventional way of life continues, Odo's inner life is confused and disturbed. An amalgam of the traditional with a smattering of the radical, Odo is beginning to test the accepted forms of thought, however quietly. His character is ripe for the intrusion of Fulvia Vivaldi.

His first encounter with Fulvia is in a context that foreshadows their future relationship. Odo has retreated to the woods, where he reads in Rosseau of "a great romantic love, subdued to duty, yet breaking forth again and again . . ." (1:120). Suddenly two figures enter Odo's reverie; they are a middle-aged man, Fulvia's father, and a young, beautiful woman, Fulvia herself. The pair, Odo thinks, "might have stepped from the pages of the romance" (1:123). They are laughing, and their conversation is a light, offhand, disrespectful discussion of current politics. Odo is fascinated. The figures do not see Odo; there is no real meeting, but Odo cannot forget the woman.

The context of the encounter is significant. Already Fulvia has been connected in Odo's mind not only with political unorthodoxy, but also with a pretty, romantic ideal. Odo would like the world he lives in to be like the books he reads, and in a sense his attempt to make it so, along with his lack of pragmatism, will lead to his failures.

Fulvia has already had another effect on Odo. After having caught a glimpse of her in the countryside, Odo immediately contrasts his conventional court love, Clarice, with this new woman. Wharton comments:

> If the ladies whom gallant gentlemen delight to serve could guess what secret touchstones of worth these same gentlemen sometimes carry into the adored presence, many a handsome head would be carried with less assurance and many a fond exaction less confidently imposed. If, for instance, the Countess Clarice . . . could have known that the Cavaliere Odo Valsecca's devoted glance saw her through the medium of a countenance compared to which her own revealed the most unexpected shortcomings, she might have received him with less easy petulance of manner. (1:130-31)

Fulvia is now Odo's "secret touchstone of worth." Not only does he draw comparisons between the two women, but he compares the two kinds of life they represent. As he sits in Clarice's rooms, he compares "the compliments to be exchanged, the silly verses to be praised, the gewgaws from Paris to be admired," with that "vision of that other life which had come to him on the hillside" (1:133). Like Newland Archer after his first visit to Ellen Olenska's home, Odo begins to be dissatisfied with his own life, feeling "no more than a puppet . . . condemned, as the strings of custom pulled, to feign the gestures of immortal passions" (1:134). Perhaps much of this discontent had been growing quietly in Odo for some time, but it is the encounter with Fulvia that crystallizes his evaluation of his old life.

Soon after his encounter with Fulvia in the woods, Odo is to meet her again and his life is to change dramatically. A friend proposes to take Odo to a secret meeting, promising to show him "the sight of a face that men have laid down their lives to see" (1:130). The meeting is a meeting of freethinkers, and Odo's friend is speaking metaphorically of the face of liberty and of free inquiry, but the "face" that Odo sees at the meeting is Fulvia's.

Fulvia's father, Professor Vivaldi, is the center of a group of learned men who meet regularly and secretly to discuss ideas forbidden in repressive Pianura. Fulvia is part of this learned circle, a woman considered by her father's friends to be brilliant enough to hold a chair of philosophy at a university. She is an object of confused admiration to Odo at this point, the kind of person who will not fit neatly into any of the social categories Odo has known so far.

Fulvia is, for one thing, a member of the middle class, "the class most inaccessible to men of Odo's rank: the only class in Italy in which the wife's fidelity was as much esteemed as the innocence of the girl" (2:120). He cannot carelessly seduce her, as he would a peasant girl, and she is not open to the ritualized flirtations of the Countess Clarice. Her learning disturbs Odo. Fulvia's habit of associating as an equal with intellectual males gives her "a self-possession disconcerting to the young blood accustomed to conquer with a glance" (ibid.).

And she is politically dangerous to Odo. Her house is watched by agents of the government; she and her father, because of their studies, are suspect persons. Odo, an heir to the throne, should not associate with Fulvia. At their first formal meeting Fulvia tries to warn Odo of his danger: "You are young and the world is fair before you. Have you considered that before risking yourself among us?" (2:139-40).

But the warning is scarcely heeded, because Odo's desire for a romance with Fulvia makes him careless about her politically dangerous status. When Fulvia offers to show Odo her father's collection of antiquities, he answers, "I should like to see whatever you will show me" (1:138), and there is irony in the reply. Fulvia will be the most significant of all Odo's teachers, but essentially he will fail as a pupil. What Odo is hoping to "see" in Fulvia, to learn from her, is a new kind of romance, with a girl who is neither a "convent-bred miss" nor a "flippant and vaporish fine lady" (1:138); what Fulvia wants to show Odo is the value of free inquiry, the possibilities of change and improvement that enlightenment may bring. She is fully committed to a political, intellectual ideal. Odo will only be committed (and never fully) to Fulvia. The results of such a mismatch will be disastrous for both people.

Odo begins to haunt the Vivaldi household, ostensibly to learn from Professor Vivaldi but in reality to see Fulvia. While he is slowly drawn to the ideas circulating among the freethinkers, his duality of vision persists. He still finds much that is pleasant in his old life: "his lurking dilettantism made him doubly alive to the elegance of the Palazzo Tournanches when he went thither from a coarse meal in the stuffy dining-parlor of one of his new acquaintances" (1:150). Ideas of change and freedom may excite Odo but he is still, at heart, happiest in his aristocratic environment.

When Odo's indiscreet visits result in the Vivaldis being driven from Pianura, Odo quickly lapses into his old ways. His life returns to a familiar pattern of travel, pleasure, and court intrigue. Odo's new beloved is Maria Clementina, a woman almost completely opposite to Fulvia in character and status. Duchess of Pianura, Maria Clementina is a distant relative of Marie Antoinette and shares many of her worst qualities, including her self-centered frivolousness and extravagance. Like May Welland in *The Age of Innocence*, Maria Clementina represents the conventional way of living, and Odo's movement toward her represents his flight from Fulvia and the disturbing ideas she embodies back to the safety of tradition.

As Maria Clementina replaces Fulvia in Odo's heart, new teachers replace her in his mind. These include the Abate Crescenti, who teaches Odo how to understand the present through studying the past, and the Abate de Crucis, a somewhat sinister Jesuit who becomes one of Odo's closest advisers. Odo thus, in a short period, jumps from seeing the world through the eyes of a revolutionary to a vision colored by the pronouncements of a much more conservative clergy and by his relationship to a shallow heiress. His aims are still unfocused, he is still "a mind not yet master of itself" (2:15), and he is even himself aware of this crippling vacillation of character. One day in the palace Odo examines the portraits of his ancestors and sees "in every countenance from that of the first Duke to that of his own peruked and cuirassed grandfather ... the same symptoms of decadency: that duality of will which, in a delicately-tempered race, is the fatal fruit of an undisturbed pre-eminence" (1:250).

Odo's next meeting with Fulvia is another study in the contrasts that fill this novel. It takes place several years after he has last seen her, in Venice, a city that Wharton calls "the essence of superficiality itself ... nowhere was the mind arrested by a question or an idea" (2:55). Odo, who finds himself falling "more and more into the habit of running with the tide" (2:59) of hedonism, is rescued by Fulvia, who has become the very symbol of asceticism — a nun. Her father's death and her struggle to publish his life's work on the origins of civilization had reduced Fulvia to a penniless, outcast state and her relatives, anxious to be rid of her, have forced her into a convent. She is trapped and desperate.

Odo now serves as Fulvia's physical rescuer, helping her to escape from the convent, while she rescues his spirit. Seeing her again, Odo "felt himself no longer a drifting spectator of life but a sharer in its gifts and renunciations" (2:76); "the strongest impression she produced was that of increasing his points of contact with life ... of letting into the circle of his nearest emotions that great tide of human longing and effort that had always faintly sounded on the shores of self" (2:94). Fulvia breaks down the barriers of Odo's egotism and reconverts him to a life of purpose and reform. The couple declare their love, flee to Geneva, and plan to marry. In Geneva the Jesuit de Crucis appears, a messenger from Pianura. Odo has been chosen the new ruler of the country.

The ensuing scene closely parallels the renunciation scene between Archer and Ellen Olenska. Odo would like very much to cast the world aside, to relinquish the throne and live as a private citizen with Fulvia, doing good work in a quiet way. Fulvia holds him to his duty. The opportunity he has been waiting for has come, she argues; now he will possess the power to reform Pianura. He must do so alone. In a speech that anticipates Ellen's renunciation of Archer, Fulvia rejects Odo's plea that she become his mistress and help him to rule. While Fulvia agrees that her greatest service would be to help Odo serve his people, she insists that "to do this I must stand aside. To be near you I must go from you. To love you I must give you up" (2:140). Odo's duty to his country must take precedence over his love for Fulvia. "If you love me," Fulvia argues, it is because we have thought the same thoughts, dreamed the same dreams, heard the same voice — in each other's voices, perhaps, as you say, but none the less a real voice, apart from us and above us, and one which would speak to us as loudly if we were apart — one which both of us must follow to the end. (2:134)

The irony is that even as Fulvia pleads for the obligations of a higher ideal than romantic love, Odo is seeing "a vision of the life he was renouncing," not a vision of what he could do for the public welfare, but of "the power, the luxury, the sumptuous background of traditional state and prerogative, in which his artistic and intellectual taste, as well as his easy impulses of benevolence, would find unchecked and immediate gratification" (2:135).

The results of this dichotomy of character are inevitable. Even as Odo makes his state entry into Pianura, he experiences a "moral lassitude" (2:157). Odo initiates some minor reforms, but he keeps the same corrupt Cabinet that had existed under the previous Duke, a Cabinet totally against change of any kind and constantly working against him. He marries Maria Clementina, now a widow, and the marriage turns into the kind of conventional and shallow partnership characteristic of Wharton's view of old New York. Odo is politically liberal in that he allows free-thinkers to live and speak openly in Pianura, but he also allows the clergy and nobility to plot against him. In essence, he is weak. Wharton defines Odo as a ruler in these terms:

Face to face with the sudden summons to action, with the necessity for prompt and not-too-curious choice of means and methods, he felt a stealing apathy of the will, an inclination toward the subtle duality of judgement that had so often weakened and diffused his energies. (2:164)

Odo's weakness must again be supported by the strong idealism of Fulvia. After Odo has ruled for several years, Fulvia returns to Pianura as his mistress and closest adviser.

While Odo was struggling to rule Pianura alone, Fulvia had enjoyed a certain personal success. She had succeeded in publishing her father's book and had become tutor to a daughter of a count, attracting around her a kind of salon populated by men of art and learning. The impact of both her father's book and her own personality can be gauged by the fact that Fulvia was finally expelled from Milan as a subversive. She returns to Pianura because she realizes that Odo needs her, "that the task for which he had given her up could after all not be accomplished without her" (2:216). Both her triumphs and sufferings have made Fulvia more committed than ever to the ideals she lives for.

The outcast Fulvia, now Odo's mistress, is thus drawn inside the power structure; as an English visitor to Pianura observes after meeting Fulvia, "Here is the hand that rules the state" (2:213). But while she may be drawn to the periphery of society, she is still basically outside of it. She does not become the conventional eighteenth-century mistress dispensing political favors, living in splendor. Instead she lives modestly, in the "frugal style of the middle class" (2:211); she refuses to accept a title and is therefore thus barred from going to court.

Yet, while she lives modestly, she makes no attempt to conceal her influence over the Duke. Believing implicitly in the goodness of her cause and the rightness of her reforms, she prefers her influence "to be so visible a factor in his relations with his people that she should come to be regarded as the ultimate pledge of his good faith" (2:217).

Ironically, this type of role makes Fulvia more of an outcast in Pianura. Fulvia is counting on the people's acceptance of Odo's reforms, and therewith their acceptance of her and her position. But the people distrust any changes that they cannot fully understand. Small tradesmen are hurt when their patrons, the nobles, are taxed heavily, and the peasants, steeped in a highly superstitious Catholicism, view any attempt to limit the power of the Church as the work of the devil. These changes, by Fulvia's own wish, are attributed to her influence. A country that expected their ruler to acquire a typically beautiful, extravagant, and mercenary mistress cannot understand the power that the modest, almost nunlike Fulvia exerts over the Duke. Fulvia begins to be regarded by many as a witch, since her influence cannot be accounted for in any traditional way, and her motivations are too idealistic to be understood.

The political situation in Pianura worsens. In 1789 Odo half-heartedly formulates a new constitution, one that will allow him to deprive the clergy of some of their privileges and that will ultimately benefit the people. As Odo becomes more oppressed by the cares of leadership, Fulvia becomes more dogmatic in pushing Odo on, pressing for the new constitution; she is, finally, almost shrill and dictatorial. Odo had brought Fulvia back to give him strength, but her presence seems only to have heightened his crippling sense of duality: "Odo remembered that he had once thought her nearness would dispel his hesitations. At first it had been so; but gradually the contact with her fixed enthusiasms has set up within him an opposing sense of the claims she ignored" (2:223). He begins to doubt the wisdom of the new constitution. Odo, whom a foreign observer considers to be better suited for "the meditations of the closet" (2:209) than for active leadership, is confronted by his mistress, who demands action, even violent action, if necessary. "When persuasion fails," Fulvia insists, "coercion must be used!" (2:226). The more Odo hesitates, the more rigid and desperate Fulvia becomes.

Finally, both Odo and Fulvia are destroyed. On the day the new constitution is proclaimed, silent crowds gather in Pianura. Odo has chosen this day for Fulvia to receive her doctorate, and her address upon the occasion concerns constitutional liberty. As Fulvia, in academic dress, leaves the assembly hall at Odo's side, the sullen mob, manipulated by the clergy and aristocrats, riots. Fulvia is killed, and with her dies Odo's impulse for reform.

Odo falls ill and in effect leaves the running of Pianura to his aristocratic cabinet. He retreats to a monastery, reluctant ever to rule Pianura again. "The old abuses persisted, the old offenses were condoned: it was as though the apathy of the sovereign had been communicated to his people" (2:297). When Odo finally reassumes the throne, he is as repressive a leader as any of his ancestors ever were. As the revolution in France moves nearer to Italy, Odo repudiates all the liberal theory he ever believed in and is finally forced to abdicate. He leaves the country to fight the French, and his last thoughts on the revolution in France reflect his bitterness and disillusion:

> The new year rose in blood and mounted to a bloodier noon. All the old defences were falling. Religion, monarchy, law, were sucked down into the whirlpool of liberated passions. Across that sanguinary scene passed, like a mocking ghost, the philosopher's vision of the perfectibility of man. Man was free at last — freer than his would-be liberators had ever dreamed of making him — and he used his freedom like a beast. (2:303)

Passages such as this (and there are several) at the end of the novel are a strong justification for interpreting *The Valley of Decision* as Wharton's commentary on the dangers of change, individual freedom, and reform. Change is revolution, and revolution is bestial, Wharton seems to be saying. However, if one considers the pattern of the novel as a whole, and especially the relationship between Odo and Fulvia, Wharton's meaning takes on a different light.

Like Archer in *The Age of Innocence*, or Darrow in *The Reef*, Odo Valsecca, the protagonist of the novel, begins as a sensitive, well-intentioned person locked into his society. While he vaguely senses that something is not right with his world, he still perceives it within the framework of his own place in society. When Odo meets and falls in love with Fulvia, he is initiated into a new way of seeing his old world; he is exposed to new options of behavior and thought. The initial reaction on Odo's part is confusion and an attempt to categorize Fulvia according to his traditional values, but eventually Odo is drawn to Fulvia's ideas, accepts her as a person unlike any other he has met, and struggles to make Fulvia's ideals into realities in Pianura.

But the duality in Odo's nature determines his fate. Blake Nevius comments that, because Wharton used Odo to dramatize the intellectual and spiritual conflicts of the age, this single representative of so many conflicts becomes a "blurred and amorphous" character, and there is never a reconciliation between his "pleasure-loving despotism" and his "intermittent passion for reform."[8] While this lack of reconciliation of the opposing drives of Odo's nature may be perceived as a literary flaw, it is as likely to be a deliberate part of the conflict of the novel. Because Odo cannot come to terms with his divided personality, can neither integrate his conflicting impulses nor decisively choose one way of dealing with life, the novel ends in Odo's bitter failure. Because Odo lives in two different worlds and constantly vacillates between them, he is weak in both. When Odo finally does choose the old world, he does so only because there is little else left to do. He does not become reactionary because, in Wharton's eyes, even repression is better than revolution, but because he has failed at living up to the ideals that Fulvia taught him. Like Newland Archer, who is exposed to a whole new world of perception through Ellen Olenska, Odo is tempted to flirt with the new, but remains a convention-bound insider at heart. And yet, ironically, even though the conventional side of both Odo and Archer wins a certain lame victory, it is a victory in which duality still persists. The values to which both Fulvia and Ellen expose their lovers make the men unable to be fully at peace in the old world. Eventually, Odo and Archer lose nearly everything, because even the past they half-heartedly embrace is lost. And, as Archer, a disappointed man, justifies his life in old age by explaining, "After all, there was good in the old ways,"[9] so Odo must find reasons outside of himself for his failures. Thus the novel ends with his horrified reactions to the French Revolution, which he can convince himself is the inevitable outgrowth of reform.

This interpretation does not deny that Wharton's reactions to the chaos in France may have been similar to her protagonist's. But it is not required that there be only two alternatives proposed in the novel, that life can only be the restricted, narrow life of tradition or the disordered one of the "sanguinary scene" in France. Wharton is not necessarily proposing that anything, even repression, is better than the horrors that may come with certain kinds of change. While, in *The Valley of Decision*, extreme horror accompanies change, another kind of change, one associated with the character of Fulvia Vivaldi, is possible.

Fulvia Vivaldi, the most sympathetic character in the novel, represents a third alternative for positive change. It is significant that Wharton never links Fulvia to any specific revolutionary philosophy or any detailed radical code, but instead gradually reveals her through her actions and through the reforms she does achieve by pressuring Odo. Far from representing any bloody and violent solution to the problems of a stagnant society, Fulvia Vivaldi embodies a compassionate and rational approach to the world's evil. Fulvia, as heroine, functions in constant opposition to the established order and beliefs of Pianura, and she does so with the greater part of the reader's (and Wharton's) sympathy.

Fulvia's character is developed through a series of contrasts. Her adventures and persecutions are woven between portraits of shallow, spoiled women — Odo's greedy and unprincipled mother, his conventionally coquettish mistress, his superficial and selfish wife. All these insiders are placed in direct opposition to Fulvia, the quintessential outsider. Her intelligence, her frank and open appraisal of the world she lives in, her willingness to sacrifice herself for ideals all make her different from, and more admirable than the stereotyped women Wharton juxtaposes with her. Fulvia's independent successes, getting her father's book published despite all opposition, supporting herself as a tutor to nobility, and attracting a salon of the best minds in Milan, make Fulvia even more an object of admiration. And society's cruelty to Fulvia, her forced flight, her loss of home and rank and family, her imprisonment — all put the reader firmly on her side.

If Fulvia is continually contrasted to the typical aristocratic women of her world, she is placed in even more direct contrast to her lover, Odo. Her strength only emphasizes his weakness; her commitment, his vacillation. And yet, paradoxically, Fulvia also represents one aspect of Odo, that hidden part of him which is his best self. Fulvia nourishes and develops in Odo that concern for the poor, that hunger for justice which might otherwise lie dormant.

Her revolutionary principles are revealed as not very revolutionary at all when one examines exactly what Fulvia asks of Odo. She desires constitutional reforms, freedom from the more superstitious elements of the Church, a better life for the poor, and a little more humanity from the rich. These are all things that Odo, in his best self, knows are important, but they are things that Odo, because he is weak, fails to provide. Thus Fulvia, who begs them of her lover, is a symbol of Odo's "best aims" and also of his "deepest failures."

The fact that Fulvia, a sympathetic character for most of the novel, ends as a shrill and dogmatic one, must be considered. *The Valley of Decision*, like *Ethan Frome*, is a novel about destruction, not only about the destruction of a country, but about the warping and distortion of personalities through imprisonment in a static, nightmare world. Mattie Silver, whose lover is too weak to escape the nightmare with her, ends as a crippled, malicious hag, her true self obliterated because her man has failed her. Similarly, Fulvia, having invested everything — emotion, independence, ideals — in her lover, must watch helplessly as her dispirited hero betrays her ideals. Odo's weakness loses him not only his kingdom but also his beloved; it transforms the once gentle Fulvia into a shrew. Only in death can Fulvia regain the reader's admiration — as a memory of what might have been.

And essentially Fulvia functions as this possibility, as a symbol of what might have occurred instead of catastrophe and bloodshed, instead of bestial revolution. The thrust of *The Valley of Decision*, whether one accepts it as a story of Italy or as a veiled comment on New York, is this: change is inevitable. Properly anticipated and planned for by good men, it can be positive and beneficial. But if decent men fight change, or ignore it, or shrink from it and retreat into the past, evil and disorder will follow. The old order will go, whatever happens, but if nothing is done to fight bravely for the future, for a better world, tragedy is as inevitable as change itself.

In contrast to Odo's appalled comments on revolution at the end of the novel, one must consider the last insight that Odo gained from Fulvia. As she delivered her thesis on liberty, Odo reflected on the centuries of men of the past who had fought battles — many of them futile or based on illusions — for the sake of ideas. "And as the vision of the inveterate conflict rose before him, Odo saw that that beauty, the power, the immortality, dwelt not in the idea but in the struggle for it" (2:278).

The character in *The Valley of Decision* who shines in the beauty of commitment to an ideal is Fulvia Vivaldi. Her struggle is to create a better and wider society and she is the strong, hard fighter needed in a changing world. But the old world kills her, and the one man of good will who could have helped her failed her. Fulvia is the first in a long line of Wharton heroines who try to make their men see reality, and, after seeing it, to act. Other heroines, like Fulvia, fail, and are punished for their attempts; some have a degree of success. But all, like Fulvia, are intruders, and they continue the struggle.

NOTES

1. Edith Wharton, *The Valley of Decision*, 2 vols. (New York: Charles Scribner's Sons, 1902), 1:138. Citations in the text are to this edition.

2. An earlier novella, *The Touchstone* (1900), also contains elements of the pattern of the female intruder, but it is a very short work and thus does not treat the conflict of the intruder, in society in any great detail. *The Touchstone* will be discussed later.

3. *Edith Wharton: A Study of Her Fiction*, p. 48.

4. Ibid., pp. 49-50. Other critics have drawn the parallel between Pianura and old New York. Among them are Marilyn Jones Lyde (*Edith Wharton: Convention and Morality in the Work of a Novelist*, p. 85) and Geoffrey Walton (*Edith Wharton: A Critical Interpretation*, p. 38). R. W. B. Lewis in *Edith Wharton* says that in the novel Wharton

was working out her own conflict concerning how to preserve the best of the past while risking the new and unorthodox (p. 104). Cynthia Griffin Wolff (*A Feast of Words*) also stresses that the novel reflects Wharton's attempt to come to terms with her own need for individual freedom and for passion (p. 97).

5. Gary Lindberg, *Edith Wharton and the Novel of Manners*, p. 45.

6. Ibid., p. 58.

7. This alliance with a married woman characterizes many of Wharton's male figures: Selden, Newland Archer, Martin Boyne, Ralph Marvell.

8. *Edith Wharton: A Study of Her Fiction*, p. 41.

9. Edith Wharton, *The Age of Innocence*, Intro. by R. W. B. Lewis (1920; reprint ed. New York: Charles Scribner's Sons, 1970), p. 347.

2

Social Falls and Social Climbs: *The House of Mirth* and *The Custom of the Country*

While Fulvia Vivaldi fought a political struggle in eighteenth-century Italy, two other Wharton heroines, Lily Bart and Undine Spragg, do battle in another arena, the social one. Although the heroines of *The House of Mirth* and *The Custom of the Country* are extremely different from one another, they are similar in one way: both are fighting for a secure status in the upper classes of twentieth-century New York society, and the struggle is nearly as violent as that of *The Valley of Decision*. And, although Lily Bart's story traces a fall from the upper levels of that society and Undine Spragg's life may be charted as a series of steps up the social ladder, their contrasting social movements create one complete picture: a vision of a corrupt, hypocritical society that forces all those in it to conform or be destroyed. Lily's failures and Undine's successes are two sides of the same coin; together their stories expose a debased and debasing world in which money is the only standard by which all other virtues and values are judged.

Lily Bart is a woman who has been trained from childhood to work for one thing: to use her beauty as a tool to gain social acceptance and the financial security that an approved and wealthy marriage will bring. Her extravagant mother taught her to see her beauty as "the last asset in their fortunes,"[1] and Lily herself "could not figure herself as anywhere but in a drawing room, diffusing elegance as a flower sheds perfume" (p. 100). Given this ambition, Lily seems to have the capacity to fulfill it; she is lovely, charming, flexible enough to adapt herself to another's egotism, able to move smoothly and seemingly effortlessly toward a conventional marriage.

Yet, even before the action of the novel begins, Lily has repeatedly jeopardized her social standing and her chances for marriage. As her friend Carry Fisher describes her, "she works like a slave preparing the ground and sowing her seed; but the day she ought to be reaping the harvest she oversleeps herself or goes off on a picnic .... Sometimes ... I think it's just flightiness — and sometimes I think it's because, at heart, she despises the things she's trying for'' (p. 189).

At the beginning of the novel, Lily's inability to avail herself of good marriage ''deals'' is a combination of both flightiness and contempt for the prize she has been trained to work for. The interest in the story grows as Lily develops as a character who loses more of the luxury and status she once craved, but who gains, in the process, insight into herself and the world.[2] This movement of the novel, then, traces Lily's progress away from New York society and toward a new sense of communion with those who suffer and gain moral stature through their pain.[3] The title of the book is taken from a passage in Ecclesiastes: ''Sorrow is better than laughter for by sadness of countenance the heart is made better. The heart of the wise is in the house of mourning. but the heart of fools is in the house of mirth.''[4] And Lily, who begins as indeed a foolish, superficial heroine, must move, through pain, humiliation, and rejection to a kind of bitter wisdom by the end of the novel. As Margaret McDowell says, ''At the same time that Lily moves toward tragedy, she moves toward understanding of herself and others and reveals that she is in essence superior to those who had formerly represented to her all the social graces.''[5] But the movement is a halting one, as Lily fights insight every step of the way; yet eventually (almost against her will) Lily can see, and thus reveal to the reader, exactly how little she has lost and how much more, morally, she has gained.

It is important to note that Lily does not begin the novel as one secure in the world of wealth and convention. Although she travels and lives with the rich and although her flexibility and eagerness to please are useful to the people she associates with, she is not one of them. Her intruder status can be attributed not only to her lack of funds necessary for permanent membership in this world, but also to the very qualities that make Lily welcome to the group. Louis Auchincloss says that ''Lily's beauty is the light in which each of her different groups would like to shine, but when they find that it illuminates their ugliness they want to put it out.''[6] Even the vulgar Rosedale, who sees in the early Lily a way to gain his own social acceptance, is attracted to her because of her difference from the group, because of ''an external rarity, an air of being impossible to match'' (pp. 299-300). And Lily herself sees that her suitor, the staid collector of Americana Percy Gryce, would like to, in effect, add her to his collection, not because she is like him, but because she is ''a creature of a different race . . . with all sorts of intuitions, sensations, and perceptions that they [people like Gryce] don't even guess the existence of'' (p. 48).

Another movement of the novel, one that adds depth and complexity to the social criticism, begins when the intruder, Lily, is placed in contact with another character, Lawrence Selden. Selden congratulates himself on his ability to enjoy himself within the confines of society and yet to maintain a fastidious distance from it. Yet Selden is no outsider. First attracted and puzzled by Lily, Selden is drawn to her and briefly considers a commitment to her, but, as she falls from grace and is cast out of the social world, Selden himself moves within the golden cage of societal prejudices and attitudes.[7] As the conflicts of the novel develop and when Lily needs Selden most, he becomes at times what Cynthia Griffin Wolff calls him: "the unthinking mouthpiece of the worst of society's prejudices."[8] Only Lily's death awakens Selden to his own character and, at least in part, redeems him.

Both Lily's journey from society and Selden's less conscious retreat toward it can be traced through their encounters in the novel. At each significant moment in Lily's downfall Selden is present. In each encounter between the two there is a great deal of learning taking place, as Selden "instructs" Lily in the rigors of an ideal he cannot live up to and as he himself faces some unpleasant truths about himself and his world. And what Selden cannot see or refuses to acknowledge about society and his imprisonment in it is made quite plain to the reader, who does not view the world of the novel through Selden's eyes.

The novel itself begins with a picture seen through Selden's eyes, and from the beginning, then, the reader must differentiate between what Selden sees and what is actually being presented, as Wharton differentiates, through irony, between Selden's point of view and the reality of situations. Because Selden, already a prisoner of the society he disdains, accuses Lily of sins he is blind to in himself, it is important that the reader constantly separate Selden's judgments from his own.

In the first scene of the novel, in which Selden and Lily have tea at his flat, Selden observes Lily and speculates on what makes her different.

> Everything about her was at once vigorous and exquisite, at once strong and fine. He had a confused sense that she must have cost a great deal to make, that a great many dull and ugly people must, in some mysterious way, have been sacrificed to produce her. He was aware that the qualities distinguishing her from the herd of her sex were chiefly external: as though a fine glaze of beauty and fastidiousness had been applied to vulgar clay. Yet the analogy left him unsatisfied, for a coarse texture will not take a high finish; and was it not possible that the material was fine, but that circumstances had fashioned it into a futile shape? (P. 5)

Commenting on this passage, Cynthia Griffin Wolff says that "Selden's musings might almost pass for social criticism were it not for the fact that the 'futile shape' he seems to deplore is a shape he obviously and exten-sively admires and that his admiration is part of the continuing 'circumstance' that fashions it.''[9] Granted, Selden lacks the perception to see himself as part of the environment that formed Lily, but the social criticism remains, whether Selden is fully aware of all of it or not. This description of Lily provides a kind of clue to the reader that her environment will increasingly attempt to disfigure the "fine material" Lily is made of, and that perhaps it has already forced her into a mold she cannot break. And Lily's presence has also stimulated Selden to question the sacrifice (of herself and of others) necessary to make and maintain a creature like Lily Bart. Lily puzzles Selden because he cannot situate her either fully within or without "the herd of her sex," and thus he is forced to think about her. This is the first of many times when Selden will try to categorize Lily, and in these attempts Selden will learn from her.

At this point Lily herself is actively seeking guidance. In the rare moments when she cannot evade her own worries she is aware that she is no longer a member-in-completely-good-standing of her set. She confides to Selden, "I've been about too long — people are getting tired of me; they are beginning to say I ought to marry" (p. 9). And she appeals to him, "Don't you see ... that there are men enough to say pleasant things to me, and that what I want is a friend who won't be afraid to say disagreeable things when I need them?" (p. 9). But as Lily reaches out to Selden for help, "he noted, with a purely impersonal enjoyment, how evenly the black lashes were set in her smooth white lids" (p. 9). Lily's plea for friendship reaches the ear of a man who regards her as a connoisseur would, from a distanced, uninvolved perspective. Selden, who lives in a building called the Benedick, "an old word for bachelor" (p. 15), will not easily relinquish his detached stance.

While Selden offers Lily very little in the way of real friendship here, he does have an effect on her. His greater independence and ability to enter and withdraw from society at will increase Lily's dissatisfaction with her own state. In Selden's library Lily sees the sanctuary she has never been permitted to have. "How delicious to have a place like this all to one's self!" (p. 7) she sighs, for Lily has neither an equivalent refuge nor a secure place in society.

The contrast between the freer life Selden lives and the one she is trying to secure for herself haunts Lily. It colors all her manipulations of the eligible Percy Gryce. Marriage to Gryce, whose family fortune came, appropriately, from "a patent device for excluding fresh air from hotels" (p. 22), would suffocate Lily, and she knows it. Yet a part of Lily sees Gryce as her last chance. After a successful day at Bellomont, in which her plans for the entrapment of Gryce have been working well, Lily reflects on how bored she is by her potential husband. But she also knows that "she must follow up on her success, must submit to more boredom, must be ready with fresh compliances and adaptabilities, and all on the bare chance that he might ultimately decide to do her the honor of boring her for life'' (p. 25). Lily knows well the role she has to play in order to acquire the setting she needs for her talents, and she has decided to accept Gryce. For although Lily has ''fits of angry rebellion against fate, when she longed to drop out of the race and make an independent life for herself'' (p. 39), she also knows that an atmosphere of luxury is ''the only climate she could breathe in'' (p. 26), even if the atmosphere is the stuffy one provided by Gryce.

All Lily's good (and mercenary) intentions disappear when Selden arrives at Bellomont. Lily begins to see the Trenor house party she had so recently admired in a new light: ''That very afternoon they had seemed full of brilliant qualities; now she saw that they were merely dull in a loud way. Under the glitter of their opportunities she saw the poverty of their achievement'' (p. 55).

Selden further tempts Lily from her chosen purpose with a vision of a ''republic of the spirit'' that she can aspire to, a republic that he says offers freedom ''from everything — from money, from poverty, from ease and anxiety, from all the material accidents'' (p. 68). He attacks her ambitions, and predicts a miserable future for her if she continues with her present goals. Selden reinforces the doubts Lily already has, increasing her own self-mistrust. And yet Lily is right when she asks Selden, ''Why do you make the things I have chosen seem hateful to me, if you have nothing to give me instead?'' (p. 72).

What Selden does is to offer Lily a standard he himself does not live by. Advising her that very few of the rich can ever enter the ''republic of the spirit,'' Selden is himself exposed by Lily's reply: ''It seems to me . . . that you spend a good deal of your time in the element you disapprove of'' (p. 70), and Selden's very presence at Bellomont, an environment he is teaching Lily to despise, indicates that Lily's criticism is a valid one. Louis Auchincloss says that Selden strikes the reader as ''a sort of Ward McAllister posing as a Thoreau,''[10] and he apparently strikes Lily in the same way here.

Like Beatrice and Benedick, Lily and Selden now move from verbal sparring to the banter of love. Like ''adventurous children who have climbed to a forbidden height from which they discover a new world'' (p. 73), Lily and Selden play with the idea of their marriage. But as they come close to an outright declaration, both back away. The intimacy is over. Selden, who had allowed his attraction to Lily to take him into that ''new world,'' is shaken, and ''it took him a moment to regain his usual view'' of her (p. 74).

Neither Selden nor Lily gains much from the meeting and Lily, in fact, suffers a significant loss as a result of it. Her afternoon in the woods has lost her Percy Gryce and made a permanent enemy of Selden's former mistress, Bertha Dorset. While Selden can retreat into the safety of his library, Lily has to face the consequences of her impulsiveness. Her expectations of a wealthy marriage destroyed, Lily must deal with her mounting debts. She does so by allowing Gus Trenor to "invest" money for her, refusing to consider where the high dividends he provides her with are coming from. Lily convinces herself that, because she now has money to spend, she can still maintain her social standing. But she has began her descent of the social ladder, although she is not fully aware of it yet: "If she slipped she recovered her footing, and it was only afterward that she was aware of having recovered it each time on a slightly lower level" (p. 262).

Yet, as Lily begins to fall, she develops an understanding of those outside her narrow little world and begins to see them as human beings like herself. Even early in the novel, when Lily enjoys playing "great lady" roles, she possesses a certain ironic ability to identify with some of those "dull and ugly people" sacrificed to maintain the way of life she clings to. Lily never makes her maid wait up for her at night, for example, because she herself "had been long enough in bondage to other people's pleasure to be considerate of those who depended on hers, and in her bitter moods it sometimes struck her that she and her maid were in the same position, except that the latter received her wages more regularly" (pp. 27-28). Despite this evidence of consideration, Lily still possessed a belief that "dingy people" could have only one attitude toward her: "admiration for brilliancy" (p. 122), and "she had always accepted with philosophic calm the fact that such existences as hers were pedestalled on foundations of obscure humanity. . . . this was in the natural order of things" (p. 150).

Now Lily gives some of Trenor's money to Gerty Farish's refuge for working girls and she visits the place, feeling virtuous about her philanthropy. The experience enables her to see poverty not in the abstract but as "individual lives, innumerable separate centres of sensation, with her own eager reachings for pleasure, her own fierce revulsion from pain" (p. 151). Lily begins to feel for those beyond her immediate circle, ironically, at the moment when the material and social distance between her and the working girls begins to narrow.

Evidence of her precarious social status is Lily's association with the Wellington Brys, social newcomers not fully accepted by the Trenor-Dorset set. At the Bry's ballroom a central scene of the novel occurs, a scene that brings together all the conflicts, patterns, and themes of the book.

To attain a quick entry into society, the Brys plan an extravagant entertainment, that of *tableaux vivants*, in which a dozen fashionable women exhibit themselves in a series of pictures. Lily performs in one of the tableaux, and Selden, Gus Trenor, Rosedale, and many others of Lily's set are in the audience. The tableau becomes symbolic of Lily's greatest virtue and her fatal flaw.

As the curtain rises to reveal scene after scene in which the women skillfully subdue their personalities to the setting, Selden is already entranced. But when Lily appears, Selden receives an impression quite different from that conveyed by the other women:

> even the least imaginative of the audience must have felt a thrill of contrast when the curtain suddenly parted on a picture which was simply and undisguisedly the portrait of Miss Bart.
>
> Here there could be no mistaking the predominance of a personality — the unanimous "Oh!" of the spectators was a tribute, not to the brush-work of Reynold's "Mrs. Lloyd," but to the flesh and blood loveliness of Miss Bart. . . . The impulse to show herself in a splendid setting . . . had yielded to the truer instinct of trusting to her unarrested beauty, and she had purposely chosen a picture without distracting accessories of dress or surroundings. (P. 134)

What Lily is here is what she is throughout the novel — an outsider, someone who, unlike the other women of her group, cannot efface her personality and blend into her surroundings. To show her own beauty Lily has dispensed with a sumptuous setting and has become purely herself, the "real" Lily. Lily is thus a character who will not fit into her environment but who is, because of her difference, more admirable. The scene anticipates the second half of the novel, in which Lily, gradually stripped of the "distracting accessories" of luxurious surroundings, will become more outcast, and therefore more herself. It parallels Selden's last scene with Lily, when she is dead, and when, too late, Selden again sees the "real" Lily.

Seeing Lily in the tableau, Selden is finally able to "place" her. Earlier he had puzzled over her genuineness, over whether she was totally a creature of her milieu, but now his doubts about Lily fall away. For the first time "he seemed to see before him the real Lily Bart, divested of the trivialities of her little world, and catching for a moment a note of that eternal harmony of which her beauty was a part" (p. 135).

This is a scene packed with irony, for as Selden sees the "soaring grace," the "touch of poetry" (p. 134) in Lily's beauty, the rest of her observers are seeing Lily as the object she is presumed to be; they cannot see past the role Lily has been living for years. What strikes the other observers is not so much Lily's grace as the scantiness of her draperies. Ned Van Alstyne sums up the reaction of the crowd when he exclaims, "Deuced bold thing to show herself in that get-up; but gad, there isn't a break in the lines anywhere, and I suppose she wanted us to know it!" (p. 135).

The comment affects Selden, and the combination of his own vision of Lily and the reaction of the crowd forces him to perform an act of faith. Caught between the world of Van Alstyne and the isolated Lily, Selden sees the cheapness of the New York set: "This was the world she lived in, these were the standards by which she was fated to be measured! Does one go to Caliban for a judgment on Miranda?" (p. 135). Seeing his class as they are, Selden separates himself from them and commits himself to Lily: " It was as though her beauty, thus detached from all that cheapened and vulgarized it, had held out suppliant hands to him from the world in which he and she had once met for a moment . . ." (p. 135). For a short time Selden wants to enter Lily's world, the world of the outsider.

The impact of the tableau on Lily herself is also ironic. She sees the evening as a great personal triumph, indiscriminately accepting all the compliments Van Alstyne and others shower upon her. She cannot know how the audience perceived her, as "a girl standing up there as if she was up at auction" (p. 157), and thus she is spared humiliation for at least one day. Lily does not realize that by making herself stand out she is casting herself out, and that by appearing different, even superior in her beauty, she has made herself an object of hatred and scorn.

Lily thinks she is shining before friends; instead she has surrounded herself with enemies. In *The American Adam*, R. W. B. Lewis comments on a scene that he calls "the paradigm dramatic image in American literature,"[11] the opening scene of *The Scarlet Letter*, with Hester Prynne on the scaffold:

> It was the tableau of the solitary figure set over against the inimical society, in a village which hovers on the edge of the inviting and perilous wilderness; a handsome young woman standing on a raised platform, confronting in silence and pride a hostile crowd whose menace is deepened by its order and dignity.[12]

Lily Bart is a similar solitary figure, herself on the edge of a perilous wilderness, a world of poverty and shame, facing her enemies — Trenor, Dorset, Rosedale — and appealing to a weak lover — not Dimmesdale, but Selden. And, just as Hester Prynne's "delicate, evanescent and indescribable grace"[13] does not save her but serves only to increase her accusers' fury, so too Lily's beauty only lends credence to the charges made against her. As the Puritans' treatment of Hester illuminates the cruelty of their beliefs, so will Lily's fate reflect upon the brutality of the rich toward those who violate their rules.

But, of course, Lily is as yet not even conscious of her own position, much less of her fate. One day of deluded joy remains. Not until the following evening must Lily face herself. For then Gus Trenor, who had interpreted Lily in the tableau as Lily on sale, demands that he get his money's worth from her. Trenor wants a return on his investment: "There's such a thing as fair play — and interest on one's money — and hang me if I've had as much as a look from you" (p. 146). Lily realizes that, by taking money from Trenor, she has become a dishonest prostitute. She cries to Gerty Farish: "I've sunk lower than the lowest, for I've taken what they take, and not paid as they pay!" (p. 166). Happy the previous day, Lily now "seemed a stranger to herself, or rather there were two selves in her, the one she had always known, and a new abhorrent being to which it found itself chained" (p. 146). The realization weakens Lily's ties to her despised self, a self she gradually breaks free of as society moves away from her.

As Lily is pushed away from society, Selden moves farther into its confines. His egotistic fantasy of taking Lily "beyond — beyond the ugliness, the pettiness, the attrition and corrosion of the soul" (p. 154) is destroyed when he sees Lily leave the Trenor house, and all the rumors about Lily are confirmed in his mind. Rather than face her Selden runs away, judging Lily by appearances and by the words of those he so recently disdained. "It was so much simpler for him to judge Lily Bart by her habitual conduct than by the rare deviations from it which had thrown her so disturbingly in his way" (p. 272).

Selden runs from Lily, and Lily runs from herself. They meet again on the Riviera, where Lily is earning her keep by distracting George Dorset from his wife's affair. Selden, seeing Lily at the fatal dinner at which Bertha Dorset will expel her from their yacht, again notes how Lily "detached herself, by a hundred undefinable shades, from the persons who most abounded in her own style" (p. 215). As Selden compares Lily to his former mistress and the others, he observes "her grace cheapening the other women's smartness as her finely discriminated silences made their chatter dull" (p. 215). But Selden has given up on his dream of redeeming Lily, since he believes that she has finally, deliberately, chosen this world "where conspicuousness passed for distinction and the society column has become the roll of fame" (p. 216). Again, Selden is perceptive enough to judge the group, but too obtuse to speculate on why he is at the dinner table; he is content to rest in the "stupid costliness of the food," and "the showy dullness of the talk, in the freedom of speech which never arrived at wit and the freedom of act which never made for romance" (p. 216).

Selden again witnesses a significant moment in Lily's destruction. When Bertha Dorset publicly casts Lily from the Dorset circle, Selden admires how "the faint disdain" of Lily's smile "seemed to lift her high above her antagonist's reach" (p. 218), but he does little to help Lily. Selden now judges Lily as society does, for his reason "obstinately harped

on the proverbial relation between smoke and fire'' (p. 219), and he feels
that Lily must have been guilty of something to deserve this treatment.

The pace of Lily's downfall accelerates. Lily loses her aunt's money and
moves from the Brys to the Gormers to the dubious world of Norma
Hatch, forever pursued by the Furies, Gus Trenor and Bertha Dorset.
Selden remains distant, appearing only as the voice of society to chide Lily
about her association with Norma Hatch. Selden feels a sense of relief as
he returns to the conventional view of Lily, and he is no longer even her
friend. When Selden comes to warn Lily about Norma Hatch, Lily is ''on
the alert for the note of personal sympathy,'' but instead Selden greets her
with an ''attitude of sober impartiality'' (p. 281). Hurt and proud, she
ignores his advice and thus stays with Norma too long to salvage her own
reputation.

But as the distance between Selden and Lily widens and she no longer
has his constant criticism to deal with, Lily develops her own moral
strength. Lily had once told Selden that ''a girl who has no one to think
for her is obliged to think for herself'' (p. 67), and in her isolation Lily
shows a new moral strength. She refuses to marry either Rosedale or
George Dorset, because to do so would involve making use of Bertha
Dorset's letters to Selden. And, ironically, in Selden's presence, when he
is embarrassed by her misery and openness, Lily performs her noblest act:
she burns those letters, which are the key to her social rehabilitation.

Lily's fall is a learning process for her in many ways. Separated from
her society, she begins to judge it more harshly. When Selden lectures
Lily on her ''false position'' at the Hatch establishment, she counters
with ''I suppose . . . that by a false position you mean outside of what we
call society; but you must remember that I had been excluded from those
sacred precincts long before I met Mrs. Hatch. As far as I can see, there is
very little difference in being inside or out, and I remember your once
telling me that it was only those inside who take the difference seriously''
(pp. 280-81). Lily's remarks are both a judgment on her former set and on
Selden's need to be a part of it.

When Lily resorts to working in a milliner's, she is surrounded by the
working girls whom she had once imagined to have nothing but ''admiration for [the] brilliance'' (p. 122) of her former world. Now that Lily is
''behind the social tapestry'' (p. 276), she can see ''the fragmentary and
distorted image of the world she had lived in reflected in the mirror of the
working-girls' minds.'' What surprises her is the blend of ''insatiable
curiosity and contemptuous freedom with which she and her kind were
discussed in this underworld of tailors who lived on their vanity and self-
indulgence'' (p. 285).

One of the poor herself now, Lily's values begin to change. Lily's
mother had raised her to believe that ''if people lived like pigs it was from

choice, and through lack of any proper standard of conduct'' (p. 30), and she had mentally equated wealth with elegance, beauty, and goodness, while poverty, the ''dinginess'' she abhorred, seemed somehow morally repulsive. But when Lily becomes poor herself, the equations are broken, because her most moral decisions occur in an atmosphere of squalor. And, finally, just before Lily's death, she is presented with a picture of beauty that has nothing to do with wealth.

Early in the novel, when Lily had accused herself of being ''the lowest of the low,'' she had asked Gerty Farish, ''There are bad girls in your slums. Tell me — do they ever pick themselves up?'' (p. 165). The answer to Lily's question is the scene with Nettie Struther, which reveals a drama of redemption achieved through another's love and trust. Nettie, who had once been helped by Lily's charitable donations, tells a story of seduction, abandonment, sickness, and then rescue by a man who loved her. Explaining her feelings when her lover proposed, Nettie says,

> At first I thought I couldn't [marry him], because we'd been brought up together, and I knew he knew about me. But after a while I began to see that that made it easier. I never could have told another man, and I'd never have married without telling; but if George cared for me enough to have me as I was, I didn't see why I shouldn't begin over again — and I did. (p. 315)

As Cynthia Griffin Wolff notes, Nettie's story provides an ironic contrast to Selden's faithlessness.[14] But the scene provides more than that. Lily's last human contact before her death is an intimate connection to a poor girl, and the meeting gives Lily ''a surprised sense of human fellowship'' (p. 316). While Lily's physical environment has narrowed from the open vistas of Bellemont to a stuffy room in a boarding house, her capacity for understanding of self and others has widened so that she can appreciate and learn from this moment with a girl from the slums. Now, as Geoffrey Walton says, able to see ''nearly everything that her creator sees,''[15] Lily can compare her early life to the life Nettie leads and decide that

> it was indeed miserable to be poor. ... But there was something more miserable still ... the sense of being swept like a stray uprooted growth down the heedless current of the years. ... All the men and women she knew were like atoms whirling away from each other in some wild centrifugal dance; her first glimpse of the continuity of life had come to her that evening in Nettie Struther's kitchen. (P. 319)

The episode provides one of Lily's final insights,[16] but it does not change her fate. Holding Nettie's baby, Lily is thrilled by ''a sense of warmth and returning life,'' and the child becomes symbolic of Lily's own potential rebirth. But the weight of the child on her lap increases;

"penetrating her with a strange sense of weakness" (p. 316). For Lily is not strong enough to begin her life again alone, and there is no lover who will take her as she is. She performs one more good action by paying her debt to Trenor, and then dies, intentionally or accidentally, of an overdose of chloral.

It is left to Selden to learn the final "lesson" of the book. Too late, he rushes to Lily, having finally "found the word he meant to say to her" (p. 324). But when Selden is left alone with the dead woman and begins to go through her few possessions, he again suffers a loss of faith. Discovering a letter to Trenor, he feels himself "flung back on all the ugly uncertainties from which he thought he had cast loose forever" (p. 327). Not until he realizes that Lily had carefully saved a note he had written her after the tableaux does Selden link the "real" Lily he had perceived that evening to the Lily "still there" on the bed, "close to him, yet invisible and inaccessible" (p. 326), and face his own complicity in her destruction. He is forced to acknowledge "the cowardice which had driven him from her at the very moment of attainment" (p. 328).[17]

Selden's last thoughts of Lily Bart are, at least in part, an attempt to justify his own actions. He comforts himself with the thought that

at least he *had* loved her — had been willing to stake his future on his faith in her — and if the moment had been fated to pass from them before they could seize it, he now saw that, for both, it had been saved whole out of the ruin of their lives. (P. 329)

Considering Selden's capacity for self-deception and cowardice, it is not likely that he will salvage much from the ruin of his life, but whatever he saves will be due to Lily Bart. Selden's involvement with Lily has taught him some unpleasant truths about himself. In a grotesque short story, "After Holbein," Wharton creates a macabre character named Anson Warley, an old, obsessive diner-out who eventually dies because he braves a blizzard in a senile search for a dinner party. Anson Warley begins much like Selden, splitting his time between his books and his little flat and his social engagements, but in time he is overcome by the need to "warm the shivering soul within him at all the passing bonfires of success."[18] Warley represents what Selden might one day become, if he does not learn from his encounters with Lily Bart.

Aside from Selden's sermons and Lily's insights, *The House of Mirth* is filled with other social criticism. What happens to Lily Bart is a comment not only on her own weakness, but on the society she lived in. Discussing *The House of Mirth*, Edith Wharton said that one problem she faced in writing the novel was the problem of injecting human significance into the story of "irresponsible pleasure-seekers." She solved this problem by concluding that "a frivolous society can acquire dramatic significance only through what its frivolity destroys. Its tragic implication lies in its power of debasing people and ideas."[19] Thus Lily Bart's experiences illuminate not only her own flaws but the quality of the world she desperately wants to be a part of.

By injecting an outsider, someone who does not possess the necessary qualifications for membership in this society of "irresponsible pleasure-seekers," Wharton can achieve two goals at once. She can tell the story of the moral growth of that outsider and she can reveal the moral bankruptcy of the people who reject Lily Bart. Similarly, the intruder herself functions in two ways: to awaken, as much as possible, the man she loves to the nature of the world he lives in, and, on a larger scale, to expose the cruelty and emptiness of that world to the reader. Lily can widen the perceptions of Selden only so far; his vision remains a limited one, but by the end of the novel Lily's experiences have awakened the reader to all that is corrupt in the domain of the rich.

The world of New York society, whether it be the old New York of the Van Alstynes and Pennistons or the "invader's" world of Rosedale and the Sam Gormers, is one in which money is the supreme good. Diana Trilling says that "*The House of Mirth* is always and passionately a money story. Money rules where God, love, charity or even force of character or distinction of personality might once have ruled."[20] Having no money, Lily cannot long survive in this world.

All of Lily's conflicts, even those which on the surface seem to involve love or jealousy, are money conflicts at heart. When Judy Trenor "cuts" Lily, it is not because she is fiercely possessive about Gus Trenor's love, but because she needs Gus Trenor's money and Lily threatens the bank account. Lily herself understands this: "If she [Judy] was careless of his affections she was plainly jealous of his pocket; and in that fact Lily read the explanation of her rebuff" (p. 229).

Similarly, Bertha Dorset becomes Lily's implacable enemy, not because she loves her husband and fears the loss of his love, but because "she doesn't want to lose her hold on him on account of the money" (p. 44). And when society has to choose between Bertha's tale of Lily's misbehavior in Monte Carlo and the truth, Lily knows what the choice will be.

> What is truth? Where a woman is concerned, it's the story that's easiest to believe. In this case, it's a great deal easier to believe Bertha Dorset's story than mine, because she has a big house and an opera box, and it's convenient to be on good terms with her. (P. 226)

If "Bertha Dorset's social credit was based on an impregnable bank-account" (p. 261), so is nearly everyone else's. Lily is still potentially acceptable to society when it looks as if she will inherit the Penniston estate, but when she is virtually cut out of her aunt's will, her old New York relations cut her out of their lives. And Rosedale, the climber, rapidly moves into the highest reaches of society because his financial success is "placing Wall Street under obligations which only Fifth Avenue could repay" (p. 240).

Given such a world, the women in it, who do not produce wealth, become commodities on sale. As Judith H. Montgomery says, "marriage has become a public market in this novel."[21] As commodities, they must be, in Thorstein Veblen's words, "useless and expensive . . . valuable as evidence of [their husbands'] pecuniary strength."[22] Thus Lily is "fashioned to adorn and delight," and when no one wants her around as an ornament any longer she is an object "as helpless out of its narrow range as the sea-anemone torn from the rock" (p. 301).

Not only are the supposedly romantic alliances in the novel truly based on monetary considerations, but they are talked about as business deals. Rosedale has a certain appeal when he makes his proposal of marriage to Lily an honest picture of what others euphemize: "I'm just giving you a plain business statement of the consequences" (p. 177), and Judy Trenor also rules out love as a motive for marriage. Discussing the fact that everyone knows that Lily has been setting a trap for Percy Gryce, she says, "we could none of us imagine your putting up with him for a moment unless you meant to marry him!" (p. 75).

The women in the novel then, "on sale" as objects, are in perpetual competition with one another for the best marital deal. This makes every woman of Lily's set a potential enemy of every other, and, in fact, Lily achieves a kind of intimacy with only three women in the novel, all to some degree outsiders. She is close only to Gerty Farish, "a parasite in the moral order . . . content to look through the window at the banquet spread for her friends" (p. 149); to Carry Fisher, who acuteness enables her to "lay a safe and pleasant course through a world of antagonistic forces," but whose real sympathies lie with "the unlucky, the unpopular, the unsuccessful" (p. 250); and to the slum girl, Nettie Struther.

The women of society all compete for one prize: a new role as consumer of their husband's wealth. As vicarious consumers of their husbands' money, they, in Veblen's words, can serve to enhance "the pecuniary repute of the master for whose behoof the consumption takes place."[23] Rosedale wants to marry Lily because, he explains, "I want my wife to make all the other women feel small. I'd never grudge a dollar that was spent on that . . . what I want is a woman who'll hold her head higher the more diamonds I put on it" (p. 176). And Lily can see that her appeal for Percy Gryce rests on her capacity to be a superb, vicarious consumer-ornament: "she determined to be to him what his Americana had hitherto been: the one possession in which he took sufficient pride to spend money on it'' (p. 49).

Having achieved a new financial status through a wealthy marriage, the woman of Lily's world thus attains a new moral license, and *The House of Mirth* therefore criticizes not only the traditional double standard of morality but another double standard as well, one that creates one rule for single women and another for married ones.[24] Bertha Dorset, secure in the protection of her husband's money, can thus indulge in affairs with Selden and Ned Silverton, but Lily's cousin disapproves of Lily's indiscretion and advises, ''When a girl's as good-looking as that she'd better marry, then no questions are asked'' (p. 157).

Such a materialistic world might still possess aesthetic value if it also uses money to create enough depth of elegance, beauty, and intelligence to give it distinction. But this is not the case of the society led by the Van Osburghs and Trenors. As Lily descends from the social heights she discovers that each new, lower level is a kind of imitation of the one above, casting an unflattering light on the upper reaches of New York. For there is, indeed, very little difference between the social insiders and the social aspirants, and what difference there is, is not entirely in the insiders' favor. Lily, reduced to moving in the Gormer circle, has a chance to evaluate this group:

> The Gormer milieu represented a social out-skirt which Lily had always fastidiously avoided; but it struck her, now that she was in it, as only a flamboyant copy of her own world. . . . The people about her were doing the same things as the Trenors, the Van Osburghs and the Dorsets: the difference lay in a hundred shades of aspect and manner, from the pattern of the men's waistcoats to the inflexion of the women's voices. Everything was pitched in a higher key, and there was more of everything: more noise, more colour, more champagne, more familiarity — but also greater good-nature, less rivalry, and a fresher capacity for enjoyment. (P. 234)

The Gormer set, and each set below it, becomes a parody of its superior, blending all the groups and blurring any distinctions. When Lily becomes social secretary to the much-divorced Norma Hatch, she is surprised to see members of her own set frequent this world, but this is just more evidence of how all the groups are essentially the same in their attitudes and pleasures.

Lily Bart's redemption is predicated on her exclusion from the mercenary New York society, and as she sheds its false values she must discover new ones to put in their place. Even while Lily moves in society, she possesses certain good qualities that endanger her status. She has a tendency to laugh at society's small hypocrisies and to disregard its trivial restrictions and dictates, even at the expense of her own reputation. Her habit of maneuvering herself to the brink of a wealthy marriage and then of sabotaging her own plans indicates at least an unconscious rebellion against her own predetermined role as object. Yet, paradoxically, the fact that she sees herself as born to be dependent on someone else's goodwill and financial support makes Lily extremely sensitive to the needs and feelings of others.

At first this sensitivity is merely one tool with which Lily keeps her social place; she can anticipate how to please her hostess or how to flatter a potential suitor, and her capacity to gauge other's responses to herself does not imply any real concern for people. She is simply probing to protect herself. But the farther Lily falls, the more this capacity to know what others feel grows, until it develops into an ability to feel what others feel. Expelled from a place where all the men and women were like "atoms whirling away from each other" (p. 319), she begins to make human connections based not on mutual manipulation but on a recognition that other people suffer as she has suffered. Lily's contact with people outside of her set widens her moral perspective. Lily never becomes another Gerty Farish, who has "that sharpening of the moral vision which makes all human suffering so near and insistent that the other aspects of life fade into remoteness" (p. 151), but she does grow. The Lily who snubs a miserable charwoman at the beginning of the novel and considers getting her fired for insolence is not the same character who holds Nettie's baby on her lap. There is no dramatic conversion of Lily in the novel, from socialite to little sister of the poor, but there is a steady character development.

And the fact that Lily can only achieve this steady moral growth, can only attain true humanity outside of the Trenor-Dorset world, says a great deal about that "frivolous society." Lily begins the novel already an outsider because the seeds of decency keep preventing her from committing the requisite sins. But virtue can grow in Lily only when she is away from the world of wealth, for inside it decency and compassion and humanity are only impediments to getting what one wants; they are signs of weakness and vulnerability. Because the New York world punishes Lily for her innate goodness, it is exposed as more than merely frivolous and shallow. The fate of the intruder shows rich New York to be vicious and cruel, a place where success can be attained only at the expense of one's soul.

One basic reason for Lily's social fall and moral climb, then, is the fact that she is not vicious enough to survive in a debased world. Discussing whether Lily could win a battle with Bertha Dorset, Lily's friend tells her, "Everyone knows that you're a thousand times handsomer and cleverer than Bertha, but then you're not nasty. And for always getting what she wants in the long run, commend me to a nasty woman" (p. 44). Edith

Wharton gives the reader a very nasty woman indeed in the character of Undine Spragg, the heroine of *The Custom of the Country*, who often (but not always) gets what she wants. Edmund Wilson calls Undine "the prototype in fiction of the 'gold-digger,'" of the international cocktail bitch,"[25] but she is much more than this. She is a success in the same materialistic world in which Lily Bart fails. Undine must deal with the same elements that destroy Lily: a society that revolves around money, that makes women ornaments and enemies of one another, and that dehumanizes its members. By exploiting each of these elements and using them to her best advantage, Undine climbs to the top of the social world. She is the outsider who becomes the insider and at the same time the moral opposite of Lily Bart.

Lily is raised in and formed by the same world as Undine, but she never quite fits into it. Undine, on the other hand, is the "monstrously perfect result of the system"[26] that dominates this society. She is totally fitted to a world in which "all the romantic values are reversed" (p. 207). "Where does the real life of most Americans lie?" Charles Bowen, an observer of Undine, asks, and his answer to his own question describes "the custom of the country":

> in some woman's drawing-room or in their offices? The answer's obvious, isn't it? The emotional centre of gravity's not the same in the two hemispheres. In the effete societies it's love, in our new one it's business. In America the real "crime passionel" is a "big-steal" — there's more excitement in wrecking railways than homes. (P. 207)

And given this kind of world, Undine, as Blake Nevius says, "holds all the cards."[27] Because business is the only passionate experience left, Undine brings the excitement of the business deal into the drawing room. She makes herself into a valuable commodity to be traded in marriage. Undine, comments Elizabeth Ammons, has "her own stock exchange . . . in which she herself is the stock exchanged."[28]

Not only can Undine make herself into an object, but she can also deal in other human beings: she will trade custody of her child, for example, for an appropriate sum of money. She does not seek human contact or emotion from others, because she sees others only in terms of their usefulness to herself. Thus, faced with the same potential enmity of the other women on the market that Lily faces, Undine knows enough not to form friendships but to make alliances. She makes a trade, for example, with her Apex companion Indiana Rolliver: Indiana will set up a meeting with Peter Van Degen, Undine's prey, in return for Undine's promise to get Indiana into society and to keep her hands off her husband. Such a deal works for the mutual benefit of both women and has nothing to do with friendship.

One particular aspect of Undine's inability to feel for others is a valuable asset in her upward climb. This asset is her lack of sexuality.[29] For Undine, despite the fact that she acquires a lover and three husbands, is never diverted from her path by the lure of physical attraction. "A cool spirit seemed to watch over and regulate her sensations, and leave her capable of measuring the intensity of those she provoked" (p. 294). Undine can use her sexual attractiveness as another weapon in the battle to become an insider, calculating its effect on those who have no corresponding effect on her.

But it is Undine's adaptability, her capacity to become whatever the occasion demands, that makes her a success. *The Custom of the Country* chronicles, among other things, Undine's education, as each set she invades teaches Undine new manners and forms, and "one of the guiding principles" of her career, learned early, is "It's better to watch than to ask questions" (p. 65). The observant Undine has a " chameleon-like' nature"[30] and can become a copy of whatever superficial qualities her setting requires. Unlike Lily Bart, who, often to her detriment, remains essentially herself, Undine becomes, as Wolff says, "the perfectly commercial item, able to simulate anything the purchaser desires."[31]

All Undine's talents seek the reward that Charles Bowen describes, the "money and motors and clothes" that the American woman receives as "the big bribe she's paid for keeping out of some man's way" (p. 208). It is the reward that Undine has been brought up to expect: her father, a preoccupied businessman, has raised her to know nothing about how money is made but to know everything about how to spend it quickly. As a young girl, Undine grew absentminded when her father alluded to business: "that was man's province, and what did men go 'down-town' for but to bring back the spoils to their women?" (p. 44). What Undine wants is a man who, like her father, will provide her with unlimited funds, money to make her the supreme consumer-ornament in a lavish setting.

But there are two other things that Undine wants as well: "passionately and persistently" she desires "two things which she believed should subsist together in any well-ordered life: amusement and respectability" (p. 354). In the quest for these three things, money to spend, amusement, and respectability, the conflicts of the novel develop.

Undine's conflicts with the men who are expected to make her into a respectable consumer arise not because they do not share the same goals, but because they interpret them differently; they have definitions of amusement and respectability that vary from Undine's. In fact, the irony and the satire in this novel arise not from the contrast between Undine's shallow aims and the nobler ones of her husbands, but from the similarity of their ambitions. All the men in Undine's life — Ralph Marvell, Van Degen, de Chelles, Moffatt — want money, pleasure, and status; all share

Undine's values. And in the revelation of the similarities between these men, each from a different class, and Undine, lies a good deal of the social criticism of the novel. Unlike *The House of Mirth, The Custom of the Country* has no one male character whose movement contrasts with that of the heroine; instead, four men, whose worlds Undine invades, are the objects of Wharton's scorn.

One image associated with Undine throughout the novel is the image of light — bright, harsh, glaring light. In her opera box, under the blaze of the chandelier, Undine becomes "the core of that vast illumination, the sentient throbbing surface which gathered all the shafts of light into a centre" (p. 60). For Undine "no radiance was too strong" (p. 105), and even in her plainest dress and least vivid hat Undine is conscious of "blazing out" (p. 107) from the scene. As Undine travels through the various classes she brings that glaring radiance with her, and casts a hard light on realities carefully evaded by the members of each group.[32]

Undine's first triumph, her marriage to the "Aborigine," Ralph Marvell, raises the question: why does this son of old New York marry the girl from Apex? Undine is supposed to be beautiful, it is true, but Wharton undercuts this presumed beauty with such descriptions as this one of Undine expressing animation in society: "twisting this way and that, fanning, fidgeting, twitching at her draperies ..." (p. 22). Her beauty is described as "vivid" and "crude," with "black brows ... reddish-tawny hair, and the pure red and white of her complexion ..." (p. 21). What is there in this garish picture to attract an over-refined young man?

Certainly it is not Undine's ability as a conversationalist, for at the first dinner Ralph takes her to, Undine revives the talk

> by recalling that she had seen Sarah Burnhard in a play she called "Leg-long," and another which she pronounced "Fade"; but even this did not carry them far, as she had forgotten what both plays were about and had found the actress a good deal older than she expected. (P. 38)

What, then, is the attraction? The appeal Undine has for Ralph is the appeal to his egotism. For just as Lawrence Selden envisions his role as that of rescuer of Lily Bart, taking her "beyond" the corruption of society, so Ralph feels that his "mission," the " 'call' for which his life had obscurely waited," is "to save her [Undine] from Van Degen and Van Degenism" (p. 80). He will save her from the Invaders, and will form her supposedly virginal young mind according to the Dagonet-Marvell philosophy.[33]

While Selden has his retreat into the exclusive "republic of the spirit," Ralph, as a child, had once found a secret cave and never shared it with his friends because there were things about it they could not be expected to understand. The sense of secret superiority has followed Ralph into adulthood. "And so with his inner world. Though so coloured by outer impressions, it wove a secret curtain about him, and he came and went in it with the same joy of furtive possession. One day, of course, some one would discover it and reign there with him" (p. 76). But Undine will not like living in a secret cave. To marry Undine is to live in her world, to join the Invaders. And whether Ralph at first wishes to face this or not, he has already sold himself to an Invader.

Ralph has been raised to live " 'like a gentleman' — that is, with a tranquil disdain for more money-getting," and "a passive openness to the finer sensations" (p. 75), and his income is small. He has a certain contempt for "the daughters of his own race" who sell themselves to the Invaders, as his cousin Clare did, and for the transaction by which the female Invaders "bought their husbands as they bought an opera-box" (p. 78). Yet, when he marries Undine he does not see himself as a part of this transaction. Instead, Ralph is "loftily careless" (p. 120) of the question of how to support himself and Undine. But he does allow his grandfather, Urban Dagonet, to negotiate a marriage settlement with Abner Spragg, who thinks he is getting "a son-in-law who expected to be pensioned like a Grand Army veteran" (p. 125). Whether he knows it or not, Ralph has been bought.[34]

His marriage almost immediately begins to fall apart over questions of amusement. For Ralph's idea of a honeymoon is to be alone with Undine in obscure parts of Italy, where initially he is happy, reflecting on "four months of beauty, changeful, inexhaustible, weaving itself about him in shapes of softness and strength; and beside him, hand in hand with him, embodying that spirit of shifting magic, the radiant creature through whose eyes he saw it" (p. 139). However, Undine's air of "shifting magic" is really one of impatience and restlessness, for wandering through the Italian woods is not her idea of a good time. As Elizabeth Ammons comments, Undine "married in order to be displayed, not educated and hidden away."[35] It does not take long for Undine to make her discontent known to Ralph, who suffers his first moment of disillusion when he realizes that "a crowd was what she wanted . . . she was sick to death of being alone with him" (p. 146). He begins to realize that Undine's mind, which he had perceived as so open to the finer sensations, is "as destitute of beauty and mystery as the prairie schoolhouse in which she had been educated" (p. 147), but Ralph distorts even these new perceptions of his wife to fit his preconceived image of her, for he decides merely to learn to "adapt himself to the narrow compass of her experience," for "the task of opening new windows in her mind was inspiring enough to give him infinite patience; and he would not yet own to himself that her pliancy and variety were imitative rather than spontaneous'' (pp. 147-48).

What Ralph really needs in order to deal with Undine and survive is strength, not a paternalistic ''patience.'' And this is indicated by the fact that Undine wins the first round of the marital battles: the couple abandon their isolation for the crush of the rich in St. Moritz and Paris. There a movement that is to characterize their marriage begins, as Undine moves farther and farther into the Invader camp of Van Degen and questionable types like the Baroness Adelschein, and Ralph tries to caution his wife about the loss of reputation she might suffer from such a move. The battle now is over each partner's definition of respectability, with Ralph again attempting the role of educator and upholding old New York principles, warning Undine, ''you know nothing of the society you're in; of its antecedents, its rules, its conventions; and it's my affair to look after you, and warn you when you're on the wrong track'' (pp. 161-62). There is a certain hypocrisy in Ralph's cautions about the dangers of indiscriminate socializing, for he himself had once mingled with the Baroness Adelschein and her set ''in his unmarried days'' (p. 159). But whether Ralph lives by a double standard matters very little, since Undine refuses to live by his standard at all.

The real battle, even on the honeymoon, is over money. For journeys, whether to unfashionable Italy or fashionable St. Moritz, cost money, and the Marvells have been spending a great deal of it. Ralph, who had once admired what he felt was Undine's lack of concern about money, soon learns that ''a disregard for money may imply blind confidence that it will somehow be provided. If Undine, like the lilies of the field, took no care, it was not because her wants were few but because she assumed that care would be taken for her'' (p. 149). Actually, this attitude that dismays Ralph is pretty much the same as his own when he married Undine, but he is beginning to realize that *he* must be the one to satisfy her appetite for cash. Ralph is now faced with the fact that he must fulfill the role that ''the custom of the country'' decrees for him: he must become a good provider.

Yet somehow Ralph still believes that bills will be paid by someone else, preferably not of his family. In St. Moritz, when the couple are low on funds, Undine asks Ralph, ''Couldn't your people do something — help us out just this once, I mean?'' Since the Spraggs have made a lifelong commitment to ''helping out'' Ralph, this hardly seems an audacious request, yet Ralph's reaction to it is extreme. ''He flushed to the forehead: it seemed inconceivable that she should make such a suggestion'' (p. 165). This incident hardly puts Ralph in a favorable light, and, subtly, is one more proof of his having ''sold out,'' because payment is expected to come only from the Spragg side of the family.

The conflicts of the honeymoon foreshadow the conflicts that characterize Undine's entire married life with Ralph. Ralph had expected his bride to enhance only the limited precincts of his home and a few select places where the new Undine he had formed would shine, but Undine prefers the studio of Claude Walsingham Popple and the company of Peter Van Degen to such domestic pleasures as a family birthday party for her little boy. Undine quickly learns the mistake she made in marrying Ralph; she has won respectability but it suffocates her, and she prefers to trade a degree of respectability for more exciting pleasures. She discovers that "she had given herself to the exclusive and the dowdy when the future belonged to the showy and the promiscuous" (p. 193), and the limited audience that the Marvell group can provide is simply not large enough for a display of Undine's charms. Undine married Ralph to gain entry into a set that she now finds he wants to keep her from. As she asked herself earlier, "What was the use of being beautiful and attracting attention if one were perpetually doomed to relapse again into the obscure mass of the uninvited?" (p. 50).

But the major conflict remains the money conflict. Ralph goes into business to make money for Undine, but he is ineffectual in his efforts to pay her ever-increasing bills. The very attempt to enter the world of Wall Street has its corrupting influences on Ralph; he first considers channeling his literary talents into the creation of a potboiler that will bring in a great deal of money, but Ralph is essentially a dilettante. Finally, desperate for money to placate Undine, Ralph involves himself in a shady real estate deal with Elmer Moffatt, whom he begins to admire. "It had been stimulating to work with Moffatt, and to study at close range the large powerful instrument of his intelligence" (p. 262), Ralph thinks, concealing from himself the fact that he and Moffatt are doing something not quite honest.

Even Ralph's corruptibility does not make him a successful entrepreneur. Undine, vexed by lack of funds, moves farther and farther away from Ralph into the Invader circle, while Ralph reacts in a way characteristic of the Wharton hero. Faced by a woman he can neither control nor fully understand, Ralph, like Selden, retreats into the safety of his familiar old world,[36] in this novel a retreat symbolized by Ralph's return to the family home, to his boyhood bedroom where he first dreamed his dreams of molding the impressionable Undine. And while Undine tells her troubles to Peter Van Degen, Ralph shares his secret cave of thoughts with Van Degen's wife Clare, another Aborigine who sold out. He has finally given up on the wife who is different from his expectations of her and who puzzles him, and returned to his own kind, for he and Clare "were of the same blood and had the same traditions" (p. 215).

And yet, after Undine has divorced Ralph and moved on in search of a bigger bankroll, Ralph must accept some unsettling truths. Back in his own room at Washington Square, everything seems on a much smaller scale than he had remembered, and Ralph asks himself, "Had the Dagonet boundaries really narrowed, or had the breach in the walls of his own life let in a wider vision?" (p. 305). Undine has caused this breach and thus caused this vision, but it is her last attack on Ralph, the game of extortion over custody of their child, that fully breaks down the walls of his sanctuary. For then Ralph must acknowledge that it was his own distaste for the vulgar transactions of divorce, a distaste and avoidance born of his old New York background, that is losing him custody of his son:

> Ralph's whole body throbbed with rage against the influences that had reduced him to such weakness. Then, gradually, he saw that the weakness was innate in him. He had been eloquent enough, in his free youth, against the conventions of his class; yet when the moment came to show his contempt for them they had mysteriously mastered him, deflecting his course like some hidden hereditary failing. As he looked back, it seemed as though even his great disaster had been conventionalized and sentimentalized by this inherited attitude: that the thoughts he had thought about it were only those of generations of Dagonets, and that there had been nothing real and his own in his life but the foolish passion he had been trying so hard to think out of existence. (P. 437)

Ralph has been dealing, with Undine, with the prime weakness of his class, the weakness of evasion. Confronted by the only "real" thing in his life, Undine, he has been defeated because he has chosen to deal with her from the safety of his own illusions, illusions about her and about himself. And yet Undine's reality is inescapable, for she reflects the real evil, the materialism and compromise, hidden under the polite veneer of old New York. In choosing Undine, Ralph chose the worst of his world and himself, and Undine has drawn what little poison there is in Ralph's nature to the surface. Once Ralph sees Undine as she really is, he sees what he took for his mate, and "he felt himself miserably diminished by the smallness of what had filled *his* world" (p. 449; emphasis added).[37] Unable to live with his new vision of himself, Ralph chooses instead to die.

Having destroyed one man, Undine now moves on, briefly, to another, one who would seem an ideal mate for her. Peter Van Degen is described in extremely unflattering terms; he has a "grotesque saurian head, with eye-lids as thick as lips and lips as thick as ear-lobes" (p. 49), and his face is also "the face of a covetous bullying boy, with a large appetite for primitive satisfactions and a sturdy belief in his intrinsic right to them" (p. 228). But it is, of course, not Van Degen's appearance that attracts Undine to him; it is his enormous wealth and his attitudes. For Van Degen personifies the very worst of the Invader class, its ignorance, its infantile satisfactions, its utter materialism. As such, he appears ideal for Undine, who approvingly "felt the strength of Van Degen's contempt for everything he did not understand or could not buy: that was the only kind of 'exclusiveness' that impressed her" (p. 192).

So Peter Van Degen becomes the next object of Undine's desire, and she works hard to manipulate him into a proposal of marriage. But even Van Degen becomes frightened by Undine's inhuman qualities. He discovers that Undine had refused to return to her critically ill husband, preferring instead to remain in Europe with Peter. And the realization of what this action of Undine's could mean to him "came over him gradually. One day when he was not feeling too well he thought to himself: 'Would she act like that to *me* as I was dying?' " (p. 360), and that ends Peter's affection for Undine.

But the shock of this discovery of Peter's is only the ostensible reason for his leaving Undine. Another reason Peter runs from Undine is that she threatens his respectability. Marriage to Undine would necessitate her divorce, his divorce, and an ensuing period of social ostracism. And while Van Degen enjoys being notorious, he enjoys his notoriety only when it stays within the framework of his social set. Van Degen runs from Undine, then, in the direction characteristic of the Wharton male, back to the safety of Clare, the tradition-bound old New Yorker. As Undine learns from the experience, she failed to trap Peter because she had not sufficiently calculated "the strength of the social considerations that restrained him" (p. 433).

Having failed to detach Van Degen from his background of convention, Undine moves on to her next victim, Count Raymond de Chelles. One of Undine's first reactions to Raymond is to note that "it was odd how he reminded her of Ralph" (p. 480), and the conflicts of this new marriage will be very much like those of her previous one. The seeds of the conflict can be seen in Raymond's first encounter with Undine, at the Nouveau Luxe hotel, a place where an international crowd of pleasure-seekers meets. When Raymond happens upon his friend Charles Bowen in this setting, Bowen is surprised that the upright nobleman would mix in such a group. Raymond explains that he likes the Nouveau Luxe because it is " 'such a refreshing change from our institutions — which are, nevertheless, the necessary foundations of society. But just as one may have an infinite admiration for one's wife, and yet occasionally —' he waved a light hand toward the spectacle" (p. 274). Raymond is a representative of the old seeking amusement in the new, as a married man may occasionally seek variety in an extramarital fling. The irony, of course, is that the man who is married to French tradition here meets a woman whom he would like to make his mistress, and he winds up making his "diversion" his wife.

For while Raymond might consider Undine as a mistress, she is hardly a potential wife for a French aristocrat. She has, it is true, learned to moderate her writhings and preenings, and her beauty has been somewhat subdued since her pre-Ralph days, but she has been divorced in a highly publicized manner and has been openly involved with the married Van Degen. Raymond's fatal mistake is to turn what could have been a temporary enjoyment into a permanent tie. Why, then, does he do so?

One motive that cannot be ignored is that Undine has learned not to trade sex for anything but the best bargain: "her demeanor to Chelles was that of the incorruptible but fearless American woman who cannot even conceive of love outside of marriage" (p. 404), and this pose keeps Chelles frustrated but interested. And it also infuriates Raymond's rigid family, who are afraid of Undine's "spoiling his [Raymond's] other chances" (p. 410). And in that phrase, in the attitude that marriage is a chance to make a good deal, lies one reason for Raymond's marriage to Undine. For like Ralph, Raymond de Chelles can be bought. The divorced Undine, living on whatever her parents can send her, is not a suitable bride for Chelles. But the widowed Undine, trustee of the considerable estate that Ralph (through dealing with Moffatt) left to his son, is in another category altogether. The Chelles family soon discovers in the widow "the moral and financial merits necessary to justify their change of front" (p. 483).

Once again like Ralph, Raymond attempts to form his bride into the kind of ornament he desires. He tries to initiate her into the ways of the family business, which, as Elmer Moffatt shrewdly says, is "ancestors" (p. 574), and to make her a more intelligent conversationalist. What Raymond wants to make of Undine is not an independent thinker, but rather one whose *bons mots* will reflect well on his choice of partner. She will fit better into society if her patter is more informed, for, as another Invader married to nobility tells Undine, "a woman has got to be something more than good-looking to have a chance to be intimate with them [the French aristocrats]: she's got to know what's being said about things" (p. 541). This is a type of ornament that Undine finds it difficult to be, and her reaction is merely to work harder on her looks: "she prolonged her hours at the dress-maker's and gave up the rest of the day to the scientific cultivation of her beauty" (p. 542).

The fact that Undine is empty-headed, bored, and incautious about her friends is not, however, what destroys this marriage. Again money is the real problem. Raymond, unlike Ralph, is a careful and dedicated businessman, maintaining and developing the family estates. He expects Undine to share his concern for the family property and to accept his frequent economizing. Undine, who has been taught only to spend money and to expect to receive large amounts of it as her natural right, simply thinks that Raymond is not fulfilling his part of the marital bargain, for "it was impossible for Undine to understand a social organization which did not regard the indulging of woman as its first purpose'' (p. 543). Once again Undine merely concludes that she has married a poor provider. Bored, trapped, and frustrated when Raymond finally refuses to pay her debts, Undine retaliates in the only way she knows how — by spending more money. She becomes obsessed with decorating herself — ''her dresses were more than ever her chief preoccupation'' (p. 502), and ''she scanned the fashion-papers for new scents and powders, and experimented in facial bandaging, electric massage and other processes of renovation'' (p. 521).

Confronted by this woman who has proved both a trial and disappointment to him, Raymond de Chelles makes the expected move — backward. Charles Bowen, seeing Chelles at the Nouveau Luxe, had predicted that he ''was the kind of man who would inevitably 'revert' when he married'' (p. 276), and the more Undine troubles him, the more Raymond withdraws into his family traditions and sanctions, making Undine again an outsider in his world. Undine senses her loss of power over Raymond, for whenever she sees him after an absence she has ''a curious sense of his coming back from unknown distances and not belonging to her or to any state of things she understood'' (p. 497). She has ceased to exist for Raymond; in one particular argument ''he looked at her as though the place where she stood were empty'' (p. 527).

This is a terrible punishment for Undine, who can define herself only through other people's eyes. And there is a certain amount of sympathy for Undine in this part of the novel, not only because Raymond ignores her, but because of the particularly cold and imprisoning nature of the trap Undine has married into. For Undine's passage through this aristocratic French milieu has illuminated its baser aspects.

Because the reader never sees Chelle's point of view, it is difficult to gauge exactly what, if anything, Raymond learns from his relationship with Undine. But the contrast of the American outsider and the French insider reveals not only the errors of American attitudes but the hypocrisies of French ways and their resemblances to certain American attitudes. Chief among the similarities of the two groups is the mercenary nature of their supposed romances. The marriage of Raymond and Undine is one of mutual exploitation, for Chelles expects to profit by it financially, as his brother Hubert does when he marries another American heiress, aptly named Miss Looty Arlington.

Whatever money is gained by these marriages, it is certainly not spent in enlivening the gloom of the family chateau, which supplies the boundaries of the narrow, suffocating world Undine has married into. If, as Elizabeth Ammons comments, Raymond is but a ''nightmarish exaggeration'' of Ralph Marvell,[38] there is also a ''nightmare quality,'' as Geoffrey Walton says,[39] to the detailed descriptions of St. Desert, which is an even narrower and more repressive environment than Washington Square. And Chelle's genteel surveillance of Undine, with its veiled threats and quiet edicts, has its sinister side.

There is considerable hypocrisy in this restrictive world, for while Undine is carefully limited in her social life and acquaintances, others do as they please. Bored by Undine, Raymond seeks amusement elsewhere, enacting the scenario he had joked about at the Nouveau Luxe. And this is not just one more example of the double standard, for Raymond's cousin, the Princess Estradina, frequently shocks Undine with her tales of sentimental adventure. It is the Princess, with her frank, careless amorality, who represents a side of the Chelles family they would prefer to keep hidden.

There is not only a measure of hypocrisy in Chelle's actions, but a certain spurious quality to the man himself. The "lean, fatigued and finished" (p. 275) Count seems something of a *poseur*, for, just as Undine played the role of virtuous American during their courtship, so Raymond took the part of ardent suitor, and Undine seemed to sense that he was acting. Raymond's devotion to her before marriage "gave Undine the thrilling sense of breathing the very air of French fiction" (p. 404), and Undine does not easily lapse into fantasy without some stimulus. The sense of an innate phoniness continues. When the Chelles marriage is nearly over, Raymond delivers an empassioned tirade, accusing Undine of being like all other boorish Americans: "You come among us speaking our language and not knowing what we mean; wanting the things we want and not knowing why we want them; aping our weaknesses, exaggerating our follies, ignoring all we care about —" (p. 543), and this long and angry speech seems to come straight from Chelles's wounded, outraged core. However, the impact of it is somewhat distorted by the description of Chelles's face as he delivers it; he has "the look of an extremely distinguished actor in a fine part" (p. 546). Like Ralph Marvell, Raymond de Chelles likes to assume noble and superior attitudes, but in fact, he and his world are most vulnerable to the attacks of an intruder like Undine, who can imitate and exaggerate his weaknesses until they become apparent to all.

It is most fitting that Undine, having traveled so far through the worlds of old New York, parvenue society, and Faubourg France, should wind up back at Apex — with Elmer Moffatt. Her marriage to Moffatt brings her full circle, back to her double, her twin; back, in a sense, to herself. For the ubiquitous Moffatt, who, like Selden, has been moving in and out of the heroine's life and been present at all her periods of crisis, is an ideal mate for her. Her first husband and (presumably) her last, Moffatt has the power to arouse what little sexuality exists in Undine, to "set her blood beating with curiosity" (p. 353). When Undine is most frustrated by her life in the chateau, Moffatt enters her life again, and she feels "the instinctive yearning of her nature to be one with his" (p. 568).

Moffatt is in many ways Undine's double, and the attraction Undine feels to him suggests a passion for herself. "Here was someone who spoke her language, who knew her meanings, who understood instinctively all the deep-seated wants for which her acquired vocabulary had no terms" (p. 536); he "used life exactly as she would have used it in his place" (p. 565). To marry Moffatt is to reinforce her own beliefs and desires.

What moves Undine to a near-passion for Moffatt is, of course, his wealth, and thus his power to make Undine the supreme consumer. Gary Lindberg describes the marriage of the two as the union of "endless erratic desire . . . with boundless means for gratification."[40] For the out-cast from Apex has become a billionaire, "the greatest American collector — he buys only the best" (p. 530), and "under the circle of baldness on top of that carefully brushed head lay the solution of every monetary problem that could beset the soul of man" (p. 459). At last Undine has found a good provider.

And she has found a strong man, capable of controlling her. The sinuous, eternally twisting Undine has given herself to a man who handles his affairs "like a snake-charmer spinning the deadly reptiles about his head" (p. 563), and Moffatt will not find it hard to handle the female serpent in the same way. Having no illusions to protect, proud of his open materialism, Moffatt is not threatened by Undine.

On the surface, then, it appears to be the perfect match, but the two in-truders from the Midwest are not identical twins.[41] Moffatt, in his climb upward, has acquired a taste for and a sensitivity to beauty that Undine will never comprehend: "the things he looked at moved him in a way she could not understand" (p. 563), and although she herself is a most beautiful object in his collection, she cannot appreciate the other pieces he acquires.

Similarly, Moffatt falls short of Undine's expectations. His endless wealth can provide her with endless amusement, but Moffatt can never give her enough respectability. Even his money cannot make her an ambassadress, and Undine is repelled by her husband's "loudness and redness, his misplaced joviality, his familiarity with the servants, his alter-nating swagger and ceremony with her friends" (p. 591). Moffatt has bought Undine a certain status in society, and she needs his money to maintain that position, but because "Moffatt did not fit into the picture" (p. 591) himself, her position will never be so high or so secure as she desires. And thus Undine, who had begun her career wanting "*every-thing!*" (p. 96), is left eternally wanting more.

The tone of *The Custom of the Country* is bitterly satirical, and no example of human folly is safe from Wharton's scorn. As Cynthia Griffin

Wolff comments, there is "no moral center within the world of the novel";[42] in fact, no one character possesses or, like Lily Bart, gradually acquires, a set of admirable, positive qualities. Instead, the reader's revulsion at the evil qualities of this world forces him to construct the needed, but missing, moral structure himself. The strongest reactions to Undine, for example, occur when she is most inhuman, when she most blatantly violates the sanctity of another's feelings, and thus this world is revealed as particularly lacking humanity. Undine's actions, like those of the other climbers, Indiana Frusk and Mabel Lipscomb, are an outgrowth of the system that perceives the world in commercial terms. Wolff notes that

> the women all seem more hideously disfigured than their male counterparts in the money game. After all, the women sell directly; and the flesh that they deal in is, — by "custom of the country" — always in the first instance their own. Having been dehumanized, they act with inhuman indifference to the feelings of others.[43]

Lacking any inner sense of self, the women of this world cannot respect the selfhood of another.

Undine's victims, as has been demonstrated, receive their own share of criticism. For they too play by the rules of the "money game." "One cannot feel sorry for Undine Spragg's victims," explains Elizabeth Monroe, "because they barter everything in life for a beautiful but hard and graceless woman."[44] In choosing Undine, in welcoming her into their world, they debase the values they supposedly live by, and demean themselves. When Undine Spragg intrudes into the lives of conventional males she does not, like Lily Bart, bring the promise of a finer, more intensely lived life. Other Wharton intruders — Lily Bart, Fulvia Vivaldi, Ellen Olenska — remain outsiders because of their essential difference from the world they confront and their refusal to remake themselves to meet society's standards. Their struggle to retain their sense of self and their own values makes them at once superior to the society they face and a living alternative to a conformist life within it. But Undine is another kind of intruder, one who merely begins with outsider status because she has not yet learned the standards she must conform to. With her capacity to become anything the buyer wishes, Undine soon sells what little selfhood she has to become whatever her lover and his world wishes. And, in transforming herself into the perfect commodity, Undine reveals the tawdriness of her men's desires and the essential cheapness of the world they inhabit. Rather than tempt her lovers away from their society, Undine invades it, triumphs in it, and thus exposes it for what it is.

Yet, while Lily Bart and Undine Spragg have contrasting effects on society, one bringing positive values, the other illuminating hidden vice, their stories may be perceived as two halves of one picture, a composite vision of a world dedicated to the spurious and the superficial. Metaphors of place are significant in both novels. At the center of *The Custom of the Country* is the Nouveau Luxe, the glamorous European hotel that Wharton uses as a symbol of "human nature's passion for the factitious, its incorrigible habit of imitating the imitation" (p. 273). The Nouveau Luxe attracts all society, European and American, for there they can amuse themselves among their own kind. Its symbolic parallel in Lily Bart's story is the house of mirth itself, the house of the foolish and sanctuary of the artificial — from the feigned jealousy of Judy Trenor to the spurious marital fidelity of Bertha Dorset to the general hypocrisy of a world professing high moral and aesthetic standards but secretly worshiping the "big steal."

Both novels then, *The Custom of the Country* and *The House of Mirth*, are set in the same world. It is the success of the two intruders who seek acceptance within this world that makes for the major difference between the books. For Undine Spragg, the consummate imitator, is quickly embraced by the inhabitants of the Nouveau Luxe, and she thrives in an atmosphere at once glittering and empty. Her story becomes a chronicle of acquisition: of husbands, lovers, wealth, status, and of that veneer of culture and class, that "fine glaze of beauty" which her experiences give her and which conceals the "vulgar clay" of the woman beneath. Undine essentially becomes what she wants to be, amused, rich, and respectable. The story of Lily Bart, on the other hand, is a tale of ostracism and above all of loss: of suitors, of money, of social standing, of all the rewards that come to those who conform in the house of mirth. It is also a story of the gradual shedding of the layers of vanity, superficiality, and egotism that insulate Lily from the real world of suffering, caring humanity. As Undine acquires layers of mannerisms, of style, of continental or New York chic, Lily loses them, becoming more and more herself. And therein lies the paradox. For while *The Custom of the Country* may be seen as the story of Undine's gains, it is also a story of great loss, of the denial of self and humanity that is a necessary part of survival in the world of the Nouveau Luxe. And it is Lily Bart's downward journey, filled with disappointment, humiliation, and despair, that ends in a great triumph: the attainment of the "real" Lily, the formation of a genuine, human self. It is a triumph that, Wharton indicates, can never occur if one remains within the house of mirth.

These two intruders, then, with such different fates and contrasting victories, function in essentially the same way. Through their battles in a mercenary world, they expose it as a place where all relationships are at bottom financial transactions, and where great wealth is the only virtue that matters. In different ways the careers of both Undine Spragg and Lily

Bart indicate that the price of success in such a world is one's integrity, that to become an insider in this world is to become in large part a monster.

NOTES

1. *The House of Mirth* (1905: reprint ed. New York: Charles Scribner's Sons, 1933), p. 34. Citations in the text are to this edition.

2. Irving Howe comments that "the meanings of the book emerge through a series of contrasts between a fixed scale of social place and an evolving measure of moral value." "A Reading of the House of Mirth," Intro. to *The House of Mirth* (New York: Holt, Rinehart and Winston, 1962), rpt. in *Edith Wharton: A Collection of Critical Essays*, p. 121.

3. Judith H. Montgomery says that Lily learns to appreciate and extend human kindness as she falls. "The American Galatea," *College English* 32 (May 1971):897.

4. Ecclesiastes 7:34.

5. *Edith Wharton*, pp. 43-44.

6. "Afterword," *The House of Mirth* (New York: New American Library, 1964), p. 347.

7. Margaret McDowell says that by the end of the book Selden has become "enmeshed in the social values which constrict his ability to love." "Viewing the Custom of Her Country: "Edith Wharton's Feminism," p. 527.

8. *A Feast of Words*, p. 111.

9. Ibid., p. 122.

10. "Afterword," *The House of Mirth*, p. 348.

11. *The American Adam*, p. 111.

12. Ibid., p. 112.

13. Nathaniel Hawthorne, *The Scarlet Letter*, Norton Critical Edition, ed. Sculley Bradley, Richmond Croom Beatty, and E. Hudson Long (New York: W. W. Norton and Co., 1961), p. 42.

14. *A Feast of Words*, p. 132.

15. *Edith Wharton: A Critical Interpretation*, p. 61.

16. James Tuttleton cites the Nettie Struther episode as a judgment upon wealth. "Leisure, Wealth, and Luxury: Edith Wharton's Old New York," *Midwest Quarterly* 7, no. 4. (1965):351.

17. Blake Nevius compares Selden to Winterbourne of *Daisy Miller*, "betrayed by his aloofness, his hesitations, his careful discriminations." *Edith Wharton: A Study of Her Fiction*, p. 59.

18. "After Holbein," *Certain People* (1930), rpt. *The Best Short Stories of Edith Wharton*, ed. with intro. by Wayne Andrews (New York: Charles Scribners Sons, 1958), p. 164.

19. *A Backward Glance*, p. 207.

20. "*The House of Mirth* Revisited," *Edith Wharton: A Collection of Critical Essays*, p. 111. A different version of this article has appeared in *Harper's Bazaar* and this revised version has also appeared in *The American Scholar* (Winter 1962-63).

21. "The American Galatea," p. 897.

22. *The Theory of the Leisure Class. An Economic Study of Institutions* (1899; reprinted. New York: Modern Library, 1934), p. 149.

23. Ibid., p. 121.

24. Marie Bristol makes this point. "Life among the Ungentle Genteel: Edith Wharton's *The House of Mirth* Revisited," *Western Humanities Review* 16 (1962):373.

25. "Justice to Edith Wharton," *The Wound and the Bow* (New York: Oxford Univ. Press, 1947), rpt. in *Edith Wharton: A Collection of Critical Essays*, p. 24.

26. Edith Wharton, *The Custom of the Country* (1913; reprint ed. New York: Charles Scribner's Sons, 1941), p. 208. Citations in the text are to this edition.

27. *Edith Wharton: A Study of Her Fiction*, p. 149.

28. *Edith Wharton's Heroines: Studies in Aspiration and Compliance*, p. 80. Both chap. 3 of this dissertation and Ammon's article, "The Business of Marriage in Edith Wharton's *The Custom of the Country*" in *Criticism* 16 (1974): 326-38, are excellent analyses of the business motif in the novel.

29. Cynthia Griffin Wolff says that Undine "is by no means repressed in the usual sense; rather, all of the energies that might normally find sexual expression or even the expression of spontaneous affection have been channeled elsewhere, sublimated in the service of acquisition." *A Feast of Words*, p. 241.

30. Blake Nevius, *Edith Wharton: A Study of Her Fiction*, p. 150.

31. *A Feast of Words*, p. 249.

32. Margaret McDowell makes a similar point. She says that Undine, in assimilating the values of each group she enters, illuminates the weaknesses of each group as she mirrors it. *Edith Wharton*, p. 79. And Louis Auchincloss says much the same thing in commenting that Undine's success "speaks more for the weakness of the patient than for the virulence of the microbe." *Edith Wharton: A Woman in Her Time*, p. 102.

33. Elizabeth Ammons says that Ralph marries Undine to satisfy his Pygmalion impulse. *Edith Wharton's Heroines: Studies in Aspiration and Compliance*, p. 82.

34. Louis Auchincloss says that Wharton's particular insight is that "the old and new, having at heart the same materialist philosophy, were bound to be reconciled." *Edith Wharton: A Woman in Her Time*, p. 69. Elizabeth N. Monroe makes much the same point, specifically about Ralph. *The Novel and Society: A Critical Study of the Modern Novel* (Chapel Hill: Univ. of North Carolina Press, 1941), p. 130.

35. *Edith Wharton's Heroines: Studies in Aspiration and Compliance*, p. 86.

36. Geoffrey Walton notes Ralph's increasing regression into the world of old New York. *Edith Wharton: A Critical Interpretation*, p. 123.

37. Margaret McDowell says that Ralph eventually "recognizes in himself, in latent form, those qualities he most hates" in Undine. *Edith Wharton*, p. 81.

38. *Edith Wharton's Heroines: Studies in Aspirations and Compliance*, p. 87.

39. *Edith Wharton: A Critical Interpretation*, p. 124.

40. *Edith Wharton and the Novel of Manners*, p. 70.

41. Geoffrey Walton calls the marriage an "alliance of two ʿmegalomaniacs whose values and manners will never quite coincide with or complement each other." *Edith Wharton: A Critical Interpretation*, p. 124.

42. *A Feast of Words*, p. 232.

43. Ibid., p. 249.

44. *The Novel and Society: A Critical Study of the Modern Novel*, p. 115.

3

Old New York and the Valley of Childish Things: *The Age of Innocence*

In the novels discussed so far, the intruder has been seen confronting society as represented by various male and female characters, and changing, or being changed by, a significant male (or males, in Undine's case) with whom she has a romantic relationship. A different twist to the pattern of the female intruder, however, occurs in three novels by Wharton published over a span of sixteen years: *The Reef* (1912), *The Age of Innocence* (1920) and *The Children* (1928). In these novels the female intruder becomes part of a romantic triangle, in which a hero, similar to Lawrence Selden or Ralph Marvell, must choose between a conventional woman and an intruder who cannot fit into a conventional world.[1] The presence of a second major female character serves to heighten the contrast between the outsider and the world that rejects her, and the choice that the male protagonist is forced to make between the two women creates the major conflict of the novel.

The best known and perhaps most representative of these "triangle" novels is *The Age of Innocence*. Its plot was anticipated in a curious little fairy tale, "The Valley of Childish Things," published in 1896 as a parable of old New York and its attitudes:[2]

> Once upon a time a number of children lived together in the Valley of Childish Things, playing all manner of delightful games, and studying the same lesson books. But one day a little girl, one of their number, decided that it was time to see something of the world about which the lesson books had taught her; and as none of the other children cared to leave their games, she set out alone to climb the pass which led out of the valley.

"It was a hard climb," the story continues, but once out of the valley the little girl saw cities and men and "learned many useful arts, and in so doing grew to be a woman." But the world outside the valley was bleak and cold, so the woman decided to return home to work with her childhood companions instead of with strangers.

The way back was a weary, bruising one, but halfway down the woman met a man who helped her over the roughest places. As soon as he spoke, the woman recognized this man as one of her old playmates. He, too, had been out in the world and was going back to the valley, and as they returned the woman and the man spoke of their plans to work in the valley. "He had been a dull boy, and she had never taken much notice of him," but as he told her of his great plans for building bridges and cutting roads through the jungle, she thought, "Since he has grown into such a fine fellow, what splendid men and women my other playmates must have become:"

> But what was her surprise to find, on reaching the valley, that her former companions, instead of growing into men and women, had all remained little children. Most of them were playing the same old games, and the few who affected to be working were engaged in such strenuous occupations as building mudpies and sailing paper boats in basins. . . .
> At first the children seemed glad to have her back, but soon she saw that her presence interfered with their games; and when she tried to tell them of the great things that were being done on the tableland beyond the mountains, they picked up their toys and went farther down the valley to play.
> Then she turned to her fellow traveler, who was the only grown man in the valley; but he was on his knees before a dear little girl with blue eyes and a coral necklace, for whom he was making a garden out of cockleshells and bits of glass and broken flowers stuck in sand.[3]

The woman whose presence interfered with the childish games in the valley becomes, in *The Age of Innocence*, Ellen Olenska, back from Europe to disrupt New York. Her kind helper becomes Newland Archer, and the "dear little girl with blue eyes" is transformed into Ellen's foil, May Welland. But it is the children, with their mudpies and toy boats, who remain essentially untransformed, since in *The Age of Innocence* they are still children, still playing their foolish and often cruel games.

The focus of Wharton's criticism in *The Age of Innocence* is the infantile quality of the New York world. It is innocence that characterizes this society, a dangerous, destructive innocence, most apparent in the women of this world. Cynthia Griffin Wolff notes that *The Age of Innocence* is the title of a well-known portrait by Reynolds, the portrait of a little girl,[4] and the women of Wharton's novel are all, with one important exception, little girls, never permitted to grow up. From May Welland, whose face has "the vacant serenity of a young marble athlete,"[5] to May's mother, a "middle-aged image of invincible ignorance" (p. 142), the women, once pressed into the mold of "factitious purity . . . cunningly manufactured by a conspiracy of mothers and aunts and grandmothers and long-dead ancestresses" (p. 46), never change. This "artificial product" (p. 46) designed to gratify the male by allowing him to "exercise his lordly pleasure in smashing it like an image made of snow" (p. 46) is, in fact, indestructible.[6] This kind of innocence remains untouchable and untouched by experience, so that young girls, their mothers, and their grandmothers, all blend together in a kind of repellent, negative virginity. Janey Archer, the old maid, thus becomes a copy of her own, supposedly more "experienced" mother, and all become hardened into perpetual childhood. Consequently, when Archer observes Ellen Olenska, the only "noninnocent" woman he knows, at dinner with a group of aging women, the older women's "plump elderly faces" strike him as "curiously immature" (p. 63) compared to Ellen's. Married women become old maids, and the virginal wedding dress is aptly worn for years after the honeymoon.

Not merely the women remain children, however. All of New York lives in the Valley of Childish Things. In this society Archer, at a weekend house-party given by a married couple, "assisted in putting a goldfish in one visitor's bed, dressed up like a burglar in the bathroom of a nervous aunt, and saw in the small hours by joining a pillow fight" (p. 130). Living in this world, nonmember Ellen Olenska feels, "is like being taken on a holiday when one has been a good little girl and done all one's lessons" (p. 75).

The quality of their amusements is not all that makes the New Yorkers perpetual children, however. Their women and their pastimes are only symbols of the "innocence" that pervades New York, "the innocence that seals the mind against imagination and the heart against experience" (p. 145). It is the terror of the real, the fear of the truth, of the unpleasant, that keeps New York in a state of arrested development.[7] For, Wharton said, in *French Ways and Their Meaning*, "Intellectual honesty, the courage to look at things as they are, is the first test of mental maturity. Till a society ceases to be afraid of the truth, in the domain of ideas it is in leading-strings, morally and mentally."[8]

This fear of the truth and evasion of the unpleasant extends so far that people in old New York never even speak of their deepest feelings or anxieties; instead, "they all lived in a kind of hieroglyphic world, where the real thing was never said or done or even thought, but only represented by a set of arbitrary signs" (p. 45). This lack of frank, open communication locks each person into the loneliness of his own fearful self, unable to find solace in sharing fear or pain with another. Every person is doubly trapped: by the paralysis of the refusal to grow up, and by the alienation of the hieroglyphic world.

In fact, images of entrapment, of suffocation, of a kind of death-in-life, pervade the novel. On his round of betrothal visits, for example, Archer is left with "the feeling that he had been shown off like a wild animal cunningly trapped'' (p. 69), and after his marriage, Archer, alone with May in the drawing room, rushes to open a window, crying, ''The room is stifling: I want a little air.'' When May warns him that he'll ''catch his death,'' Archer must suppress his reply: ''But I've caught it already. I *am* dead — I've been dead for months and months'' (p. 295).

But it is not only the main characters, who suffer most obviously, who are described as trapped. All those who do not grow and who hide from reality are similarly imprisoned. The social leader of old New York, that somewhat pathetic aristocrat, Mrs. van der Luyden, is described as having been ''rather gruesomely preserved in the airless atmosphere of a perfectly irreproachable existence, as bodies caught in glaciers keep for years a rosy life-in-death'' (p. 53), and a happy summer archery contest at the Beaufort estate in Newport becomes a picture of ''children playing in a graveyard'' (p. 207), linking the image of death to the atmosphere of eternal childhood.

This picture of New York in the 1870s, with its retreat from the real and consequent imprisonment of the self, becomes clear only when New York is threatened by an outsider, someone who is not of its own kind. The intrusion of Ellen Olenska, who is a very unpleasant reality to old New York, exposes New York as a fortress of evasion. Ellen, who has been out in the real world, who has ''had to look at the Gorgon'' (p. 288),[9] frightens and disturbs New York society, and *The Age of Innocence* is the story of how society deals with her.

Caught in the middle of the battle between Ellen and New York is Newland Archer, who at the beginning of the novel is firmly on the side of his society. His is the sole point of view of the novel, although it is one that Wharton distances herself from by irony and supplements with authorial comment.[10] Archer is one of the most likable of Wharton's heroes because, although he begins as a complacent member of society, he grows and learns a great deal from the outsider, Ellen. As Wolff says, ''Ellen is the catalyst that forces Newland's self-confrontation'';[11] she makes him see his world as it is, and also makes him see beyond it. Archer himself tells Ellen that she is ''opening my eyes to things I'd looked at so long that I'd ceased to see them'' (p. 75), and as the book progresses Archer himself becomes more sympathetic as his perceptions widen.

But while Ellen is an attractive alternative to Archer's way of seeing, she is also a frightening one. For the very mention of Ellen's name threatens to make all Archer's ''carefully built-up world ... tumble about him like a house of cards'' (p. 189), and Archer has certain allegiances to that world.[12] Chief among them is May Welland, the conventional virginal girl Archer is to marry. And if Ellen fascinates and attracts Archer, she also disturbs him. Ellen represents freedom to Archer, but freedom is risky. May, in contrast, may be dull and predic-

table, but her world is a safe one. Torn between the security and mono-
tony of life with May and the stimulation and danger of life with Ellen,
Archer is forced to make choices. His choices and their consequences are
the story of the novel as Archer moves from one side of the battle to the
other.

The novel begins with the juxtaposition of the two women and the
worlds they represent. As it opens, Archer, a rather pompous and self-
satisfied young man, has just declared his allegiance to the conventional
world by proposing marriage to May Welland.

Now, arriving fashionably late at the opera, he gazes across the room at
May, "a young girl in white with eyes ecstatically fixed on the stage
lovers" (p. 5), and he draws "a breath of satisfied vanity" (p. 6) as he
watches her blush and finger the lilies-of-the-valley he sent her. He
realizes that she does not understand the seduction scene being played
onstage, and he feels "a thrill of possessorship in which pride in his own
masculine initiation was mingled with a tender reverence for her abysmal
purity" (p. 7). Like Ralph Marvell dreaming of Undine Spragg, Archer
has visions of forming and educating his innocent bride. "We'll read
Faust together . . . by the Italian lakes . . ." (p. 7).

Archer has ambitious plans for the development of his fiancée into the
woman he wants her to be.

> He did not in the least wish the future Mrs. Newland Archer to be a
> simpleton. He meant her (thanks to his enlightening companionship) to
> develop a social tact and readiness of wit enabling her to hold her own with
> the most popular married women of the "younger set," in which it was the
> recognized custom to attract masculine homage while playfully discouraging
> it. If he had probed to the bottom of his vanity (as he sometimes nearly did) he
> would have found there the wish that his wife should be as worldly-wise and
> as eager to please as the married lady whose charms had held his fancy
> through two mildly agitated years; without, of course, any hint of the frailty
> which had so nearly marred that unhappy being's life, and had disarranged
> his own plans for a whole winter. (P. 7)

The irony in this passage creates an impression of a fatuous, egotistical
young man who blithely adheres to the double standard. The irony
continues, for how "this miracle of fire and ice was to be created" (p. 7)
and sustained in a harsh world Archer has never really considered, but he
is happy to hold this view without analyzing it, "since he knew it was that
of all the carefully-brushed, white-waistcoated, button-hole-flowered
gentlemen who succeeded each other into the club box" (p. 7). Although
Archer is superior to these gentlemen in intellectual and artistic matters,
and although he has probably "read more, thought more, and even seen a
good deal more of the world" than his friends in the opera box, he accepts

"their doctrine on all the issues called moral. He instinctively felt that in this respect it would be troublesome — and also rather bad form — to strike out for himself" (p. 8).

Into this fantasy of marital bliss, and into May Welland's box, comes May's cousin, Ellen Olenska. Ellen, who had been born to New York parents, had, even as a childhood playmate of Archer's, been "a fearless and familiar little thing, who asked disconcerting questions" and "made precocious comments and possessed outlandish arts" (p. 60). From childhood she went from bad to worse, for her parents, continental wanderers, died and left her in the care of her eccentric aunt Medora, another wanderer who let her wear black satin at her debut and who had married her off to "an immensely rich Polish nobleman of legendary fame" (p. 60). When Ellen appears in May's box she is a runaway from that marriage, trailing rumors of an affair with her husband's secretary behind her.

Archer's first reaction to Ellen's appearance is one of annoyance, for it seems distasteful for the Welland-Mingott clan to drag the family scandal out in public, and "few things seemed to Newland Archer more awful than an offense against 'Taste,' that far-off divinity," and though "Madame Olenska's pale and serious face appealed to his fancy as suited to the occasion and to the unhappy situation . . . the way her dress (which had no tucker) sloped away from her thin shoulders shocked and troubled him. He hated to think of May Welland's being exposed to the influence of a young woman so careless of the dictates of Taste" (p. 15).

His next reaction is a gallant one, for he immediately goes to May, to proclaim his engagement to her at once, "to see her through whatever difficulties her cousin's anomalous situation might involve her in" (p. 17). While the gesture may be a noble one, it is also the first of many times that Archer, somehow threatened or troubled by Ellen, runs to the safety of May.

This time, however, joining May in her box means encountering Ellen. Ellen's first words to Archer are a comment, however unintentional, on the more childish qualities of New York, for Ellen, remembering Archer as a child, says, "We *did* use to play together, didn't we? . . . Ah, how this brings it all back to me — I see everybody here in knickerbockers and pantalettes" (p. 18). Archer is irritated by such a flippant remark about "the august tribunal before which, at that very moment, her case was being tried" (p. 18). Archer cannot yet see anything that Ellen sees; "Taste" and "Form" are his gods, and Archer, like everyone else he knows, would much prefer not to have to deal with Ellen Olenska. He is happy that May avoids discussion of Ellen and her problems at the Beaufort ball after the opera; "nothing about his betrothed pleased him more than her resolute determination to carry to its utmost limit that ritual of ignoring the "unpleasant' in which they had both been brought up'' (p. 26). Archer's initial reaction to Ellen is to thank heaven "that he was a New Yorker, and about to ally himself with one of his own kind'' (p. 32).

And yet, almost in spite of himself, Archer soon begins to assume the role of Ellen's defender. Irritated to the breaking point by the malicious gossip that his mother and sister exchange eagerly with Sillerton Jackson, the prissy, self-appointed guardian of New York's moral standards, Archer supports Ellen's public appearances. While the others admit that the Count might be a brute who made Ellen's life miserable, they would prefer not to be reminded of her problems or even of her existence by her presence at the opera or at balls. But Archer thinks differently: "Madame Olenska has had an unhappy life: that doesn't make her an outcast'' (p. 41). And yet, of course, given New York's terror of the unpleasant, it does. Archer comes nearer to seeing his set for what it is when he cries out, "I'm sick of the hypocrisy that would bury alive a woman of her age if her husband prefers to live with harlots. . . . Women ought to be free — as free as we are'' (p. 42).

Newland Archer is forgiven for making such heretical pronouncements because his hearers assume that he is merely doing his duty in making the best of an awkward situation in his fiancée's family. But when he is alone that night, his impulsive words about May's cousin lead Archer to a reevaluation of May herself and of his anticipated marriage, for the "case of the Countess Olenska had stirred up old settled convictions and set them drifting dangerously through his mind'' (p. 43). As Archer stares at May's photograph,

> that terrifying product of the social system he belonged to, the young girl who knew nothing and expected everything, looked back at him like a stranger through May Welland's features. . . . What could he and she really know of each other, since it was his duty, as a "decent'' fellow, to conceal his past from her, and hers, as a marriageable girl, to have no past to conceal? (Pp. 43-44)

The innocence that had seemed such an asset in his bride only a few days before now seems likely to ruin Archer's dreams, since the "passionate and tender comradeship'' he had envisioned that his marriage would be "presupposed, on her part, the experience, the versatility, the freedom of judgment, which she had been carefully trained not to possess'' (p. 44).

Archer for the first time imagines his marriage to May becoming "what most of the other marriages about him were: a dull association of material and social interests held together by ignorance on the one side and hypocrisy on the other'' (pp. 44-45); he sees himself transformed into another Lawrence Lefferts, a man who "had formed a wife to completely to his own convenience that, in the most conspicuous moments of his frequent love affairs with other men's wives, she went about in smiling unconsciousness" (p. 45). Only a few days earlier Archer had considered Ellen Olenska's arrival in New York only in terms of "the faint shadow that her unhappy past seemed to shed on their [his and May's] radiant future" (p. 29); now a discussion of that unhappy woman has prompted Archer to reexamine that future itself.

The novel continues with a series of contrasts between Ellen and May. On a visit to Ellen's little house in an unfashionable neighborhood in the city, Archer is entranced by "the faded shadowy charm of a room unlike any room he had known," by "some small slender tables of dark wood, a delicate little Greek bronze on the chimney-piece, and a stretch of red damask nailed on the discolored wallpaper behind a couple of Italian-looking pictures in old frames" (p. 70). To Archer the "atmosphere of the room was so different from any he had ever breathed that self-consciousness vanished in the sense of adventure" (p. 71), and the contrast between this room and the drawing-room that May will select for their married life comes to his mind. For May "submitted cheerfully to the purple satin and yellow tuftings of the Welland drawing room, to its sham buhl tables and gilt vitrines. . . . He saw no reason to suppose that she would want anything different in her own house" (p. 72).

Ironically, just as Archer is noticing how different Ellen is from all those around her, Ellen is pleading with him, "I want to do what you all do — I want to feel cared for and safe!" (p. 75). But Ellen will be a diffi-cult person to assimilate into New York, because she cannot be made to take its pretensions seriously. Archer lectures her on the great favor that the van der Luydens did her in giving her a dinner, explaining that they are "the most powerful influence in New York society. Unfortunately — owing to her health — they receive very seldom." Ellen looks at him thoughtfully and replies, "Isn't that perhaps the reason? . . . For their great influence; that they make themselves so rare." It is Archer who blushes, struck by the "penetration of the remark. At a stroke she had pricked the van der Luydens and they collapsed. He laughed, and sacrificed them" (pp. 75-76). From disapproval of Ellen's flippant attitudes, Archer has moved to complicity in her irreverence.[13]

Ellen also speaks openly of the evasion of New York. When Archer advises her to follow the counsel of the older women of their set, because they "like and admire you — they want to help you," Ellen cries, "Oh, I know — I know! But on condition that they don't hear anything un-pleasant. . . . Does no one want to know the truth here, Mr. Archer? The real loneliness is living among all these kind people who only ask one to pretend!" (p. 78). Ellen cries; Archer soothes her and then feels guilty. To relieve that feeling of guilt he hurries to the florist to send May the expected daily box of lilies-of-the-valley, which New York lovers send their intendeds. Once at the florist, he sees a beautiful bouquet of golden roses and "his first impulse was to send them to May instead of the lilies. But they didn't look like her — there was something too rich, too strong, in their fiery beauty" (p. 80). The white, fragile flowers are sent to May, and the sensual roses are also sent — to Ellen. It seems that Archer has found a woman with the "experience, the versatility, the freedom of judgment" (p. 44) necessary for a happy married life, but the woman is not the one he is engaged to.

Archer may laugh at Ellen's lack of respect for New York, and he may be charmed by her house and conversation, but he is still not fully committed to her. He continues to find much to disapprove of in her, and he is puzzled by a woman he cannot easily categorize. There is her association with the "shoe polish queen," Mrs. Lemuel Struthers, for example, which Archer cannot understand. Mrs. Struthers, a parvenue with a scandalous past who is trying to entice New York society to her Sunday evening cultural entertainments, is shunned by Archer's group, yet Ellen visits her, taking along an English duke. Rather than accepting this action as an example of true aristocrats secure enough to cross social boundaries, Archer is again irritated by Ellen's flagrant violation of the New York code.

What bothers him even more than Ellen's association with Mrs. Struthers is her friendship with Julius Beaufort, a banker whom New York accepts with reservations. Beautfort, who came from nowhere and made a lot of money, has a reputation for dubious financial deals as well as for having a mistress whom he makes little attempt to hide. And if, Archer reasons, Beaufort is interested in Ellen Olenska, he could have "only one object in view in his pursuit of pretty women" (p. 137). Archer's reaction to Beaufort's interest in Ellen is a mixture of jealousy and doubt about Ellen: like Ralph Marvell, who wants to rescue Undine from Van Degen, Archer wants to make Ellen "see Beaufort as he really was, with all he represented — and abhor it" (p. 78), and yet he fears that Ellen will not abhor Beaufort because she already knows what he is. The question tormenting Archer is that of Ellen's innocence. Accustomed to the simplicity of a world with two kinds of women in it, "the women one loved and respected and those one enjoyed — and pitied" (p. 97), Archer does not know which group Ellen belongs to. Did she have an affair with her husband's secretary, the man who helped her run away? It is important to Archer to find the answer to this question, for, although he has begun to deplore the innocence of May, he is uneasy dealing with a woman who may possibly be more experienced.

Archer's obsession with that supposed affair leads him to counsel Ellen

against divorcing her husband.[14] At first Archer is reluctant to agree to
the request of Ellen's family that he advise her about the consequences of
a divorce action. His sympathies are with Ellen, especially when his senior
law partner urges him to prevent the divorce, for to Archer, Mr.
Letterblair "suddenly became the Pharisaic voice of a society wholly
absorbed in barricading itself against the unpleasant" (p. 99). Archer has
even begun to see Ellen's case as an individual one, one not easily judged
by New York's rigid dicta. He is almost ready to condone Ellen's having
had an affair, for, he thinks, in the "complicated old European communi-
ties," there could be a situation "in which a woman naturally sensitive
and aloof would yet, from the force of circumstances, from sheer defense-
lessness and loneliness, be drawn into a tie inexcusable by conventional
standards" (p. 97).

But Archer is still so firmly entrenched in New York ways of thinking
that at heart he wants to hear Ellen protest her innocence before he allies
himself with her in her struggle for freedom. He tests her, in the
"hieroglyphic" manner of New York, by outlining the dangers of
divorce for a woman who is not pure: "if the woman, however injured,
however irreproachable, has appearances in the least degree against her,
has exposed herself by an unconventional alliance to — to offensive
insinuations" (p. 111), the divorce will destroy her reputation. What
Archer wants to hear, at this point, is Ellen defending herself and
proclaiming her conduct irreproachable. When Ellen does not do this,
Archer reverts to the empty words the family expected him to say; he
asks her to sacrifice her freedom for the good of her family, for "what
should you gain that would compensate for the possibility — the certainty
— of a lot of beastly talk?" (p. 111). His lack of faith in Ellen has led him
to join the ranks of New York in their attempt to cover up any potential
scandal.

But Archer's attitude to Ellen remains ambivalent. Immediately after
he counsels her to give up her desire for a divorce, he regrets his words.
Once again the problem is that Ellen defies stereotyping; it is not easy to
"place" her and deal with her accordingly.[15] Ned Winsett, a poor writer
whom Archer knows, tells him of Ellen's kindness to his little boy, who
fell down in the street, and Archer is moved, for although "any woman
would have done as much for a neighbor's child . . . it was just like Ellen
. . . to have rushed in bareheaded, carrying the boy in her arms" (p. 123).
Although it supersedes the conventions Archer lives by, the spontaneous
charity that Ellen practices appeals to him in spite of himself.

On the other hand, Archer worries about the ever-present Beaufort,
troubled by the possibility that Ellen will become his mistress. At times
Archer sees Ellen as "an exposed and pitiful figure" (p. 96) whom he will
save, and other times he feels that "she knew how to take care of herself a

good deal better than the ingenuous May imagined. She had Beaufort at her feet, Mr. van der Luyden hovering above her like a protecting deity, and any number of candidates . . . waiting their opportunity in the middle distance'' (p. 121).

Ellen's ''mysterious faculty of suggesting tragic and moving possibilities outside the daily run of experience'' (p. 115) appeals to Archer, but the very fact that he sees Ellen as ''outside the daily run of experience'' makes it inevitable that he will abandon her and choose May. For to Archer marriage to Ellen is never a real possibility. Ellen has a place in Archer's life, in the area where his books, his intellectual friends, his cultural interests reside. All these are an escape from the mediocre life of New York, but they are not an integral part of *real* life. Ellen cannot fit into Archer's world;[16] he can only imagine her as a fantasy woman, someone he could have had if circumstances had been different. In fact, Archer could make the fantasy into reality, he could break his engagement to May, but the key to Archer's nature is given in the first pages of the novel: ''thinking over a pleasure to come often gave him a subtler satisfaction than its realization'' (p. 4); the fantasy is better than the reality. Thus Archer spends an evening reading *The House of Life* and pursuing ''through those enchanted pages the vision of a woman who had the face of Ellen Olenska'' (p. 139), and only days later, when he and Ellen are closest to declaring their love, he runs away to Florida, to May, for here ''was truth, here was reality, here was the life that belonged to him'' (p. 141).

The sense of frustration that fills this novel occurs because Archer, like Selden, finally commits himself to the intruder — too late. And even then, Archer's avowal of love is made in terms that imply its futility: ''you are the woman I would have married if it had been possible for either of us'' (p. 169). Ellen's reply is ironic, for just as Lily Bart takes Selden's counsel and becomes the free and moral self that eludes him, so Ellen has heeded Archer's empty words and lived by them.[17] '' 'Possible for either of us? . . . you say that — when it's you who've made it impossible? . . . Isn't it you who made me give up divorcing — give it up because you showed me how selfish and wicked it was, how one must sacrifice one's self to preserve the dignity of marriage. . . . I did what you told me, what you proved to me that I ought to do. Oh,' she broke out with a sudden laugh, 'I've made no secret of having done it for you!' '' (p. 169).

Ellen, the intruder, embodies those values of loyalty and decency, of sacrifice of the individual for the good of others, which New York gives lip service to but does not live by. And now Ellen holds Archer to his own words, for by denying Ellen the freedom of a divorce, Archer has chosen to live by the standards of New York. Ellen holds him to the consequences of that choice.

Archer and May's wedding, which begins Book 2, is only a public enactment of the renunciation of Ellen that Archer has still, privately, to make. The rest of the novel becomes a description of the nature of the cage Archer has constructed for himself (and May), of his attempts to free himself, and of the freeing of Ellen. It is filled with criticism of New York as Archer becomes more and more aware of his lifelong imprisonment.

The images of an infantile life and of entrapment in that life multiply as the story moves forward. On his wedding day Archer is aware of how alien all that he had once respected seems to him now, for the "things that had filled his days seemed now like a nursery parody of life" (p. 182), and Archer envisions a "black abyss" yawning before him and pictures himself "sinking into it, deeper and deeper" (p. 186).

To Archer, May becomes the symbol of all that he wishes to escape. He sees her as the eternal child, incapable of growth, and on their wedding day, traveling toward what he anticipates as her sexual initiation, May seems a girl who will never become a woman:

> She was alone for the first time with her husband, but her husband was only the charming comrade of yesterday. There was no one whom she liked as much, no one whom she trusted as completely, and the culminating "lark" of the whole delightful adventure of engagement and marriage was to be off with him alone on a journey, like a grown-up person, like a "married woman," in fact. (P. 188)

Two years later Archer observes his wife at the opera, wearing her wedding dress, and he notes the hardening of May's innocence: "but for the slight languor that Archer had lately noticed in her she would have been the exact image of the girl playing with the bouquet of lilies-of-the-valley on her betrothal evening" (p. 321). Life with May has become "a perpetual tepid honeymoon, without the temperature of passion yet with all its exactions" (p. 293), and Archer naturally resents May, whom he had made "the tutelary divinity of all his old traditions and reverences" (p. 196), because he now despises those traditions. Married and firmly established in the ways of old New York, he feels buried alive: "His whole future seemed suddenly to be unrolled before him; and passing down its endless emptiness he saw the dwindling figure of a man to whom nothing was ever to happen" (p. 227).[18]

Archer struggles against the life he has chosen by turning to Ellen, whom he in some way blames for his predicament, for he tells her, "You gave me my first glimpse of a real life, and at the same moment you asked me to go on with a sham one" (p. 242). But the "real life" Archer dreams of with Ellen is still just a dream, for Archer can come up with no practical way to make it a reality. What Archer wants, he tells Ellen, is

"somehow to get away with you into a world where words like that —
[words like *mistress* and *adultery*] categories like that — won't exist.
Where we shall be simply two human beings who love each other, who
are the whole of life to each other; and nothing else on earth will matter"
(p. 290). This, of course, is only a fantasy, like Ellen or the Blessed
Damozel, and Ellen, who has seen "the Gorgon" of reality, must tell him
so: "She drew a deep sigh that ended in another laugh. 'Oh, my dear —
where is that country?'" (p. 290).

The only practical solution to the problem of the lovers, then, is the
New York way of the secret affair, and it is again Ellen, the realist, who
voices the real objections to a clandestine affair: "We're near each other
only if we stay far from each other. Then we can be ourselves. Otherwise
we're only Newland Archer, the husband of Ellen Olenska's cousin, and
Ellen Olenska, the cousin of Newland Archer's wife, trying to be happy
behind the backs of the people who trust them" (pp. 290-91). Ellen
refuses to cover up the truth of what adultery would mean; she knows
that it would transform the idealistic lovers into hypocrites of the New
York order.

Archer, then, is permanently trapped. And, ironically, his choice of
marriage to May also traps his wife in an existence of dullness and
emptiness. For although Archer had once dreamed of forming and
educating May, he finds after marriage that "it was less trouble to
conform with the tradition and treat May exactly as all his friends treated
their wives than to try to put into practice the theories with which his un-
trammeled bachelorhood had dallied" (p. 193). The tragedy is that May is
not the cardboard stereotype that Archer perceives;[19] just as Ellen Olenska
has opened his eyes to a larger world, Archer could, if he chose, do the
same for May. May has the potential for growth and change, which was
revealed to Archer even before their marriage when May offered to break
their engagement if Archer loved another: "I couldn't have my happiness
made out of a wrong — an unfairness — to somebody else. . . . what sort
of a life could we build on such foundations?" May had asked. She even
acknowledged that "when two people really love each other, I understand
that there may be situations which make it right that they should —
should go against public opinion" (p. 149). There is a potential, if weak,
rebel hidden in May, for she pleaded to Archer that she is not so
hopelessly innocent: "You mustn't think that a girl knows as little as her
parents imagine. One hears and one notices — one has one's feelings and
ideas" (p. 149). The new self that Ellen has helped to create for Archer
could be created for May, but Archer will not free her from the bonds of
New York. He is too concerned with his own situation, and thus, even
after marriage, will not make the best of what he considers a bad bargain.
Even when Archer recognizes in his wife "the same reaching toward

something beyond the usual range of her vision'' (p. 315) that he had seen in his fiancée, and remembers ''the passionate generosity latent under that incurious calm'' (p. 321), he ignores it. If he could only release his wife from her imprisonment in innocence, Archer could make her a mate to share his new world, could bring her out of her New York childhood. But ''he had long given up trying to disengage her real self from the shape into which tradition and training had moulded her'' (p. 327).

The farewell dinner for Ellen Olenska, at which the outsider is finally cast out of New York and the husband and wife left to their fate, is an inevitable but bitter scene. It is here that all the inherent viciousness in New York rises to new heights of cruelty. Although Ellen has been moving farther and farther outside of society by her own choice, although she ''had grown tired of what people called 'society' . . . had found herself, as she phrased it, too 'different,' to care for the things it cared about'' (p. 239), her attachment to Archer still makes her presence in New York a threat to the group. She must therefore be cast out, but the casting out must be done in the ''pleasant'' New York manner. As Archer sits at the table at the fine dinner, the realization of what the occasion represents is brought home to him: ''There were certain things that had to be done, and if done at all, done handsomely and thoroughly; and one of these, in the old New York code, was the tribal rally around a kinswoman about to be eliminated from the tribe'' (p. 334). He understands that all of New York assumes that he and Ellen are lovers, that for months he has been ''the center of countless silently observing eyes and patiently listening ears,'' and that ''now the whole tribe had rallied about his wife'' (p. 335) to expel the intruder.

Archer is desperate for a private word with the woman he loves, but he is carefully maneuvered away from her during the evening; he is not even permitted to see her to her carriage. All is done, of course, with smiles and a pretense of ''unalterable affection for the Countess Olenska now that her passage for Europe was engaged'' (p. 334), and Archer understands that

> it was the old New York way of taking life ''without effusion of blood''; the way of people who dreaded scandal more than disease, who placed decency above courage, and who considered that nothing was more ill-bred than ''scenes,'' except the behavior of those who gave rise to them. (P. 335)

New York has marshaled all its forces to eliminate the vulgarity in its midst, and the battle has been fought with finesse and subtlety. With Ellen finally gone for good, New York can be restored to its original state of innocence.

It is left to Archer to make a life for himself in his old world. And the final chapter of the novel, set nearly thirty years after the farewell dinner, indicates what Archer has managed to salvage from the wreckage of his existence. It is not much.[20] Due largely to his experience with Ellen Olenska, Archer has managed to face the upheavals of a changing order with a certain dignity and adaptability.[21] He has briefly gone into politics, something previously unheard of for a man of his class, and "every new movement, philanthropic, municipal, or artistic, had taken account of his opinion and wanted his name. . . . His days were full, and they were filled decently. He supposed it was all a man ought to ask" (pp. 346-47).

And yet, examining his life critically, as Ellen taught him to do, Archer realizes that "he would always be by nature a contemplative and a dilettante" (p. 346), and he knows that he has missed "the full flower of life" (p. 347). His reflections on his marriage become a kind of defense of it:

> Their long years together had shown him that it did not so much matter if marriage was a dull duty, as long as it kept the dignity of a duty: lapsing from that, it became a mere battle of ugly appetites. Looking about him, he honored his own past, and mourned for it. After all, there was good in the old ways. (P. 347)

But these "old ways" created a union that locked May into the traditional ways of thinking, in which Archer and his children engaged in a family conspiracy to keep reality from May, who was thought to be "so lacking in imagination, so incapable of growth" (p. 348) that she could not deal with change. May was thus cut off from an authentic relationship not only with Archer, but with her children as well:

> Her incapacity to recognize change made her children conceal their views from her as Archer concealed his; there had been, from the first, a joint pretense of sameness, a kind of innocent family hypocrisy, in which father and children had unconsciously collaborated. (P. 348)

One of the final ironies in the novel is Archer's realization, after May's death, that she was a person of greater depth than he thought. On her deathbed May had confided to her oldest son that she had lived the years of her marriage knowing of Archer's sacrifice, aware that Archer, for her, had given up the thing he most wanted. Of what good then was the sacrifice? It had been made, Ellen believed, to spare May. It was May's happiness that Ellen placed above her own:

> if it's not worthwhile to have given up, to have missed things, so that others may be saved from disillusionment and misery — then everything I came home for, everything that made my other life seem by contrast so bare and so poor because no one there took account of them — all these things are a sham or a dream — (P. 242)

May had kept her husband, but she had been spared little disillusionment and had become a kind of tolerated burden to her own family, a child to her own children. Considered in the light of what happens to May, the sacrifice of the lovers seems a romantic but futile one.

Yet, given Newland Archer's nature, the pattern of his life and marriage are the only course he could have taken, for during the years of his separation from Ellen she remained to him what she was from the beginning: a fantasy, beautiful to dream of but never to become real. "When he thought of Ellen Olenska, it was abstractly, serenely, as one might think of some imaginary beloved in a book or a picture: she had become the composite vision of all that he had missed" (p. 347). In essence this is what Ellen had always been to Archer; she had freed his thoughts and filled his imagination, but Ellen could never give Archer the strength to act against his New York upbringing. The final scene of the novel reinforces this picture of Archer,[22] because, widowed and with his children grown, Archer now faces no real obstacle in finally attaining his vision. Yet he prefers to keep Ellen a dream; he sits meditatively outside her apartment, thinking, "It's more real to me here than if I went up" (p. 361). Once again the anticipation of a pleasure, the fantasy, is safer and more enjoyable than the realization (and risk) of the pleasure itself.

The novel thus ends with a pair of gentle negatives: Archer's life not entirely wasted, thanks to his widening perceptions; May's marriage intact if stultifying, and with a positive new world in which, now, intruders like Fanny Beaufort are taken "joyfully for granted" (p. 352). The most satisfying final impression is that of a free Ellen Olenska, who, having been expelled from New York, has lived as an independent woman, safe from her husband, surrounded by the culture and variety of Paris. The apartment that Archer gazes at, at the end of the novel, is "many windowed . . . pleasantly balconied" (p. 360), and it seems as though the sun has just left it. The expulsion of Ellen from the suffocation of New York has released her to the light and openness of a new life.

Many critics tend to view this novel, especially the lovers' renunciation and its consequences, as at least in part a vindication of the values of old New York.[23] There are certain passages in the book that could give this impression. Ellen Olenska, for example, explains her willingness to sacrifice her own happiness for the good of May by saying, "under the dullness [of New York] there are things so fine and sensitive and delicate that even those I most cared for in my other life look cheap in comparison" (p. 241), and the statement seems an endorsement of the conventional way of life by one of the novel's most sympathetic characters. However, it must be remembered that not one fully "New York" character practices the virtues that Ellen feels she has learned from New York. Newland Archer relinquishes his own desires for the benefit of another, certainly, but he does so at the insistence of Ellen, the intruder, and when he has become something of a rebel himself. And May's capacity for generosity and tolerance is demonstrated only when she is least "innocent" and most ready to depart from conventional ways of thinking. New York society does not contain one wholly admirable person who sincerely lives by the values of loyalty, duty to family, and moral uprightness, which supposedly characterize old New York. Those who most strongly profess these values and most rigidly demand them in others are seen as malicious, like the gossip Sillerton Jackson; or hypocritical, like Lawrence Lefferts; or coldly tyrannical, like Mrs. Manson Mingott. And each of these New York types violates his own standards repeatedly — Jackson's slander is disloyal, Lefferts's infidelity threatens the family unit, and Mrs. Mingott's tyranny over her clan can hardly be termed moral.

There is only a quiet irony in Ellen's belief that New York's inner goodness has made her a better person, because the result of society's passion for avoiding the unpleasant is a world filled with hypocrisy and cruelty, devoid of intellectual development.

Representative of the hypocrisy of the New York world is Lawrence Lefferts, whose marriage Archer considered to be a typical New York one, who covers up his many affairs by pontificating about the holiness of the marriage bond. Wharton increases the reader's sympathy for Ellen and anger at old New York by placing Lefferts in certain key scenes in which Ellen is being most maligned. At the farewell dinner, for example, Archer, despite his own pain, notices that "never had Lefferts so abounded in the sentiments that adorn Christian manhood and exalt the sanctity of the home" (p. 337), and Sillerton Jackson explains, "I hear there are pressing reasons for our friend Lawrence's diatribe: — typewriter this time, I understand" (p. 337). Lefferts's adultery is tolerated by New York because it is hidden, and, unlike the activities of the more open Ellen, does not threaten to disrupt the pleasurable life. It is therefore not marital fidelity that is a value in New York, but rather the appearance of it.

Similarly, although the social tribe ostensibly "exacted a limpid and impeccable honesty" (p. 258) in business matters, it is quite willing to accept Julius Beaufort with his disreputable past, as long as his dishonesty is kept quiet, because Beaufort gives his friends a good time. The Beauforts have a ballroom where they regularly give splendid balls, and "this undoubted superiority was felt to compensate for whatever was regrettable in the Beaufort past" (p. 19). Therefore, when the rumors of Beaufort's scandalous financial failure circulate, New York hopes that they are not true, for the "disappearance of the Beauforts would leave a considerable void in their compact little circle; and those who were too ignorant or too careless to shudder at the moral catastrophe bewailed in advance the loss of the best ballroom in New York'' (p. 268).

However, when Beaufort's empire does crash, publicly and dishonorably, New York's reaction is swift: Beaufort simply ceases to exist, socially. When his wife pleads with her kinswoman, the powerful Mrs. Manson Mingott, for support and refuge, Mrs. Mingott replies, ''Honor's always been honor, and honesty honesty, in Manson Mingott's house'' (p. 272). Mrs. Mingott had, of course, known of Beaufort's dishonorable business methods since he had come to New York, but since his banking practices appeared to be in order, reality could be ignored. Mrs. Mingott now attempts to adhere to the same policy that had worked so well in the past: push reality away. She drives Regina Beaufort from her house and gives orders that no one should mention the Beauforts to her again. Even family members must be sacrificed so that New York will not have to look upon, or deal with, pain or dishonor.

As has already been discussed, Ellen Olenska is the most obvious victim of the cruelty of evasion. And yet the cruelty is ''innocent'' in a certain sense, for all the pressure applied to make Ellen return to her husband is employed without a full knowledge of what such a reconciliation would mean. Monsieur Riviere, the Count's secretary, explains to Archer that return to her husband would subject Ellen to certain ''unthinkable'' things and he is in one sense right when he says that ''if Madame Olenska's relations understood what these things were, their opposition to her returning would no doubt be as unconditional as her own'' (pp. 253-54). But their deliberate, calculated ignorance, their refusal to hear of her sufferings, makes it morally acceptable, in their eyes, to send her back to the unthinkable, and to view her case as merely one of a woman's duty to her husband.

New York fears the real then, and this fear has many consequences. One of them is the elimination from society of any intellectual or creative individuals, for such persons might introduce something new and therefore dangerous into a safe environment. Society feels a ''certain timidity'' about artists, musicians, and writers. ''They were odd, they were uncertain, they had things one didn't know about in the backgrounds of their lives and minds'' (p. 102). Society considers it bizarre that one of their own, Emerson Sillerton, ''a man who had had 'every advantage,' . . . wealth and position,'' should become an archaeologist, ''or indeed a Professor of any sort . . . live in Newport in winter, or do any of the other revolutionary things that he did'' (pp. 219-20). It is not surprising, then, that Ellen can say of New York society that ''except the other evening at Mrs. Struthers's, I've not met a single artist since I've been here'' (p. 106).

While New York observed in action seems to live by no admirable values, this is not to say that *The Age of Innocence* contains no moral positives at all. The most explicit statement of values of the novel is made by Monsieur Riviere, the man rumored to have been Ellen's lover: "it's worth everything, isn't it, to keep one's intellectual liberty, not to enslave one's powers of appreciation, one's critical independence?" A person must, he says, preserve his "moral freedom, . . . one's 'quant à soi.' . . . The air of ideas is the only air worth breathing. . . . Voyezvous, monsieur, to be able to look life in the face: that's worth living in a garret for, isn't it?" (p. 200). This statement stands in direct opposition to the attitudes and behavior of old New York, and is a code that only one character in the novel besides Riviere himself lives by. Only Ellen Olenska can fully "look life in the face," and only she escapes from New York with her identity intact.

She is the outsider whose decency and loyalty and generosity of spirit put her critics within society to shame. Her compassion encompasses a child in the street, the outcast Regina Beaufort, and the woman her lover married in place of her. Ellen's openness and honesty enable her to share her fine, free vision with an insider, and she gives him what little he is capable of taking from her. Because Ellen has faced pain and has not run from life, she is an adult, and thus it is most fitting that Ellen be cast out of New York. As a grown-up she can find no place in a world of evasion.

As in *The House of Mirth*, Edith Wharton has described a society that is inferior to the woman it rejects: the intruder is unacceptable inside this world because she is different from it, but the difference is in her favor. Ellen Olenska's conflicts with old New York contrast her vitality, her freedom of spirit, with a timid and repressive society that is so fearful of the unpleasant in life it has shut itself away from all of life. Safe inside this shelter, protected by elaborate taboos from the intrusion of the real, New York remains a sanctuary for those who will never grow up. A safe place, where nothing can happen and thus no one truly lives, old New York is the Valley of Childish Things.

NOTES

1. Cynthia Griffin Wolff links *The Reef* and *The Age of Innocence*, commenting that each contains "a man torn between two women — one the self-conscious product of 'old New York,' the other an elusive outsider," but her interpretations of the novels, particularly of *The Age of Innocence*, differ from mine. *A Feast of Words*, p. 220.

2. Wolff cites this parable as an expression of the personal conflicts Wharton was experiencing at the time she wrote it, and connects it to *The Reef*, but she does not link its story to *The Age of Innocence*. *A Feast of Words*, pp. 82-83.

3. "The Valley of Childish Things, and Other Emblems," *The Century Magazine*

52 (July 1896), rpt. in *The Collected Short Stories of Edith Wharton*, ed. and intro. R. W. B. Lewis (New York: Charles Scribner's Sons, 1968), 1:58-59. There is an interesting, parallel between Wharton's little tale and Samuel Johnson's fable *Rasselas*, with its Happy Valley where "revelry and merriment was the business of every hour, from the dawn of morning to the close of even." *The Norton Anthology of English Literature*, ed. M. H. Abrams (New York: W. W. Norton and Co., 1968), 1:1818. The journey of Johnson's young prince and his sister and the lessons learned about the illusory nature of total happiness are also similar to the experiences of the pair in *The Valley of Childish Things*.

4. Wolff, *A Feast of Words*, p. 312.

5. *The Age of Innocence* (1920; reprint ed. New York: Charles Scribner's Sons, 1970, with intro. by R. W. B. Lewis), p. 142. Citations in the text are to this edition.

6. In *French Ways and Their Meaning* (New York: D. Appleton and Company, 1919) Edith Wharton says that "it is possible to have a ruling caste of grown-up men and women only in a civilisation where the power of each sex is balanced by that of the other" (p. 113). According to this belief the creation of the "innocent" bride as a toy for the egoistic male may help to keep New York infantile.

7. Blake Nevius rightly links Wharton's criticism of this evasion of pain and responsibility in *The Age of Innocence* to her later novels, which attack the same failing of the twenties. *Edith Wharton: A Study of Her Fiction*, p. 189.

8. *French Ways and Their Meaning*, p. 58. A comment from Thorstein Veblen is also appropriate here: "The proximate tendency of the institution of the leisure class in shaping human character runs in the direction of spiritual survival and reversion. Its effect upon the temper of a community is of the nature of an arrested spiritual development." *The Theory of the Leisure Class: An Economic Study of Institutions*, p. 213.

9. Wharton uses this image for facing reality, in different variations, several times. In the introduction to *French Ways and Their Meaning*, Wharton says that the French have "gone up to the Medusa and the Sphinx with a cool eye and a penetrating question," pp. ix-x. And in the novel *A Son at the Front*, a rather trivial woman is suddenly ennobled through pain: "But she's magnificent! She's seen the Medusa!" (New York: Charles Scribner's Sons, 1923), p. 9.

10. Both Louis Auchincloss (*Edith Wharton: A Woman in Her Time*, p. 133) and Cynthia Griffin Wolff (*A Feast of Words*, p. 314) make this point.

11. Wolff, *A Feast of Words*, p. 316.

12. Irving Jacobson, in "Perception, Communication, and Growth as Correlative Themes in Edith Wharton's *The Age of Innocence*," says that the novel is about "an Outsider . . . who cannot be accepted into the Tribe . . . and an Insider . . . who cannot break out." *Agora* 2, no. 2 (1973):69.

13. "Reverence and irreverence are both needed to help the world along, and each is most needed where the other most naturally abounds." *French Ways and Their Meaning*, p. 31.

14. Geoffrey Walton says that Archer's subjection to convention comes out in his advice to Ellen to avoid divorce and his decision to stay engaged to May because he is not sure of Ellen's innocence. *Edith Wharton: A Critical Interpretation*, p. 135.

15. Cynthia Griffin Wolff says that in the earlier portions of the novel Archer drastically simplifies his notions of Ellen "so that he need not deal with the complexities of the complete person." *A Feast of Words*, p. 319.

16. "His yearning for Ellen is indescribably intense, yet for the most part it belongs to another world." Cynthia Griffin Wolff, *A Feast of Words*. Wolff also says that Wharton's earlier outlines of the novel had Archer marry Ellen, but the two are not happy together (p. 327).

17. Constance Carlson (*Heroines in Certain American Novels*, p. 107) says that Ellen "carries out the simple ethics New York professes but cannot live by."

18. Blake Nevius makes the connection between this realization and John Marcher's discovery in Henry James's "The Beast in the Jungle." *Edith Wharton: A Study of Her Fiction*, p. 187.

19. This point is made by Irving Jacobson ("Perception, Communication, and Growth as Correlative Themes in Edith Wharton's *The Age of Innocence*, p. 76); Louis O. Coxe ("What Edith Wharton Saw in Innocence," *New Republic*, 27 June, 1955, p. 16); Gary Lindberg (*Edith Wharton and the Novel of Manners*, p. 107); and Cynthia Griffin Wolff (*A Feast of Words*, p. 322).

20. Brenda Niall comments that Archer is a study of "moral timidity in an individual and in the class he represents, of wasted possibilities in private and public life." "Prufrock in Brownstone: Edith Wharton's *The Age of Innocence,*" *Southern Review: An Australian Journal of Literary Studies* 4 (1971):206.

21. Gary Lindberg says that Ellen, having released Archer from both his conventions and their mere inverse, has enabled him "to discover states of feeling he could not have anticipated," and it is this that he saves from their "doomed affair." *Edith Wharton and the Novel of Manners*, p. 84. Charles C. Doyle, in "Emblems of Innocence: Imagery Patterns in Wharton's *The Age of Innocence,*" *Xavier University Studies* 10, no. 2 (1971):25, also believes that Archer is left with a new capacity for vision.

22. Irving Jacobson says that in this last scene Archer "reinforces the refusals of his lifetime to break out of the limitations of time, place, and experience imposed upon him by an already moribund culture." "Perception, Communication, and Growth as Correlative Themes in Edith Wharton's *The Age of Innocence*," p. 81.

23. See, for example: Joseph Warren Beach, *The Twentieth Century Novel* (New York: Appleton-Century-Crofts, 1932), p. 295; Louis Auchincloss, *Edith Wharton* (Minneapolis: Univ. of Minnesota Press, 1961), p. 30, and *Edith Wharton: A Woman in Her Time*, pp. 126-28; James A. Robinson, "Psychological Determinism in *The Age of Innocence*," *Markham Review* 5(1975):4; Margaret McDowell, *Edith Wharton*, p. 92; Gary Lindberg, *Edith Wharton and the Novel of Manners*, pp. 85, 100; Blake Nevius, *Edith Wharton: A Study of Her Fiction*, pp. 22-23; R. W. B. Lewis, "Introduction," *The Age of Innocence* (New York: Charles Scribner's Sons, 1968), p. xiii; and Cynthia Griffin Wolff, *A Feast of Words*, pp. 331, 341.

Constance Carlson disagrees. *Heroines in Certain American Novels*, p. 108.

4

More Triangles of Innocence: *The Reef* and *The Children*

The Age of Innocence is not the only novel by Edith Wharton in which the theme of entrapment in an infantile world is a dominant one. The theme is equally important in two other novels, both of which are also structured around a triangular romantic conflict: *The Reef* and *The Children*. These two novels differ from *The Age of Innocence* in time period and locale, yet they share a major conflict: the struggle of the intruder both to maintain an adult sense of self in a childish society and to rescue a trapped male from that society. Less well known than *The Age of Innocence*, both *The Reef* and *The Children* echo its conern about the dangers of evading life out of fear of experiencing life's pain.

The Reef, the second "triangle" novel, has often been called the most Jamesian of Wharton's novels, perhaps because of its detailed analysis of the psychological problems of its characters and its limited social setting. Cynthia Griffin Wolff says that the main characters of the novel "are rendered with a chiaroscuro sharpness that articulates them almost as if they were specimens mounted against a backdrop,"[1] and indeed the relatives sparseness of social scenery and absence of a large cast of supporting characters like the Mingotts and van der Luydens make the novel a sharp contrast to *The Age of Innocence* or *The House of Mirth*. Most of the major conflicts of *The Reef* take placĕ in one setting, a French chateau, Givré, peopled by a very small group of characters. Givré is more than a stark background putting its inhabitants into sharper focus, however; it is a symbol of the isolated, safe world of the novel's main characters, George Darrow and Anna Leath. It is Anna's home and Darrow's refuge, and significantly, when Anna is forced out of the secure simplicity of her previous ways of thinking, she leaves Givré and travels to Paris. The novel both begins and ends with the "real" life of Paris, but the major portion of the book concerns the impact of reality on that fortress of innocence, Givré.

Once again Edith Wharton examines the life that seals itself off from experience, but in *The Reef* the focus of the criticism is somewhat narrowed. The novel analyzes in great detail the pain and misery that ensue when society establishes the false polarities of "good" and "bad" in dealing with its women.

It is Anna Leath, one of the three main characters of the novel, who has attempted to live the role of the "good" woman and who has suffered from the restrictions of the role. Brought up in the typical old New York way, Anna has been schooled in reticence, evasion, and a kind of artificial serenity that have denied her any sexuality and caused her to suffocate in a boring marriage to a dilettante. The novel chronicles, among other things, Anna's struggle to free herself from the prison of her existence, and it is unique among Wharton's works in that half of the book is from the point of view of the trapped woman herself.[2] For Anna, life at Givré was "like a walk through a carefully classified museum, where, in moments of doubt, one had only to look at the number and refer to one's catalogue,"[3] and now that Fraser Leath, her husband, has died, she is looking for love to "release her from this spell of unreality" (p. 86).

Ironically, Anna seeks this release from a man as conventional as herself, one who is also, as Margaret McDowell says, "trapped in the conventional pattern of thinking that categorizes women as either 'fallen' or 'pure.' "[4] While Anna looks to George Darrow, her youthful love, for a sexual and emotional awakening and for entry into the world outside of Givré, Darrow, who has already enjoyed the company of "bad" women, is looking to Anna for the consolations of a "good" one. Her very narrowness and her limitations make Anna appeal to Darrow, for his imagination is struck by "the quality of reticence in her beauty. She suggested a fine portrait kept down to a few tones, or a Greek vase on which the play of light is the only pattern" (p. 126). What Darrow sees in Anna is an exquisite aesthetic object that he will keep unsullied from contact with real life. Thus, although he dreams of putting "warmth in her veins and light in her eyes," of making her "a woman through and through" (p. 29), this sexual initiation will only serve to make Anna more exclusively his, even more "like a picture so hung that it can be seen only at a certain angle: an angle known to no one but its possessor" (p. 129). For Darrow, Anna will always be the limited "good" woman, and Givré a "pure sequestered shrine" (p. 146), a suitable throne for her and a refuge for him.

Given the conflicting fantasies of Anna and Darrow, there would seem to be little possibility of romance between them. And yet such a romance does evolve, because Anna, despite all her visions of a larger life, is at heart the childlike and innocent woman Darrow seeks. The early days of their love are characterized by Darrow's recurring "thrill of youthful wonder at the coincidence of their views and their experiences, at the way their minds leapt to the same point in the same instant" (p. 130). Since both Darrow and Anna live by the same safe attitudes, no disparity between their philosophies or needs separates them; what does divide them is the intrusion into their lives of Sophy Viner, a person who defies their easy categorizations.

As a free spirit and a woman neither conventionally "good" nor "bad," Sophy Viner shatters the complacency of the lovers. Her involvement in their lives introduces elements of the real world into the sanctuary of Givré and requires that the pair examine their lives, their love, and their inmost selves. Cynthia Griffin Wolff comments that "the essence of Sophy Viner eludes us," and that the novel fails because Sophy is never presented to the reader directly; rather, "Wharton attempts to fix our attention instead on the mediating terms by which Darrow and Anna Leath perceive her,"[5] but this exclusion of Sophy's point of view from the novel is not a flaw. It is an elimination designed to focus the reader's interests on the main pattern of the novel: the conflict that develops when two people who live by stereotyped ways of thought are forced into contact with a person whose behavior challenges those stereotypes.

Sophy Viner is "the reef" of the novel, the hidden obstacle that wrecks the "deep and tranquil current" (p. 233) of love that is growing between Anna and Darrow.[6] Water and sea imagery is frequently associated with the lovers' affair: Anna, planning her marriage to Darrow, feels that she is "floating on a mid-current of felicity, on a tide so bright and buoyant that she seemed to be one with the warm waves" (p. 177), and Darrow exults in Anna's gaze, which is like "a deep pool into which he could plunge and hide himself" (p. 270). But Sophy, who has made her own plunge "into the wide bright sea of life" (p. 22), is responsible for the storm that develops over the tranquil chateau. She wrecks the fairy-tale romance[7] of Anna and Darrow, creating shame and misery for Darrow, who has treated her as a "bad" woman, and horror for Anna, who has acted as if she were a "good" one.

As the novel begins, Anna and Darrow have resumed their youthful romance, which had ended rather abruptly with Anna's marriage to Fraser Leath. Darrow, looking back on their earlier courtship, cannot understand exactly why he and Anna had ever parted. But Anna remembers. What destroyed the love between the couple, and what will help to destroy it again, was Anna's repression of her deepest feelings and her overwhelming jealousy.

Anna, raised in the world of New York society, where "the unusual was regarded· as either immoral or ill-bred," and where "people with emotions were not visited" (p. 85), had been formed to be the perfect young girl, another May Welland,[8] cited by envious mothers as "a model of ladylike repression" (p. 86). Anna is not fully content in this role, but her only escape is into "the passions and sensations which formed the stuff of great poetry and memorable action," and she does not see "how the magnificent things one read about could ever have happened'' (p. 85) in a world like the one in which she lives. Anna escapes from the dullness of her world into the "world of hidden beauty" of her books, but she dimly senses that other girls, "leading outwardly the same life as herself," possess "some vital secret" (p. 86) that makes life more real to them. The secret is the knowledge of their own sexuality, a knowledge that "good" girls like Anna are not supposed to have, and the lack of which helps to destroy Anna's first romance with Darrow. For when Anna is with Darrow he wants to kiss her, but she is longing to "talk to him about books and pictures, and have him insinuate the eternal theme of their love into every subject they discussed" (p. 87).

After each such encounter with her lover, Anna "wondered how she could have been so cold, called herself a prude and an idiot, questioned if any man could really care for her," and, in short, resented what her "good girl's" training had made her. But Anna, afraid to step past the boundaries set for the young innocent, cannot break the pattern: every time Darrow reappears "her head straightened itself on her slim neck and she sped her little shaft of irony, or flew her little kites of erudition, while hot and cold waves swept over her, and the things she really wanted to say choked in her throat" (p. 87).

Only dimly aware of her own sexuality, Anna will not allow herself to use it to attract a man, for only "bad" women are supposed to do this, and thus, when she sees one of her own set doing it to Darrow, her reaction is one of fury and almost savage jealousy. At a dinner party Anna observes Darrow's conversation with Kitty Mayne, a girl of her own class who had recently shocked society by her elopement but who has since been readmitted into the fold: "Miss Summers [Anna's maiden name] perceived that she [Kitty] had somehow grown luminous, perilous, obscurely menacing to nice girls and the young men they intended eventually to accept. Suddenly, at the sight, a rage of possessorship awoke in her. She must save Darrow, assert her right to him at any price. Pride and reticence went down in a hurricane of jealousy" (p. 88).

Anna, lacking sexual appeal, grows furious at seeing another use an enticement she does not possess. Yet her feelings are ambivalent, for part of her would desperately like to imitate Kitty Mayne, to use the tactics of the "bad" girl and to reap her rewards: "It would have offended her once if he [Darrow] had looked at her like that. Now her one thought was that none but she had a right to be so looked at" (p. 88). All night she wonders, "What was she saying to him? How shall I learn to say such things?" (p. 88), but when she asks Darrow about Kitty the next day, he says only, "she's rather good fun," but "suddenly Anna saw in his eyes the look she had seen there the previous evening" (p. 89). Anna cannot understand how Darrow, who is supposed to love her for her purity, can flirt with her opposite and find satisfaction in doing so. She can only conclude that her beloved is not what she had fancied, but somehow alien to her deepest self. "She felt as if he were leagues and leagues away from her. All her hopes dissolved" (p. 89). For Anna, trapped by her own repressed desires, afraid of sex yet longing to be fearless, cannot excuse what Darrow has done. She does not understand that in her society, with its rigid categories, a man who must satisfy the needs of both spirit and flesh will rarely be faithful to a "good" woman.

When Darrow does indulge in a brief affair with Kitty Mayne, Anna retaliates by marrying the ultra-conventional Fraser Leath. After fourteen years of marriage Fraser Leath dies, and Anna reencounters Darrow in London, where their attraction to one another develops again. In the first chapter of the novel Darrow is on his way to France to ask Anna to marry him when he receives a cable from her: "Unexpected obstacle. Please don't come till thirtieth. Anna" (p. 1). As he sits at the train station at Dover, cable in hand, Darrow is angry and hurt. "She didn't want him, and had taken the shortest way to tell him so" (p. 8). His attention is then diverted by the sight of a young woman whom he seems vaguely to remember, struggling with her umbrella. He comes to her aid and the girl, who recognizes him, reintroduces herself. She is Sophy Viner, an American, something of a waif, having just left her position at Mrs. Murrett's, whom Darrow remembers as a "shrieking inescapable" woman "into whose talons he had fallen in the course of his pursuit of Lady Ulrica Crispin" (p. 14). Although Darrow remembers with distaste his episodes with the "bad" Lady Ulrica, he cannot remember Sophy, who reminds him that he used to pass her on the stairs. Sophy also explains that she was Mrs. Murrett's "reader": "I wrote notes, and made up the visiting-book, and walked the dogs, and saw bores for her" (p. 15). After a quarrel with her employer Sophy has left, "without my dinner — and without my salary. . . . And without a character!" (p. 20).

Darrow, having nothing better to do, his ego wounded and his love seemingly scorned, befriends Sophy, who seems to him to be "loveliness in distress" (p. 12), and decides to cross to Paris with her. He is drawn to Sophy's frankness and naturalness, and is both shocked and amused by her stories of the underside of the Murrett world. "It was odd" to him "to discover suddenly that the blurred tapestry of Mrs. Murrett's background had all the while been alive and full of eyes" (p. 16).

The girl who has emerged from the shadows of the Murrett world puzzles Darrow, and he is unable to place Sophy with any certainty.[9] For although Darrow "had had a fairly varied experience of feminine types."

the women he had frequented had either been pronouncedly "ladies" or they had not. Grateful to both for ministering to the more complex masculine nature, and disposed to assume that they had been evolved, if not designed, to that end, he had instinctively kept the two groups apart in his mind, avoiding that intermediate society which attempts to conciliate both theories of life. (P. 25)

Just as Archer attempts to classify Ellen, Darrow tries to label Sophy: "She might be any one of a dozen defineable types, or she might — more disconcertingly to her companion and more perilously to herself — be a shifting and uncrystallized mixture of them all" (p. 60). Darrow can only determine that Sophy is different from "the daughters of wealth" because she has an "acquaintance with the real business of living," and yet he does not feel that reality has corrupted her; rather, "her experience had made her free without hardness and self-assured without assertiveness" (p. 26).

As he watches Sophy asleep on the train, Darrow, in part because he is angry at Anna, is moved to compare the two women and to find Sophy the more appealing. When Sophy wakes, she shakes the hair out of her eyes, smiles, and then goes back to sleep, as relaxed and natural as a child. If Anna were in a similar situation, Darrow muses bitterly, the "oddness of the situation would have made sleep impossible, or, if weariness had overcome her for a moment, she would have waked with a start, wondering where she was, and how she had come there, and if her hair were tidy; and nothing short of hairpins and a glass would have restored her self-possession" (p. 27).

The open, natural manners of the working girl beside him lead Darrow to other criticisms of his intended. In a meditation similar to Newland Archer's over the photograph of his fiancée, Darrow wonders whether the "sheltered" girl's training might not make her unfit "for all subsequent contact with life."

How much nearer to it had Mrs. Leath been brought by marriage and motherhood, and the passage of fourteen years? What were all her reticences and evasions but the result of the deadening process of forming a "lady"? The freshness he had marvelled at was like the unnatural whiteness of flowers forced in the dark. (P. 28)

Anna Leath, Darrow senses, is very little different from Anna Summers. In their new romance as in the old one, "her eyes had made promises which her lips were afraid to keep. She was still afraid of life, of its ruthlessness, its danger and mystery. She was still the petted little girl who cannot be left alone in the dark" (p. 28).

In contrast there is Sophy Viner, only possibly a "lady," but most definitely a brave soul, leaving a despised position with no security and no money, to make her way alone in Paris.

But Sophy is not to be left to face Paris alone, for Darrow, moved partly by pity and partly by his attraction to her, offers Sophy a chance, "just for a few days, to have all the things you've never had" (p. 66). Sophy's grateful and trusting acceptance of the offer sets the tone of the arrangement and Darrow, perceiving that Sophy is "a child after all," determines that "all he could do — all he had ever meant to do — was to give her a child's holiday to look back to" (p. 71). Having classed Sophy as a child, Darrow thus resolves to keep the interlude with her a platonic one. And although this innocent vacation "was not like anything that had ever happened to him before, or in which he had pictured himself as likely to be involved," Darrow sees no reason to question "his fitness to deal with it" (p. 75).

Almost inevitably, Darrow does not "deal with" the situation as he had promised himself he would. He initiates an affair with Sophy for several reasons, almost all of which he hides from himself. Darrow's motives in the episode include anger at Anna for betraying his ideal of her, wounded vanity, and a genuine attraction to Sophy.

Throughout his stay in Paris, Darrow has been anxiously waiting for a letter from Anna to explain her canceling of his visit. When such a letter does not arrive Darrow feels pain, and much of the pain is caused by the fact that Anna's silence casts a shadow over his bright image of her. A fine woman such as Mrs. Leath would surely explain her conduct, Darrow reasons, but her neglecting to do so makes her less fine, and Darrow "could not bear to think of her as trivial or insincere. The thought was so intolerable that he felt a blind desire to punish someone else for the pain it caused him" (p. 54). The most available person to punish is Sophy, and the most severe punishment for her, given Darrow's attitude, is to "ruin" her, to seduce her. If the "good" woman he cares for has disappointed him by not behaving according to his high standards, then the girl with him, who may quite possibly be "bad," must pay.

There is, of course, the additional reason that Sophy is a convenient salve to Darrow's bruised ego. Starved for life and lonely, Sophy reacts to even the smallest kindness with an overwhelming gratitude and appreciation. How much more, Darrow reasons, would she respond to his affections? There is a cruel detachment in Darrow as he observes Sophy's happiness in Paris: "He had not often had the opportunity of studying the effects of a perfectly fresh impression on so responsive a temperament, and he felt a fleeting desire to make its chords vibrate for his own amusement" (p. 50). To bolster his own image of himself, then, and to lash out against his damaged image of Anna, Darrow turns to Sophy Viner. Aside from these two motives, Darrow becomes sexually involved with Sophy for another, much less complex reason. He likes her. Her naturalness is a refreshing change from the studied poise of Anna Leath. Sophy's spontaneity leads Darrow to reflect that "mankind would never have needed to invent tact if it had not first invented social complications" (p. 34). Sophy's courage in the face of a dismal future, her enormous enjoyment of even the simplest pleasures, her total lack of pretense, contrast favorably with Anna's fears, reticences, and sophisticated responses. The long-awaited letter from Anna finally does come to Darrow. But when it arrives Darrow throws it, unopened, into the fire. This action, as Geoffrey Walton remarks, suggests that the affair with Sophy "means more to Darrow than he later admits to himself."[10]

The affair is soon over, and within a few months Darrow has returned to his "good" woman. Book Two opens with Anna at Givré, awaiting the arrival of Darrow. Finally, Anna feels, she is to enter the real world. "She felt, saw, breathed the shining world as though a thin impenetrable veil had suddenly been removed from it" (p. 82). Darrow is equally happy, having found "the kind of woman with whom one would like to be seen in public" (p. 130), and having relegated Sophy to the status of "a memory which had no place in his present picture of himself" (p. 129).

This pretty picture of himself and his beloved, which Darrow so complacently cherishes, is soon destroyed by the intrusion into Givré of Sophy Viner. Unknown to Darrow, she has become the governess of Anna's daughter, and is soon to announce her engagement to Anna's stepson, Owen Leath.

In a series of subtle and complex scenes, the truth about Sophy and Darrow is gradually revealed by what Anna calls "the force of its irresistible pressure" (p. 353). Each stage in these painful revelations is used to further explore the hidden recesses of personality of the three main characters.

When Darrow learns of Sophy's engagement to a member of the Leath family, his reaction is the ignoble and hypocritical one of a man who lives by the double standard.[11] A disreputable woman like Sophy must not be permitted to taint the sacred atmosphere of Givré. Such a person must be removed. Quietly, so that his own complicity in Sophy's fall will not be exposed, Darrow tries to bribe, coax, and cajole Sophy into breaking her engagement. His final argument with Sophy is an attempt to convince her that "you'll be wretched if you marry a man you're not in love with" (p. 206).

The argument has almost more effect than Darrow could wish,[12] for Sophy, out of love for Darrow, acts with such generosity that she puts him to shame. When she is finally told of Darrow's engagement to Anna, Sophy breaks her own engagement and leaves Givré, to give her lover the happiness that will be denied her. What she will salvage out of this tangled set of circumstances, Sophy tells Darrow, is the memory of her days with him.

"I don't want to forget — to rub out. At first I imagined I did; but that was a foolish mistake. As soon as I saw you again I knew it. . . . It's not being here with you that I'm afraid of — in the sense you think. It's being here, or anywhere, with Owen!" She stood up and bent her tragic smile on him. "I want to keep you all to myself." (P. 262)

For Darrow the affair in Paris is only an unpleasant memory, because the incident "had fallen below his own standard of sentimental loyalty" (p. 152), and thus had cast an unsavory shadow on his estimate of himself. For Sophy the days with Darrow are a cherished memory, and not because she fosters any illusions about his love for her. She knows and openly admits that Darrow never loved her: "I wonder what your feeling for me was? It seems queer that I've never really known. I suppose we *don't* know much about that kind of feeling. Is it like taking a drink when you're thirsty?" (p. 262). The episode, then, is not important to Sophy because it was a fairy-tale romance, but rather because it *was* the only chance she ever had, and possibly will have, for giving her love and for receiving the kindness so lacking in her life. Sophy knew the risks she took; she understood the situation and has no regrets. As she tells Darrow:

Don't for a minute think I'm sorry! It was worth every penny it cost. My mistake was in being ashamed, just at first, of its having cost such a lot. I tried to carry it off as a joke — to talk of it to myself as an "adventure." I'd always wanted adventures, and I tried to take your attitude about it, to "play the game" and convince myself that I hand't risked any more on it than you. Then, when I met you again, I suddenly saw that I *had* risked more, but that I'd won more, too — such worlds! (P. 263)

Like Ellen Olenska in *The Age of Innocence*, it is Sophy Viner who emerges as the big "winner" in the novel, because she has taken the risks that life in the real world involve, and because she has given — given her love to Darrow without hope of reciprocation, and given up all chance of the wealthy and pleasurable life Owen Leath offers so that Darrow can be happy. The small fears, subtle withdrawals, and timid advances of Darrow and Anna are a shadowy backdrop for Sophy's glowing act of courage.[13]

Sophy's renunciation of Owen and her declaration of love have two negative effects on Darrow. Her action leaves him to face his own shallowness, for "there before him, staring him in the eyes . . . was the overwhelming fact of Sophy Viner's passion and of the act by which she had attested it" (p. 272), to reproach him forever. Darrow had made no comparable commitment, for he "hadn't spent a penny" on the affair, "which was no doubt the reason of the prodigious score it had since been rolling up" (p. 168).

The affair costs even more than Darrow expects, however, because Sophy's sudden departure from Givré tumbles the whole elaborate structure of Anna's romance like a house of cards. Humbled by Sophy's generosity, Darrow must now face the righteous anger of the "good" woman who has discovered all. Edith Wharton explores Anna's confused reactions in great detail and with considerable sympathy, but the analysis only reinforces the impression of Anna as a woman, as Walton says, "over-fastidious by nature and so molded by social training that she cannot face the realities of life."[14]

After learning the truth about Sophy and Darrow, Anna's first reaction is merely to run away from the horror of it, to block out the pain she has never been taught to deal with by dismissing Darrow. Darrow senses her motives when he tells Anna, "You're afraid. . . . You've always said you wanted, above all, to look at life, at the human problem, as it is, without fear and without hypocrisy; and it's not always a pleasant thing to look at" (p. 292). But Anna's conventional background has provided her with no way to deal with her new knowledge. "What are you?" she cried to Darrow. "What *is* she?" (p. 292). When Anna attempts to find solace in describing Sophy as a "bad" woman, Darrow, whose new admiration for Sophy has made him see things in a less simple light, discards the conventional classification. He pleads for Sophy, not himself, arguing that Sophy *is* bad "if you measure her by conventional standards," but that "she had the excuse of her loneliness, her unhappiness — of miseries and humiliations that a woman like you can't even guess. . . . She saw I was sorry for her and it touched her. . . . I ought to have seen the danger, but I didn't. There's no possible excuse for what I did" (p. 293-94). With the vision of Sophy's sacrifice still before him, Darrow becomes impatient with Anna's helplessness in the face of life; if she cannot forgive him, she can try to understand Sophy's situation. But, in her innocence, Anna cannot do this. "I don't think I understand what you've told me," she admits to Darrow.

> "No, you don't understand," he returned with sudden bitterness; and on his lips the charge of incomprehension seemed an offense to her.
> "I don't want to — about such things!"
> He answered almost harshly: "Don't be afraid . . . you never will . . . you're too high . . . to fine . . . such things are too far from you." (P. 295)

Anna, in her greatest moment of stress, becomes the epitome of the "good" woman, and Darrow realizes that the role is not entirely suitable for the occasion.

Having made the decision to give Darrow up, Anna becomes human when she realizes that she does not want to lose him. She must instead relinquish her dream of the ideal husband and reconcile herself to the real man. For although she has decided to break the engagement to "raise a mournful shrine to the memory of the Darrow she had loved, without fear that his double's shadow would desecrate it," Anna is beginning to learn that "the two men were really one" (p. 302). As in the episode with Kitty Mayne, Anna must learn that when life provides only two rigid classes of women, a man who desires both will become this dual character.

What forces Ann to cling to the man who hurt her is the duality of her own nature. For although Anna feels that there are "certain dishonours with which she had never dreamed that any pact could be made" (p. 301), her long-repressed sexuality makes her desire Darrow in spite of herself. As she had both disdained and envied Kitty Mayne, Anna condemns Sophy and yet sees in her "an intenser passion than she had ever felt" (p. 309) and she wants to know that passion. Her deepest fear is that she will "never know what that girl has known" (p. 296), and as Anna fights against her sexual needs she senses "her body and soul divided against themselves" (p. 316).

As it had done earlier in her life, jealousy makes Anna more fiercely possessive, more intensely, obsessively, in love. She does not ultimately cast Darrow out of her life because now she herself feels "restless, insecure out of his sight: she had a sense of incompleteness, of passionate dependence" (p. 319) on Darrow. The simple categories Anna had lived by begin to fall apart for her, and she even begins to identify herself with Sophy, although it is "humiliating to her pride to recognize kindred impulses in a character she would have liked to feel completely alien to her" (pp. 320-21).

Anna's identification with Sophy extends farther than her merely feeling what Sophy feels; she even acts as Sophy did: she spends the night with Darrow. Her action is a desperate one, an attempt to cling to Darrow, to narrow the distance that seems to separate them, and to force herself to a decision through this irrevocable act. But the episode does not give Anna the security she desires, for although she muses that "she was his now, for life" (p. 345), she still cannot trust Darrow. As she watches him reading the paper the next morning, she is troubled because he seems so calm, "almost indifferent to her presence. 'Will it become a matter of course so soon?' she wondered with a twinge of jealousy." Her love for Darrow has now become "a sort of suspicious tyrannical tenderness that seemed to deprive it of all serenity" (p. 346), and the doubts, the revulsion, and, paradoxically, the clinging possessiveness persist. Every encounter with Darrow becomes a scene of recrimination in which she begs him for every detail of his past affair, and she dissolves finally in pathetic tears, pleading with him not to leave.

Anna does not like what she has become, but she sees only one escape from her plight. "It was Sophy Viner only who could save her — Sophy Viner only who could give her back her lost serenity. She would seek the girl and tell her that she had given Darrow up; and that step once taken there would be no retracing it" (p. 360).

But Sophy cannot save Anna, for Sophy is gone. True to her own standards, she has withdrawn herself from Owen's life and gone back to the only alternative left her, back to Mrs. Murrett and the misery of that tawdry world. Seeking Sophy in Paris, Anna finds Sophy's sister, the only stereotypical "bad" woman in the novel. Large, blond, blowsy, she reigns in her bed with her attendant lover, small dog, masseuse, and bill-collector around her. Her glances and movements are disturbingly like her sister's, and critics have made much of this, suggesting that this last scene of the novel is Wharton's parting shot at Sophy, or Anna's justification for classifying Sophy as a sexual adventuress.[15] A much more likely interpretation, however, is Geoffrey Walton's, which describes the scene as "a scathing comment on Anna. She goes to look for Sophy and finds real coarseness and vulgarity in her sister, and one is made finally to realize beyond any doubt the distinction of Sophy's character, which has survived its environment with a simple integrity that Anna, with all her refinement, cannot achieve."[16] The scene contrasts Anna's naiveté and horror of such a setting with Sophy's ability to transcend it. It is one more contrast between the strength that life in the real world demands and the weakness fostered by a life of evasion.

As the final scene of the novel, the encounter with Sophy's sister does not provide Anna with any answer to her own problem. Having given Darrow to Anna, Sophy will not now save her from him. Anna and Darrow are thus left to one another and to a life far different from what they had dreamed. For Darrow marriage to Anna will bring the eternal surveillance of a jealous and disillusioned woman; for Anna the dream of initiation into reality has become a nightmare, because the real world is too frightening to face.

Almost all the misery in which the novel ends can be seen as a result of living by the artificial and simplistic categories that Darrow and Anna use to define women. If Darrow had not persisted in viewing Sophy as a "bad" woman, he would not have entered so casually into an affair that has such horrible consequences. And because Anna is locked into the role of "good" woman, she neither can understand her first glimpse of real life — Darrow's infidelity — nor does she have much idea of how to deal with it. As in *The Age of Innocence*, it is the intruder who emerges from the complicated triangle relatively unscathed. Because she has never been protected by the veil of innocence that separates Anna from reality,[17] Sophy is better able to handle whatever life inflicts upon her. Although she loses her chance for a wealthy marriage and is forced back to Mrs.

Murrett, this time as her lackey in India, she does emerge the winner of the book's struggles and, as Ralph Curtis said, one can only hope that she will "marry a peer's son in Simla and end up the intimate friend of the Mayfair aristocracy."[18]

Like Ellen Olenska, Sophy Viner represents the positive values of the novel. Significantly, what Sophy responds to most fully in her visit to Paris is not "the beauty and mystery of the spectacle as much as its pressure of human significance, all its hidden implications of emotion and adventure" (p. 33), for Sophy emerges as the most human of the trio of *The Reef*, the most sensitive to others' emotions, and the most honest about her own. Just as Ellen Olenska seems to perceive Archer's love for her even before he faces it himself, so Sophy Viner is honest enough to admit that the man she loves never loved her. Like Ellen, who is unafraid of such unladylike words as *mistress* and *adultery*, Sophy refuses to think in the abstract, evasive terms of Anna and Darrow. She accepts that what she had with Darrow was to him a shameful little episode; from the beginning she refuses to disguise it, even to herself, as a romantic affair. Yet, because it is the cloest thing to love that Sophy has ever been offered, she accepts the offer unashamedly. Both Ellen and Sophy have a capacity for honesty self-appraisal, which others, like Archer and Darrow and Anna, only painfully and partially acquire. And both Ellen and Sophy seem able to perceive others, not through a fog of wishful illusions, but as they are, imperfect people with emotions and needs like their own. This ability to perceive others realistically is never cynical or critical, but rather a tolerant, often loving acceptance of them as they are. Thus Ellen loves Archer despite his weaknesses and she is generous in her concern for his wife. Similarly, Sophy continues to love Darrow even when he insults and demeans her by his conduct at Givré, and is kind to her rival, Anna.

There *are* major differences between Ellen and Sophy. Sophy lacks Ellen's sophistication, her cool self-assurance, her culture and intelligence. Sophy is more impulsive, more openly defiant of society, than Ellen. Her experience of society has been different from Ellen's; she has lived the life of a genteel but nonetheless social dependent — she is a glorified servant. Sophy has never had the moments of social success or status that Ellen has enjoyed; thus she is much more careless about violating all of society's taboos. Superficially, as an adventuress at Givré, she is more of an intruder than Ellen; yet, in the qualities that matter, she and Ellen are the same.

Sophy's virtues are much like Ellen's; she is independent, brave, and ready to look life in the face. Like Ellen, she is capable of true passion and willing to sacrifice for those she loves. Sophy shares one other important quality with Ellen Olenska. Throughout the novel Darrow and Anna think of Sophy as someone much younger than themselves; she is always "the girl" while Anna is a "woman," and sometimes, to Darrow, Sophy is like a young boy: she shakes her hair back "with a movement like a boy's" (p. 14), her gaze is "as clear as a boy's" (p. 69). Such descriptions may reflect Darrow's admiration for the almost childlike openness of Sophy, but they do not make her a child in any negative sense, in the sense of an aversion to life. For in terms of negative, childish "innocence," Sophy, like Ellen Olenska, is the only adult in a world full of children.

Edith Wharton's third "triangle" novel, *The Children*, is about the struggle of a group of children, the offspring and stepchildren of the various marriages of Joyce and Cliffe Wheater, to remain together in the face of the alimony, child custody, and marital battles that threaten to separate them. But the Wheater children and their "steps" are not necessarily the "children" of the title, for as Margaret McDowell explains, the adults in the novel may also be considered children.[19] In fact, Judith Wheater, the fifteen-year-old girl who leads the children's battle to remain together, is in many ways the true adult of the book. Judith, the victim of her parents' marital misadventures, has, like Ellen Olenska, been forced to look at the Gorgon, and her painful experiences and her role as mother to the other six children have made her an adult. Her own mother, Joyce, says that Judith is "older and wiser" than any of her various parents and stepparents,[20] and her governess explains that "Judith's never been a child — there was no time" (p. 26). The story of *The Children*, then, is once again a story of a mature intruder, this time Judith Wheater, forced to deal with an immature world.

There has been considerable negative criticism of *The Children*. Published in 1928, the novel has often been classed, along with other books Wharton wrote after World War I, as one of the author's shrill attacks on the disintegration of conventional standards and life as she knew it. The supposed literary flaws of the novel, and of others of this period — sentimentality, uncontrolled railing against the jazz age, lack of the usual irony expected of Wharton and of any understanding of the new society — are often attributed to the author's alienation from the postwar world. Blake Nevius, for example, says that in her writing Edith Wharton

> demanded a fixed point of reference, which was provided by the manners of her class but which in the end proved a handicap since it limited her vision. As the manners which defined her world lost their reality and with it their moral significance, the understanding which she brought to bear on her subject, in every novel after *The Age of Innocence*, became more superficial.[21]

Louis Auchincloss joins Nevius by attacking the superficial treatment of the rich Wheater crowd in the novel, and attributes this failing to the same cause. Wharton, he says, in "the turmoil and dislocation of the post-war world . . . began to look back with a new appreciation on the quiet, settled New York of her childhood";[22] she cannot really understand the representatives of the jazz age; she "has no true insight into their lives, she stands apart like her spokesman, Mrs. Sellars, in disdain, describing the Wheaters only in terms of snobbish and disapproving suppositions."[23]

Irving Howe lumps all the later novels into a "failed" category for the same reason:

> In the novels written during the last fifteen years of her life, Mrs. Wharton's conservatism hardened into an embittered and querulous disdain for modern life; she no longer really knew what was happening in America; and she lost what had once been her main gift: the accurate location of the target she wished to destroy.[24]

One cannot deny that certain of the novels of Wharton's later life — *The Glimpses of the Moon* and *The Marne*, for example — do not meet the standards of *The House of Mirth* or *The Custom of the Country*. But is also worth noting that Wharton's work in any period of her life is uneven: *The Fruit of the Tree*, for example, published two years after *The House of Mirth*, is not nearly so good as its predecessor. Consequently, it is dangerous to group all the postwar novels together and to attribute any inferiority in them to one general cause. When *The Children* is examined carefully, and examined with the pattern of the intruder in mind, one may find in it what Geoffrey Walton notes: "a revival of her [Wharton's] old creative energy and narrative skill along with the play of irony, albeit of a rather less subtle kind, which is the distinguishing feature of her best work." As a writer, he continues, Wharton "deals as surely and decisively with the world of Scott Fitzgerald as she did with him in person at the famous tea party . . . at the Pavillon Colombe."[25]

There is considerable irony in the novel, and as usual in Wharton, much of it is directed at the male from whose point of view the story is told. As for excessive sentimentality in the book, the story of seven emotionally abused children could lend itself to a "women's fiction" treatment, but Wharton makes these children as self-centered and manipulative, as badly behaved and irritating as real children often are. Even the love story of the novel is bittersweet, not saccharine.

More important, the basis for much criticism of Wharton's later work — her supposed reactionary attitudes and her retreat into the safety of old New York ways — also becomes questionable when the role of the female intruder in *The Children* is considered. For if Judith Wheater is regarded as the heroine of the novel, it becomes clear that her enemies, and the targets of criticism within the book, are not only those who represent the jazz age, but those who represent old New York as well. There are two three-sided conflicts in the novel: the first involves the romantic choice that Martin Boyne, the male protagonist, must make between the traditional woman, Rose Sellars, and the unconventional girl, Judith Wheater; the second allies Martin with Judith Wheater in her struggle to keep her "family" of children together. In this second struggle not only do the hedonistic representatives of the twenties oppose Judith, but so does Rose Sellars, the symbol of old New York.[26] Thus both the traditional and the modern become the objects of Wharton's scorn, for both are willing to exploit or even damage Judith and the children for their own ends. Far from being a favorite or ideal character of Wharton's, as some have seen her,[27] Rose Sellars is another member of that New York which will genteelly take a life "without effusion of blood"[28] in order to insure that its own serenity will not be disturbed.

The two enemy camps in the novel are similar in many ways, not only in their opposition to the children's goal. For in reality the pleasure-seeking, mindless Wheater world is not, as Wolff describes it, the "grotesque inversion" of the New York world,[29] but rather the logical extension, the exaggeration, of the world depicted in *The Age of Innocence*. It shares the same supreme goal: pain, reality, must be avoided at any cost. Similarly infantile in its avoidance of the unpleasant, it is thus often heedlessly cruel in ridding itself of a disturbing element. And the Wheater world is as conformist as old New York, for in *The Children* the stereotyped, virginal May Welland and her conventional beau are merely replaced by the stereotyped flapper and her lover, so that, at a dinner with the Wheater group, Martin Boyne notices that

> all about them, at other tables exactly like theirs, sat other men exactly like Lord Wrench and Wheater . . . other women exactly like Joyce and Zinnie and Mrs. Lullmer. . . . Every one of the women in the vast crowded restaurant seemed to be of the same age, to be dressed by the same dress-makers, loved by the same lovers. (P. 154)

The Jazz set is the New York set with fewer restraints and newer toys. Old New York, with its "two great fundamental groups," one of which cares for "eating and clothes and money" and the other for "travel, horticulture, and the best fiction,"[30] is merely transformed into Cliffe Wheater with his enormous yacht, the Duke of Mendip with his Moroccan tent, and Syb Lullmer, "chock full of drugs" (p. 153). Both groups lead the same nonintellectual, trivialized existence; both fear reality more than anything else; but each has developed different methods of avoiding it. The rules for a "happy" life are different and less restrictive in the twenties, but the game is the same: whether it be Givré, or New York, or the Lido, one must find a Valley of Childish Things and hide in it.

Since the focus of the criticism in *The Children* is so much like that of *The Age of Innocence* and *The Reef*, it is not surprising that the book is a blend of the elements of the other two novels, with parallel characters, imagery, and incidents.

The opening of the novel is a replay of the opening of *The Reef*. A middle-aged man, Martin Boyne, is traveling to Cortina to declare his love for the recently widowed Rose Sellars, who is in many ways a copy of Anna Leath. Like Anna, Rose is refined, reticent, and subtle: "All her life had been a series of adaptations, arrangements, shifting of lights, lowering of veils, pulling about the screens and curtains" (p. 38), and, as all the veils and screens indicate, Rose, like Anna, is trapped in her world. She is "like a canary in a window facing north" (p. 39), looking out on a world she has no place in. Boyne, however, is not quite the typical Wharton hero; as a civil engineer who has spent the better part of his life on jobs in various foreign outposts, he is far more dissociated from the old New York of his childhood than Archer or Darrow. He lacks the complacency of the typical Wharton male, and as the book begins, he is bemoaning the lack of adventure in his life. "He would have loved adventure, but adventure worthy of the name perpetually eluded him, and when it has eluded a man till he is over forty it is not likely to seek him out later" (p. 2).

When adventure does come to Boyne, in the person of Judith Wheater, he is not at first sure what to do about it. He makes the expected effort to place Judith; seeing her with a baby in her arms and several other children hanging on to her, he at first classes her as a scandalously young mother and then as a governess. When she sits in a deck chair marked "Wheater," Boyne mistakenly concludes that Judith must be the most recent wife of his old college friend Cliffe Wheater. Even when the mystery of Judith's identity is solved, Boyne remains puzzled about her.

A description of Sophy Viner as "an odd mingling of precocious wisdom and disarming innocence"[31] can easily be applied to Judith, and Boyne does not know quite how to deal with this mixture. He is moved by her governess's description of Judith's background:

> Even as a little thing, Miss Scope explained, Judith couldn't bear it when her parents quarrelled. She had had to get used to that, alas; but what she couldn't get used to was, after the divorce and the two remarriages, being separated from Terry [her brother], and bundled up every year with Blanca [her sister], and sent from pillar to post, first to one Palace Hotel and then to another, wherever one parent or the other happened to be. . . . It was that, Miss Scope thought, which had given the grown-up look to her eyes. (p. 25)

Boyne admires the girl's assumption of grown-up responsibility, but is repelled by certain other adult qualities of the fifteen-year-old Judith. When Judith talks frankly of her mother's new lover, for example, Boyne blushes and averts his eyes from her, chiding, "You've said something exceedingly silly. Something I should hate to hear if you were grown-up. But at your age it's merely silly, and doesn't matter" (p. 61). To this scolding, Judith responds with justified anger. "My age? My age? What do you know about my age? I'm as old as your grandmother. I'm as old as the hills. I suppose you think I oughtn't to say things like that about mother — but what am I to do, when they're true?" (p. 61). Like Newland Archer, Martin Boyne is drawn to the intruder's difference from the stereotype, is attracted by her openness, and yet secretly wants her to be more conventional, more innocent.

> There were moments when she frightened him; when he would have given the world to believe either that she was five years older than she said, or else that she did not know the meaning of the words she used. At such moments it was always the vision of Rose Sellars which took possession of him. (Pp. 61-62)

If Judith's experience disturbs Boyne, her ignorance disappoints him. When their ship stops for a day, Boyne takes Judith to see a cathedral. She cannot appreciate it, cannot understand what he tells her about it, and Boyne reasons that "it had been stupid of him to expect that a child of fifteen or sixteen, brought up in complete ignorance of the past ... should feel anything in Monreal" (p. 35). Boyne had expected more from Judith, and this very expectation indicates his attachment to the girl he continually refers to as a "child," for his disappointment, he admits to himself, comes because "he was already busy at the masculine task of endowing the woman of the moment with every quality which made life interesting to himself" (p. 36). Boyne's conflict centers not only on whether to classify Judith as innocent or experienced, but on whether to care for her as child or woman.

While Boyne represses any sexual feelings he may have for Judith, his attachment to her, in the guise of paternal family friend, continues to grow. Although "the more Boyne saw of her the more she perplexed him, the more difficult he found it to situate her in time and space" (p. 36), he is fascinated by Judith's changefulness, her enthusiasm, her courage. Instead of parting from the Wheater clan at Venice as he had intended, Boyne agrees to spend several days there in order to investigate the uneasy truce that the reunited parents, Cliffe and Joyce Wheater, have established between them, and to plead with Cliffe for a tutor for Terry, the oldest boy. It is Cliffe Wheater's treatment of Terry that provides another insight into the Wheater world: because Terry is sickly he has been ignored by his athletic father, and he has never been educated because Cliffe, Judith explains, "can't see why people should want to be educated when they don't have to. What does it ever *lead* to, he says" (p. 59).

The success of Judith's plans for the children is dependent on the survival of the Wheater's remarriage. Signs of an impending breakup are already evident when Boyne arrives in Venice. Joyce Wheater, who is currently on her third marriage, casually explains to Boyne that she "still believed in the sanctity of marriage. But all the same, if one came to feel that by living with a man, even if he *was* one's husband, one was denying one's Ideal: that was awful too, wasn't it?" (pp. 53-54), and then proceeds to suggest, as Terry's tutor, a young man who has been taking her around the galleries, and who is "too much of an idealist" (p. 55). While Joyce is thus proposing that her lover be hired to educate her son, Cliffe Wheater is restlessly pacing the Lido because he cannot find anyone to go yachting with him. Cliffe is bored, and, as Judith says of her parents, "it's always when they've got nothing particular to do that they quarrel" (p. 62). The Wheater children are in jeopardy because of their parents' amusement, or lack of it.

The ominous situation at the Wheaters no longer concerns Boyne, however, for having fulfilled his promise to Judith to plead for a tutor, he makes the characteristic move of the Wharton hero — away from the intruder to the safety of the traditional woman.

Even on his way to Rose, however, Boyne is conscious of the ambiguity of his feelings for her. For although he "had schooled himself to think that what he most wanted was to see Rose Sellars again," Boyne also, deep inside himself, "knew that it wasn't so; at least, not certainly so. Life had given him hints of other things he might want equally, want even more; his reluctance to leave Venice and his newly-acquired friends showed that his inclinations were divided" (p. 81).

Once at Cortina and in the quiet elegance of Rose's chalet, Boyne's doubts are at first completely dispelled. He and Rose spend their evenings before the fire, talking or reading. Boyne decides that he would like to "look forward to an eternity of such evenings, in just such a hushed lamplit room, with . . . that quiet silvery-auburn head with its mass of closely woven braids bending over a book across the hearth" (p. 86).

The first hint of discord occurs when Boyne proposes to Rose and, like Newland Archer, presses for an early wedding date. When Boyne makes this request and notes Rose's reaction to it ("there were people who had to be considered, who might be offended by too great haste") (p. 92), he realizes exactly how conventional his bride-to-be really is. He observes with dismay "the recoil of the orderly deliberate woman whose life has been too vacant for hurry, too hopeless for impatience'' (p. 910). Although Boyne argues for a wedding before Rose's year of mourning is up, Rose in her subdued and rational way wins the battle, and Boyne suddenly feels ''as if they were already married — as if they had been married a long time'' (p. 96).

This disagreement has a minimal effect upon Boyne's romance in comparison to the effect that the arrival of the Wheater tribe at Cortina creates. Judith and the children have run away. Their parents are divorcing once more, and the division of the children is inevitable. Judith, desperate, has turned to Martin Boyne for help, asking him to ''swear to see us through'' (p. 11). His assent now aligns him irrevocably with the children and against both their parents and his fiancée.

One of Boyne's first concerns when Judith appears on the scene is anxiety over how Rose will react to the girl. ''If only,'' he worries, ''Judith doesn't begin by saying something that will startle her'' (p. 119), and it is clear that Boyne is becoming increasingly aware of Rose's innocence. ''Boyne did not see how any good will on either part could bridge the distance between Mrs. Sellars's conception of life, and Judith Wheater's experience of it'' (p. 124). And Rose's inability to enter or understand the world of the children makes her seem cold and unconcerned about their plight. When she hears about their situation, she can only say, ''It's too awful. I didn't know there really *were* such people'' (p. 98). Her advice to Martin is to persuade the children to return home and her lack of understanding turns to positive malice when she recognizes Judith as a rival for Boyne's love. At her first sight of Judith, Rose notes that she is ''awfully young; but still-grown up!'' (p. 116), and Rose teases Boyne about being in love with Judith. Boyne denies it, as he is still denying it in his own heart, but already he is judging Rose in terms of her difference from the intruder. In contrast to Judith's frankness, Boyne notices that Rose has ''premeditated spontaneity'' (p. 127), and when Rose is with the children he perceives, not wholly approvingly, that ''her sweetness suffused them like a silvery icing'' (p. 131).

Boyne further alienates himself from Rose by agreeing to plead for the children at Venice. The visit provides Boyne with a clearer picture of exactly what the world Judith is running from is like. The Wheaters' activities in Venice are similar to those of a perverse summer camp. Joyce Wheater has become engaged to Terry's tutor (although he prefers Judith), Cliffe has taken up with a woman whose little girl recently committed suicide, and the Wheaters and their spouses-to-be are joined by Cliffe's ex-wife, an American actress, in the battle over how to divide the children. It is very difficult for Boyne to state the children's case, however, because the negotiations are carried on ''piecemeal, desultorily, parenthetically, between swims and sun-baths, cocktails and foxtrots, poker and baccarat — and, as a rule, in the presence of all the conflicting interests'' (p. 174). As in old New York,

> in the Wheater set they could deal with things only collectively; alone, they became helpless and inarticulate. They lived so perpetually in the limelight that they required an audience — an audience made up of their own kind. . . . When all was said and done, all they asked was not to be bothered — (P. 175)

In the midst of all the battles at the Lido, Boyne discovers that ''it was not that any of these parents really wanted their children.'' Instead the children are pawns in the alimony and divorce game; they are ''a bone of contention'' and ''the taking or keeping possession of them was a matter of pride or of expediency, like fighting for a goal in some exciting game'' (p. 301).

This callous unconcern for the welfare of the children is echoed in Rose Sellars's own growing animosity toward them. When Boyne returns to her to report that he has succeeded in being appointed guardian of the children for the summer, Rose is displeased, for she is becoming increasingly concerned over Boyne's love for Judith. Her only desire is to get rid of Judith, and if that involves sending the children back to a life of misery, Rose is willing to do so. The disturbing element must be removed to insure her own security.

The incident of the gifts that Boyne brings back from Venice indicates that Rose has good reason to be nervous about Judith. In *The Age of Innocence* Archer sends exotic yellow roses to Ellen and rather tepid lilies-of-the-valley to May. In *The Children* Martin Boyne brings a sapphire ring set in diamonds for Rose, and as he places it on her finger he thinks, ''it looks like the engagement ring any other fellow would have given to any other woman'' (p. 172); it is the conventional gift for the conventional woman. To Judith, however, Boyne gives ''a curious crystal pendant in a network of worn enamel'' (p. 172), and he is certain that it ''was Judith's by right because, like her, it was odd and exquisite and unacountable'' (p. 188). When Rose and Judith, each wearing her new gift, confront each other the next day, Boyne observes that the ''mutual reconnaissance was swift and silent as the crossing of searchlights in a night sky'' (p. 190).

The battle image is appropriate because Rose Sellars does not accept her replacement by a fifteen-year-old with her characteristic grace. Like Anna Leath, she is fiercely jealous, and like May Welland, she fights with the weapons available to her. Anna Leath angrily confronts Darrow with her discovery of his affair, and Rose Sellars, desperate, accuses Boyne of being in love with Judith.[32] Boyne is indignant and also disappointed in Rose, because his image of her did not allow for such scenes. As they face each other, "guardedly, apprehensively," "something fragile and precious, which they had been carrying together . . . slipped between their fingers . . . broken" (p. 220).

For Boyne the love affair is over, but Rose tries one more tactic. Like May Welland, she finally agrees to an immediate wedding, explaining, "I've been imprisoned in my past — I see it now; I had become the slave of all those years of conformity. . . . But you've opened my eyes — you've set me free. How monstrous to have waited so long for happiness, and then to be afraid to seize it when it comes!" (p. 230). Her plan is to marry right away and then to "sail for home" (p. 231), for New York, where Boyne will be safely out of the clutches of Judith. The children must be left to take care of themselves.

This tactic creates enormous disillusion for Martin Boyne. The woman he had once seen as so fine, so rare, is now perceived in images that suggest, not the gentle and almost sacred figure he had made of Rose, but rather a black widow spider waiting for her victim. Boyne begins to understand that while he "had often mocked at himself" as a man who "had never had a real adventure,"

> he saw that he himself had been one, had been Rose Sellars's Great Adventure. . . . While she had continued, during the weary years of her marriage, to be blameless, exemplary, patient and heroically gay, the thought of Boyne was storing up treasures for her which she would one day put out her hand and take — no matter how long she might have to wait. . . . She had trained herself to go on waiting for happiness, day after day, month after month, year after year . . . like a tireless animal waiting for its prey. One day her prey, her happiness would appear, and she would snap it up; and on that day there would be no escape from her. (P. 235)

The distance between Rose and Boyne has become so wide that nothing can close it, and Rose's last plan for the children — to divide them up and, after the wedding, to adopt the two she finds least threatening — is the final disillusionment for Boyne. The engagement between the couple is broken and Rose exiles herself to Paris.

At first Boyne is happy to be alone with the children, for their spontaneous quarrels, conversations, and amusements give him a "feeling of liberation." Returning to them after a session with the refined Rose is "like getting back from a constrained bodily position into a natural one" (p. 245). Boyne can find satisfaction with the children because he is not entirely a typical Wharton male. Having been a wanderer, a waif, himself for so long, he identifies with these waifs. He knows that, even had the children not been in trouble, he would have been drawn to them; "his own restlessness and impulsiveness would have fraternized with theirs. 'The fact is, we're none of us grown up,' " he reflects (p. 247).

The childhood idyll is brief, for the summer is over and various parents are demanding their children. Boyne has only one last plan to keep the children together, a plan that he must finally see for what it is: a way to keep Judith, whom he loves, with him forever. Boyne cares for the others in a paternal way, but he has finally faced the fact that he wants Judith for his wife. Obliquely, he proposes to Judith, saying, "I'll stay with you always if you'll have me; if things go wrong I'll always be there to look after you and defend you" (p. 308), and Judith simply does not understand. "Oh, Martin," she cries, "do you really mean you're going to adopt us all, and we're all going to stay with you forever?" (p. 309). Judith, who has lived her life for "her" children, cannot envision a separate life for herself, and cannot "detach herself, even in imagination, from the others" (p. 247). Her world is simply too different[33] from Boyne's, her future as an individual, apart from her charges, too far away. Again for the Wharton hero, love has come too late, for Martin Boyne is too old to wait for the love of a girl still too young to give it.

The final scene of the novel is, as Blake Nevius and Cynthia Griffin Wolff note, reminiscent of the last scene of *The Age of Innocence*.[34] Three years after he has lost Judith and left Rose, Boyne is alone in Biarritz. One night, peering through the window into a ballroom, Boyne sees Judith.

> It was one of her moments of beauty: that fitful beauty which is so much more enchanting and perilous than the kind that gets up and lies down with its wearer. This might be — Boyne said to himself — literally the only day, the only hour, in which the queer quarrelling elements that composed her would ever join hands in a celestial harmony. It did not matter what had brought the miracle about. Perhaps she was in love with the young man who had bent over her, and was going to marry him. Or perhaps she was still a child, pleased at her new dress, and half proud, half frightened at the waking consciousness of her beauty, and the power it exercised. ... Whichever it was, Boyne would never know. He drew back into an uneit corner of the terrace, and sat there a long time in the dark, his head thrown back and his hands locked behind it. Then he got up and walked away into the night. (p. 347)

Echoes of Archer sitting in twilight outside Ellen's apartment cannot be ignored. But Boyne's life does not seem so wasted as Archer's. He has avoided the trap of the conventional marriage. And unlike Archer, who only dabbles in politics and philanthropy, Boyne has his real work. In Biarritz on leave from a job in Brazil, Boyne's eyes are "full of visions of work to be, his hands of the strength of work to be done" (p. 336). Boyne is alone and lonely, but even in his happiest days with Judith he had realized that his "highest moments had always been solitary" (p. 182), and in those days too he had been "suddenly aware of an intense, unexpected satisfaction in being for once alone, his own master, with . . . no one to be tormented or enchanted by, no one to listen to and answer" (p. 239). After his one adventure Boyne has simply returned to the life of a wanderer and a worker; he has not chosen to retreat into the secure but asphyxiating world of tradition. It is true that for Boyne the taste of that one adventure "had been too bitter" (p. 338) to risk another, but Boyne's encounter with Judith left him, if lonely, also free.

And as in *The Age of Innocence*, the final scene in the novel presents another vision: the vision of a free woman for whom life holds a great deal. In all three novels — *The Age of Innocence, The Reef, The Children* — the elusive intruder can transcend her pain and move forward, often to a future filled with risks and dangers, but always with the courage to deal with them.

The three intruders in the "triangle" novels — Ellen, Sophy, and Judith — are like three sisters, none of whom is a carbon copy of another, but all bearing a strong family resemblance. The three vary most in what may be termed their education, in the broadest sense of the term. Ellen and Judith share a knowledge about the culture of wealth; they have had the experiences of travel, luxury, and variety which money can buy. Sophy lacks this sophistication and background of wealth, yet she and Judith have both been toughened by another kind of education, by exposure to the underside of the world of the rich. Sophy knows this territory well, as a servant in it; Judith, relegated most of her life to the care of maids, governesses, and other more dubious parasites who cling to her parents, also knows this world intimately.

The intruders differ also in their acquisition and development of moral values. Ellen possesses the most consciously arrived at moral code; at the beginning of *The Age of Innocence* she already has her own characteristic set of values, which develop as the novel progresses. While Sophy Viner, at the opening of *The Reef*, does not have the same deliberately thought-out moral code, she too develops and acquires principles as she confronts various situations. Judith's sense of right and wrong is most irrational and instinctive, arising out of her fierce maternal protectiveness toward her "family" and her desire to keep them together. For Judith, stealing and lying are justifiable if her "children" require them.

And although all three women are fighters, Judith and Sophy fight their battles more openly than Ellen. They lack her finesse and polish. Ellen, on contrast, appears more refined and subtle in her battles; she is the most idealized and ethereal of these intruders.

Yet, while there are these significant differences between the women, they are obviously kin. There is one scene in *The Children* that characterizes not only Judith Wheater, but Sophy Viner and Ellen Olenska as well. It is the scene in which Boyne takes the little Wheaters on a picnic and separates Judith from her charges to show her the cathedral at Monreal. Inside the cathedral Judith is shy and ill at ease. She cannot appreciate it or understand it. Boyne quickly takes her out of there, into the sunlight, saying, "Come along: it's chilly here after our sun-bath. Gardens are best, after all" (p. 35). At the door of the cathedral Judith pauses and looks "a little wistfully down the mighty perspective they were leaving. 'Someday, I know, I shall want to come back here,' " she says. "Oh, well, we'll come back together," Boyne answers hastily (p. 36).

The scene is more than ironic foreshadowing of the novel's conclusion: there will be no "someday" for Boyne to educate Judith or for the two of them to savor the beauties of the world together. It also, with its contrasts of garden and cathedral, places Judith in her appropriate setting, the garden, the natural, open one, as opposed to the monument to civilization and the ordered past, the cathedral. "Gardens are best" for Judith because she possesses a certain kind of innocence, different from the innocence of Rose or Anna Leath or May Welland, which thrives in bright sunlight and in scenes unbounded by walls. This episode can easily be linked to certain others in *The Age of Innocence* and *The Reef*. It calls to mind Ellen Olenska racing Archer through the snow at Skuytercliff, a big dog leaping about her, or Archer's feeling that the Blenkers's "unpruned garden, the tumbledown house, and the oak-grove" are "exactly the place in which he ought to have found Madame Olenska."[35] Sophy Viner too is associated with images of nature: Darrow at one time thinks of his stay in Paris with Sophy as "a sunrise stroll with a dryad in a dew-drenched forest,"[36] and he first kisses Sophy in a forest, where "he felt her presence as a part of the charmed stillness of the summer woods."[37]

For it is not only Judith who possesses a kind of innocence[38] that is positive and endearing; all three women — Ellen, Sophy, and Judith — exemplify a natural and open attitude toward life in direct contrast to the closed society they encounter. Their innocence is born, paradoxically, of experience, for, having been exposed to some of the worst that life can inflict, they cease to fear life. Rather than hiding from the world, the intruder continues within it, enormously receptive of and sensitive to its joys, appreciating whatever is to be appreciated, unhampered by conventions that could restrain her. The intruder's innocence lies in the fact that her presence in the real world makes her eternally vulnerable; because she so bravely exposes herself to life, with trust in others and belief in human goodness, she can be hurt or corrupted. Unlike the traditional New York woman, the intruder has little wariness, few hesitations[39] about what could happen, to protect her. Her openness is her innocence, and her true innocence is the quality that appeals to her lover, which turns Sophy and Judith and Ellen each into what Charles Doyle calls Ellen: a "guileless temptress."[40] And the Wharton male, having had a great deal of the spurious and cultivated "innocence" of the traditional woman, discovers a new and natural world with the intruder.

NOTES

1. *A Feast of Words*, p. 208.
2. Although the point of view of Charity Royall, a young girl who hates her imprisonment, is used in *Summer*, Charity is far less conventional than Anna Leath.
3. *The Reef* (New York: D. Appleton and Co., 1912), p. 94. Citations in the text are to this edition.
4. *Edith Wharton*, p. 60.
5. *A Feast of Words*, p. 218, p. 210.
6. Elizabeth Ammons (*Edith Wharton's Heroines: Studies in Aspiration and Compliance*, p. 50) says that the reef of the book is the double standard on which Anna's dreams shatter.
7. Ammons's interpretation of the novel centers on the fairy-tale quality of both Anna and Sophy's dreams: Anna, as Sleeping Beauty, and Sophy, as Cinderella, both look for a Prince Charming to transform their lives. *Edith Wharton's Heroines*, p. 64.
8. Margaret McDowell also compares Anna to May. *Edith Wharton*, p. 59.
9. Cynthia Griffin Wolff makes this point (*A Feast of Words*, pp. 210-11) and also notes that after Darrow becomes sexually involved with Sophy he repeatedly offers her money "as if thus to discharge his 'debt' and rid himself of the emotional encumbrance" (pp. 212-13).
10. *Edith Wharton: A Critical Interpretation*, p. 65.
11. Constance Carlson says that Darrow's attempts to prevent Sophy's marriage are "the first step in his realization of the hypocrisy of the double standard." *Heroines in Certain American Novels*, p. 101.
12. Again, there is a similarity to *The Age of Innocence*, where Archer's advice to Ellen about divorce comes to haunt him.
13. Geoffrey Walton says that Sophy "has an absolute sincerity about her own feelings, which puts Darrow again to shame." *Edith Wharton: A Critical Interpretation*, p. 67.
14. *Edith Wharton: A Critical Interpretation*, p. 65.
15. For such interpretations see: Blake Nevius (*Edith Wharton: A Study of Her Fiction*, p. 140), Irving Howe ("Introduction: The Achievement of Edith Wharton," in *Edith Wharton: A Collection of Critical Essays*, p. 7); Louis Auchincloss (*Edith Wharton*, p. 23); and Margaret McDowell (*Edith Wharton*, p. 61). For an interpretation more sympathetic to Sophy, which views the scene as a picture of what Sophy has risen against, see Elizabeth Ammons (*Edith Wharton's Heroines: Studies in Aspiration and Compliance*), p. 57.
16. *Edith Wharton: A Critical Interpretation*, p. 70.
17. Millicent Bell makes an interesting comparison of the "experienced" Sophy to

Miriam, of Hawthorne's *The Marble Faun*, and links Anna to Hilda, whose insufficient innocence must be enriched by the dark side of experience. *Edith Wharton and Henry James: The Story of Their Friendship* (New York: George Braziller, 1965), p. 277.

18. Quoted in R. W. B. Lewis, *Edith Wharton*, p. 327.

19. *Edith Wharton*, p. 120.

20. *The Children* (New York: D. Appleton and Company, 1928), p. 53. Citations in the text are to this edition.

21. *Edith Wharton: A Study of Her Fiction*, p. 67. Although I disagree with this interpretation of Wharton's later novels and its comment on their overall quality, I agree with Nevius's linking of the social criticism of *The Age of Innocence* to the criticism in *The Children*: Wharton, he says, "found that the case she had formulated against her parents' generation was applicable to their grandchildren's. Each sought in its own way to escape the common lot; each, in its effort to avoid pain and responsibility, had weakened its moral fiber" (p. 189).

22. *Edith Wharton: A Woman in Her Time*, pp. 126-27. Auchincloss makes this statement in a discussion of *The Age of Innocence*.

23. Ibid., p. 174.

24. "Introduction: The Achievement of Edith Wharton," in *Edith Wharton: A Collection of Critical Essays*, p. 5. There are other, similar critical comments. Alfred Kazin (*On Native Grounds: An Interpretation of Modern American Prose Literature*, p. 82) calls Wharton's later work "a series of cheap novels," with "tired and forlorn courtesy," and a "smooth rendering of the smooth problems of women's magazine fiction," written as the world around Wharton "changed beyond all recognition," and as she "ignored the parvenue altogether and sought refuge in nostalgia." Marilyn Jones Lyde (*Edith Wharton: Convention and Morality in the Work of a Novelist*, p. 163) attributes the inferiority of Wharton's postwar work to the loss of all conventions and, though she does not view Wharton as a blind adherent to convention, feels that Wharton needed "a society complex enough to merit examination and a fixed moral tradition by which it may be appraised and evaluated" in order to do her best work. Elizabeth Ammons (*Edith Wharton's Heroines: Studies in Aspiration and Compliance*, p. 187) blames "the excesses in Edith Wharton's later novels" on her "hurry" to reform postwar America.

25. *Edith Wharton: A Critical Interpretation*, p. 26. The famous "tea party" Walton refers to is a visit that Fitzgerald, drunk, paid to Wharton at home in 1925, and at which she remained unperturbed when Fitzgerald told a series of dirty stories. Recounted in R. W. B. Lewis, *Edith Wharton*, p. 468.

26. Cynthia Griffin Wolff (in a reference to Boyne's calling himself "an old fogey out of the wilderness") perceives two "wildernesses" in the novel: the "wilderness of evasions and courtesies," which she links to Rose and Boyne, and the wilderness of "boundless wealth and instant gratification" of the adult Wheaters. *A Feast of Words*, p. 385. I would not link Boyne so closely to Rose Sellars.

27. See Frances Theresa Russell, "Melodramatic Mrs. Wharton," *Sewanee Review* 40 (1932): 430, and Hilton Anderson, "Edith Wharton as Fictional Heroine," *South Atlantic Quarterly* 69 (1970):120. Marilyn Jones Lyde (*Edith Wharton: Convention and Morality in the Work of a Novelist*, p. 14) characterizes Rose as representative of "all that was best in the aristocratic tradition" but also as "a prisoner of the sterile, outmoded conventions which are a concomitant of that tradition."

28. *The Age of Innocence*, p. 335.

29. *A Feast of Words*, p. 385.

30. *The Age of Innocence*, p. 34.

31. *The Reef*, p. 60.

32. Geoffrey Walton feels that animosity toward Rose grows after this accusation, but also feels that Wharton's treatment of Rose is uneven. *Edith Wharton: A Critical Interpretation*, p. 157.

33. Cynthia Griffin Wolff notes the "essential and ineradicable differences" between the two (*A Feast of Words*, p. 383) and also mentions that the original outline of *The Children* ended with the marriage of Judith and Boyne, p. 381. This proposed ending anticipates the union of the best of two worlds that will finally come in *The Buccaneers*.

34. *A Feast of Words*, p. 39; *Edith Wharton: A Study of Her Fiction*, p. 214.

35. *The Age of Innocence*, p. 227.

36. *The Reef*, p. 34.

37. Ibid., p. 34.

38. Geoffrey Walton calls Judith "an older version of Maisie who, in spite of it all, preserves a basic innocence of intention and sense of responsibility." *Edith Wharton: A Critical Interpretation*, p. 152.

39. Cynthia Griffin Wolff (*A Feast of Words*, p. 387) remarks that Judith is "young" in the sense that she does not see hazards and is free from petty hesitations.

40. "Emblems of Innocence: Imagery Patterns in Wharton's *The Age of Innocence*," p. 23. Doyle also notes that innocence in the novel can exist "in different — in fact, antithetical — states. Ellen's oblivion to the rules of New York society is as innocent as May's invariable, practically reflexive, observance of them." (ibid.).

5

Other Variations of the Pattern

The female intruder appears in many guises in Edith Wharton's work: as an eighteenth-century revolutionary, a Midwestern social climber, a beautiful ornament, a scandalous woman, a precocious child. In whatever form she appears and whatever world she enters, the intruder's function remains basically the same; she disrupts the society she has entered, usually by representing an attractive yet dangerous alternative to it.[1] In one of Edith Wharton's early novels, *The Fruit of the Tree*, the world disrupted by the intruders is not so much the physical world of Westmore, a New England mill town, as it is the inner world of a Westmore inhabitant, John Amherst. This long and intricately plotted novel deals primarily with two problems: social reform and euthanasia, and at the center of each problem is Amherst, a well-intentioned but extremely conventional man whose expectations of life and, primarily, of the women he becomes involved with are continually being challenged by the women themselves. In one sense there are two female intruders in *The Fruit of the Tree*, Amherst's first wife, the rich, spoiled Bessy Westmore, and his second wife, Justine Brent. Although it is primarily Justine, an independent, intelligent woman who defies convention, who is the intruder in the book, in certain ways Bessy, a more passive, stereotyped woman, also functions as intruder in Amherst's world because her behavior challenges both his preconceived notions of femininity and his entire world view. For Bessy Westmore, who at first appears to Amherst as a conventional society woman, much like May Welland, develops and changes into a more complicated character as the story progresses. The development of Bessy exemplifies a technique Wharton uses, which Margaret McDowell describes as follows:

> In many of her novels and stories, Wharton apparently accepts traditional clichés about the nature, function, and status of women in the early part of a work. An ironic tone later dominates as Wharton builds a satiric structure around the very stereotype which she had used in introducing the protagonist and her situation. Wharton thus uses stereotypes of women purposefully to highlight the falsity of such categorizing and to suggest the many deceptions and incongruities involved in accepting such ready-made conceptions of a woman's role in society.[2]

In *The Fruit of the Tree* it is Amherst's long-cherished and "ready-made conceptions" about woman's role that are attacked.

John Amherst, the manager of the Westmore mill, is a man of good family fallen on hard times. He basks in the adoration of his sacrificing, widowed mother, who had scrimped for years to put him through college, hoping that he would pick "a gentlemanly profession."[3] Instead Amherst, who loves machinery, chose this factory position, and he "loved the work itself as much as he hated the conditions under which it was done" (p. 56). Amherst hopes that his factory training will eventually be followed by some kind of "larger work" (p. 55) of reform, but as the novel begins he has done little to ameliorate the grim conditions in the town of Westmore. Not until he meets a nurse in the mill hospital and learns about the miserable fate of a mill hand maimed in an industrial accident is the full extent of the workers' suffering made clear to him. When Amherst finally realizes just how bad life at Westmore is for the poor, he decides to take a serious risk: to bypass the proper channels and to appeal for help directly to the mill's owner, the young widow Bessy Westmore.

Amherst is immediately drawn to Bessy. At their first meeting Amherst "felt his self-possession slipping away into the depth of a pair of eyes so dark-lashed and deeply blue that his only thought was one of wonder at his previous indifference to women's eyes" (p. 41).

Aside from the obvious attraction of her beauty, Bessy fascinates Amherst for many reasons, some of which he conceals from himself. He has a genuine desire to transform Bessy, the frivolous socialite, into a compassionate reformer, "to see the angel of pity stir the depths of those unfathomable eyes, when they rested, perhaps for the first time, on suffering that it was in their power to smile away as easily as they had smiled away of his own distrust" (p. 47). There is egotism in this desire to remake Bessy, as there is egotism in Ralph Marvell's dream of remaking Undine Spragg, but there is far more egotism in Amherst than he admits to himself in this conscious goal. For Bessy's money is at the heart of Amherst's interest in her, and money would both give him the power he craves to do good and restore him to what he feels is his proper station in life.

Amherst, like his mother, is a snob at heart. He keenly feels the loss of the family fortunes, not only because lack of money makes him unable to initiate his desired reforms, but because it places him in a position of subordination. This side of his character is brought to light when he takes Bessy on a tour of the slums of Westmore. As he conducts her through the bleak neighborhood Bessy can only exclaim, "What a good day for a gallop!" (p. 50), and, although Bessy's remark at first chills Amherst, it also "calls up thrilling memories of his own college days, when he had ridden his grandfather's horses in the famous hunting valley not a hundred miles from Hanaford'' (p. 50). Part of Amherst is deeply *like* Bessy Westmore; under his veneer of social concern lie the aristocratic traditions and notions that he, like Bessy, has been raised with. Although Amherst works for Bessy and depends on her for his livelihood, he does not see himself as her inferior; rather, he desires that ''Mrs. Westmore should not regard him as less of her own class than his connections and his up-bringing entitled him to be thought'' (p. 68).

The strongest reason for Amherst's attraction to Bessy, however, is the possibility of power that a connection to her would provide. When Bessy expresses a superficial interest in the mill workers, and begins to spend her days with Amherst under the pretext of her concern for them, Amherst begins to dream of a marriage to Bessy that would give him the money — and thus the power — to become a great philanthropist. ''Money! He had spurned the thought of it in choosing his work, yet he now saw that, without its aid, he was powerless to accomplish the object to which his personal desires had been sacrificed'' (p. 97). And Bessy, in the guise of the passive, adoring rich woman, sees the fulfillment of Amherst's dream, for she ''listened with her gentle look of trust, as though committing to him, with the good faith of a child, her ignorance, her credulity, her little rudimentary convictions and her tentative aspirations, relying on him not to abuse or misdirect them in the boundless supremacy of his masculine understanding'' (p. 100). Bessy appears to be both the perfect mate for Amherst — submissive, utterly uncritical — and the perfect financial resource, a limitless bankroll with which to do good. Like Hollingsworth in *The Blithedale Romance*, Amherst is looking for a Priscilla — a sweet and subservient source of financial and emotional support.

And Amherst is like Hollingsworth in another, more important way. His zeal for reform becomes an obsession; the subject becomes identified in his mind with his very being; an attack on his goals, or even a questioning of his methods, becomes, to Amherst, an attack on his own character. Like Hollingsworth, Amherst's life comes to illustrate Hawthorne's statement that ''admitting what is called Philanthropy, when adopted as a profession, to be often useful by its energetic impulse to society at large, it is perilous to the individual, whose ruling passion, in one exclusive channel, it thus becomes. It ruins, or is fearfully apt to ruin, the heart. . . .''[4] Amherst marries Bessy, not out of genuine love, but to further his ambitions. Bessy is the owner of Westmore, and to Amherst, Westmore is ''the special outlet offered for expression of what he was worth to the world'' (p. 276).

The marriage proves to be a disappointment to both partners. Bessy has married Amherst, not out of love of good deeds, but for love of the man himself. When she discovers that her love is not reciprocated, she retaliates with the only weapon in her command — her money. She denies Amherst the total control of finances that he had expected to be his, thwarting his objectives by spending freely and frivolously on her personal pleasures. To Amherst, who "had always conveniently supposed that the poet's line summed up the good woman's rule of ethics: 'He for God only, she for God in him' " (p. 179), Bessy's behavior is infuriating. As he explains to Bessy, "When we married I never expected you to care or know much about economics. It isn't a quality a man usually chooses a wife for. But ... I had a fancy that you might take my opinions on faith when it came to my special business — the thing I'm generally supposed to know about" (p. 200).

Amherst's conflict with Bessy centers on the fact that, as Nellie Elizabeth Monroe explains it, he wanted both to marry for money and remain a disinterested idealist at the same time.[5] Bessy's reaction to Amherst's constant demands for control of her money is more than a selfish desire to keep the money for her own amusement, however, for Bessy has realized that all she represents to her husband is a source of funds. If she played the passive role expected of her and surrendered control of the mill, she would cease to exist for Amherst at all. In their continual battles over money, Amherst, considering his wife "inaccessible to grown-up arguments and the stronger logic of experience" (p. 196), handles her "as mechanically as a nurse soothing a fitful child" (p. 198), and Bessy is aware of Amherst's attitude, once crying out, "I can't endure to be humoured like a baby!" (p. 199). Amherst simply does not know how to deal with a woman who is not as willing to sacrifice and submit as his mother was,[6] and he can only treat her as the child he expected her to be. While he cannot see it, Bessy wants, above all, to be perceived not as a silly and dependent child, but as a person. When a friend tells Bessy that she herself dreams not of "a man who made life easy," but of "some one who made it interesting," Bessy replies "with a bitterness that issued strangely from her lips: 'Don't imagine you invented that! Every girl thinks it. Afterwards she finds out that it's much pleasanter to be thought interesting herself' " (p. 226). The marriage becomes a war of wills and egos, for Amherst takes any refusal to accept his reforms as an affront to his own sense of self-worth, and Bessy clings to her money, knowing it to be the only thing she has that "interests" her husband.

Caught in the middle of this unhappy marriage is Justine Brent, the woman who, ironically, had been the catalyst for Amherst and Bessy's initial meeting. Justine, a former classmate of Bessy's, had been the nurse at the mill hospital who had violated hospital rules to plead to Amherst for the maimed worker; now she lives with the couple as nurse to Bessy's daughter, Cicely, and friend to both husband and wife. Justine is both confidante to Amherst and "a kind of outlet for Bessy's pent-up discontents" (p. 227). She is also the second intruder in the novel.

Justine Brent is very different from Bessy. Having experienced the loss of the family fortunes as a child, she has been forced to earn her own living, and her self-possession and cool control are in direct contrast with Bessy's rages. To Amherst she is a comrade in the struggle against suffering, the woman whose courage and frankness had forced him to see the misery of Westmore as it really is. Bessy, on the other hand, is especially accepting of Justice, for she senses no threat to her marriage in this woman who is intelligent, vital, and involved, but who is not so pretty as she is. To Bessy, Justine is merely a much-needed friend in this troubled time.

But Justine is herself uneasy in her role at Lynbrook, the Westmore family home. Aside from being caught in the cross fire of every argument between Amherst and Bessy, Justine has other reasons for feeling uncomfortable. Like many intruders, she does not quite fit into the upper reaches of society. Employed as a type of higher servant, Justine will not allow herself to be treated as a member of Bessy's social circle, and yet her position as Bessy's former schoolmate and her function as family peacemaker make her more than a governess. Like Lily Bart, Justine loves the luxury of the world Bessy inhabits, but the people in it, she feels, "missed the poetry of their situation" (p. 221). Justine feels trapped, for she is "a creature tingling with energy, a little floating particle of the power that moves the sun and the other stars, and the deadening influences of the life at Lynbrook roused these tendencies to greater intensity, as a suffocated person will suddenly develop abnormal strength in the struggle for air" (p. 222). An outsider in the shallow social world of Lynbrook, Justine can only long rather hopelessly for "a life in which high chances of doing should be mated with the finer forms of enjoying." (p. 223).

When Amherst, able to endure his frustration no longer, finally leaves Bessy, Justine is left to manage the household and to comfort the distraught wife. Bessy consoles herself with wild rides on a dangerous horse, appropriately named Impulse, a horse that her husband had specifically cautioned her not to ride. Bessy is critically injured and there is little hope that she will ever recover. As she lingers on in terrible pain, she tells Justine that she wants to die. Justine remembers Amherst's comment on the maimed mill worker: "In your work, don't you ever feel tempted to set a poor devil free?" (p. 428), and on the flyleaf of one of Amherst's books she reads, "Socrates used to call the opinions of the many by the name of Lamiae — bugbears to frighten children . . ." (p. 429). Because she thinks it is what Amherst would want, and because she can no longer bear to watch Bessy in torment, Justine gives her a fatal dose of morphine.

Bessy's death leaves Amherst in control of her estate, and leaves him free to begin his program of reform. As he plans the dedication ceremony of his first project, the Westmore Memorial Hospital, he looks at Justine and realizes that "among the little group who were to surround him on the morrow, she was the only one discerning enough to understand what the day meant to him, or with sufficient knowledge to judge of the use he had made of his great opportunity" (p. 445-46). Once again Amherst seeks an appreciative audience for his endeavors; he can consider Justine only in terms of himself and his obsession. It is to fulfill his need for admiration that he takes Justine as his second wife, and he considers her a more suitable mate than Bessy, for she has the intelligence necessary to make her approval valuable, and her penniless situation will make her a grateful partner.

To Justine marriage to Amherst seems the fulfillment of her desire to do good in a beautiful setting. Her immense energy, she feels, has at last found a suitable outlet, and her wish for meaningful work at first blends with Amherst's philanthropy: "their duties had the rarer quality of constituting, precisely, the deepest, finest bond between them" (p. 472). The marriage soon founders, however, for it is not long before Amherst discovers that Bessy did not just fade away conveniently, but that Justine had helped her to die more quickly. This discovery destroys the bond between Amherst and Justine, for as Justine learns, "Amherst had not understood her — worse still, he had judged her as the world might judge her!" (p. 524).

Amherst's reaction to Justine's "crime" indicates his essential conventionality, for, as Blake Nevius notes, Amherst "cannot penetrate to the clear moral atmosphere in which her decisions are formed."[7] The philanthropist who dedicates his life to alleviating the suffering of the masses cannot countenance Justine's act of charity, for hers was an act in violation of society's law. Amherst's inability to stand by and support Justine is the most negative aspect of his character and belies his radical posings.

Justine's initial response to Amherst's revulsion is one of self-examination, for she fears that her motivation in helping Bessy to die might have been her love for Bessy's husband. But she eventually rejects this thought: "No! Her motive had been normal, sane and justifiable — completely justifiable. Her fault lay in having dared to rise above conventional restrictions, her mistake in believing that her husband could rise with her" (p. 525). Rather than blame herself, Justine must instead deal with her changed relation to the man she married, for "the tie between them was forever stained and debased" (p. 526).

Amherst can never forgive Justine because not only has she acted on principles he only talked of, but, as Elizabeth Ammons explains, she acted "on her own initiative, out of her own sense of moral autonomy, and did not feel bound to seek his approval after the fact."[8] By freeing Amherst from his detested wife, Justine has also placed Amherst under a certain obligation to her; he owes, in effect, his new position to her, and she has thus doubly upset the balance of power in their marriage. All of this is too much for Amherst to take. Faced once again with a woman too independent for his tastes, Amherst retreats, like other Wharton males, from the living woman, and turns for solace to an ideal: to the memory of Bessy. The willful, selfish Bessy whom Amherst hated is now, in his mind, transformed into what Margaret McDowell describes as "a suppliant saint, a person whom he could love because he would be able to dominate her."[9] In the final irony of the book, Amherst plans for a workmen's gymnasium, convincing himself that the blueprints he discovered in Bessy's house were her plans for such a structure and that he is carrying out Bessy's last generous wishes. As Justine, who submits to this charade, well knows, the blueprints were for Bessy's own private sports center. Justine herself is now trapped, "pledged to the perpetual expiation of an act for which, in the abstract, she still refused to hold herself to blame" (p. 624). She becomes the outsider in her own marriage, while the "unreal woman, this phantom that Amherst's uneasy imagination had evoked," supplants her, "first as his wife, and then as his fellow worker ..." (p. 629).

The negative portrait of John Amherst that fills so much of *The Fruit of the Tree* is not to be interpreted as Wharton's attack on reformers. On the contrary, the novel, with its double marriage, double intruders, and double social problems of factory reform and mercy killing, is linked by one theme: the difference between true and false charity. The descriptions of the mill town in the novel indicate the need for real charity, for true reform, and Wharton does not spare the reader a picture of "the dark side of monotonous human toil, of the banquet of flesh and blood and brain perpetually served up to the monster whose insatiable jaws the looms so grimly typified" (p. 57).[10] What the novel condemns, however, is the false charity of obsessions, of egotism, of the reform done only for self-glorification.

The false philanthropist of the novel is John Amherst, to whom Justine's rather offhand remark that "philanthropy is one of the subtlest forms of self-indulgence" (p. 156) may rightly be applied. Amherst's ideal of philanthropy is like Selden's "republic of the spirit" or Ralph Marvell's secret cave shielding an image of a refined and purer life — a fantasy standard the dreamer applies to others but does not live up to himself. And, as Lily Bart and Undine Spragg each uncover the true nature of their men's standards, so too Justine's function in *The Fruit of the Tree* is to reveal Amherst's philanthropy as empty and self-indulgent. Opposing Amherst's egotistical, theoretical brand of charity is Justine's genuine, impassioned involvement with people, with the human side of philanthropy and reform. For Justine "had always taken an interest in the lives and thoughts of working-people: not so much the constructive interest of the sociological mind as the vivid imaginative concern of a heart open to every human appeal" (p. 457). The heart, the personal concern and need for human contact is what Justine possesses and Amherst lacks.[11] Unlike Amherst, Justine does not dream of reconstructing an entire town, of designing large institutional centers; rather, she reaches out, transcending convention, to those closest to her: to the individual worker, to Bessy, to Amherst himself. As a nurse she is "glad to do her part in the vast impersonal labour of easing the world's misery," but always she longs for "a special load to lift, a single hand to clasp" (p. 147). Her true charity operates in both factory and family. She is the link between the novel's two subjects, for she deals with the large and small world alike, with concern, not for abstractions or theory, but for the suffering individual. Without the core of humanity and without the heart that characterize Justine, Amherst's grandiose reform is, in contrast, the generosity of an ungenerous man.

The use of double intruders occurs again in another work by Wharton, one of her novels of the twenties, *Twilight Sleep*. The title of the novel refers specifically to a new process by which childbirth can be made painless, but it refers more generally to all the different attempts that the book's characters make to avoid pain. Like *The Age of Innocence*, *The Reef*, and *The Children*, *Twilight Sleep* is a novel about evasion. Each character in the book, with one exception, has one goal: to get through life without suffering; and each numbs his sensibility in a different way: through the pursuit of pleasure, through bad faith, through false credos, or through self-delusion.

First on the list of evaders of the real is Pauline Manford, a wealthy society woman whose whole life is "a long uninterrupted struggle against the encroachment of every form of pain. The first step, always, was to conjure it, bribe it away, by every possible expenditure — except of one's self."[12] Pauline's defenses in the battle against the unpleasant include endless philanthropic committees, a series of masseurs and rejuvenators, and, above all, a succession of spiritual "guides" ranging from a corrupt Mahatma to Alvah Loft, author of "Spiritual Vacuum-Cleaning" and "Beyond God" (p. 137), to a Russian "Scientific Initiate" with a new treatment that "absolutely wiped out wrinkles" (p. 279). It is characteristic of Pauline that she blithely supports both birth control and a National Mother's Association, for, as Elizabeth Ammons points out, in reality

Pauline has no convictions.[13] Because Pauline succeeds in avoiding pain, she fails to feel anything.[14] Sealed up in a thin bubble of unreality, living by her "smiling resolves to ignore or dominate whatever was obstructive or unpleasant" (p. 235), Pauline cuts herself off from any real contact with her family, which is falling apart before her eyes because "her glittering optimism was a hard surface for grief and failure to fling themselves on" (p. 219).

Pauline's husband, Dexter, has his own problems and his own peculiar way of dealing with them. Although he is a successful and wealthy lawyer, his days are not happy ones, for they start with "a great sense of pressure, importance and authority," but end with "a drop at the close into staleness and futility" (p. 56). Although Dexter is astute enough to recognize "the perpetual evasion, moral, mental, physical, which he heard preached, and saw practised, everywhere about him" (p. 56), he cannot recognize his own escape for what it is. Although he is seeking to regain his own youth and self-esteem in an affair with his stepson's wife, Dexter deludes himself into believing that his motives in pursuing Lita Wyant are "to help and save her for Jim's [his stepson's] sake and her own" (p. 191).

Pauline's first husband, the old New Yorker in the novel, attempts to live by a traditional code of chivalry and gentility that has become outmoded at best and actually dangerous at worst. If the quality of his beliefs may be judged by the character of the man, old New York is not to be regarded too highly, for Arthur Wyant is a gossipy, alcoholic hypochondriac, sunk into "a sort of premature old age" (p. 25), and ineffectual in times of crisis.[15] Rather than representing one clear critical voice in the wilderness, that of the outsider able to see things as they are, Wyant joins the conspiracy of evasion. For his "tradition of reticence and decency ... had always joined with Pauline's breezy optimism in relegating to silence and non-existence whatever it was painful or even awkward to discuss" (p. 165). In this linking of the old New Yorker with the "new woman," Wharton makes explicit the kinship of evasion in the two worlds, which many of her other works suggest.

The novel is crammed full of other people with other devices for escape: there are Pauline's friends, "bright elderly women, with snowy hair, eurythmic movements, and finely-wrinkled over-massaged faces ... inexorably earnest, aimlessly kind and fathomlessly pure" (p. 5), all like older May Wellands, trapped in negative innocence. There are the flappers and their lovers, occupied in "the ceaseless rush from thrill to thrill" (p. 5), and, in contrast, there is Aggie Heuston, a woman who finds solace in an exalted pseudo-religion and who denies her husband both a real marriage and a divorce.

There are two intruders, two characters who do not quite fit into this world for two quite different reasons. The first, Lita Wyant, the beautiful and amoral wife of Pauline's son, is another Undine Spragg, a symbol of all the follies of her society exaggerated and magnified until she becomes dangerous to the world that made her. There are many superficial similarities between Lita and Undine; like Undine, Lita begins as an outsider and enters society through marriage; she is also described in terms of endless movement: dancing, she is sinuous, "a small still flower on a swaying stalk" (p. 85), and she admits that "immobility was never my strong point" (p. 129). She is the ultimate consumer; of her recently (and expensively) decorated living room Lita says, "I'd like to throw everything in it into the street" (p. 34) and begin again. And, like Undine, "she wants the universe — or her idea of it" (p. 205).

Lita's resemblance to Undine Spragg is more than a matter of similar movements, ambitions, or "goldfish-coloured hair" (p. 32), however. Her function in this novel is nearly identical to Undine Spragg's in *The Custom of the Country*. Like her predecessor, Lita exists as an object lesson, as the monster that her world's vices have created. Utterly self-centered, pure surface with nothing inside, Lita Wyant is Pauline Manford distorted and exaggerated; her face, "something so complete and accomplished that one could not imagine its being altered by any ulterior disturbance" (p. 333), mirrors only the inhuman serenity of those around her.

Ironically, Lita most resembles her mother-in-law. Although Pauline is most often startled or annoyed by Lita, the two are unmistakably similar. While Pauline visits the spurious Mahatma to learn exercises to reduce the size of her hips, Lita merely goes her one better and stays at his establishment to learn semi-nude dancing, thus causing a family scandal. Pauline divorces her first husband, Arthur, because he fails to meet her stringent specifications for a partner; Lita likewise wants to divorce Pauline's son because, she casually explains, "I want a new deal" (p. 230).

Lita is not only a reflection of Pauline, however. Her perpetual cry, "Oh children — but I'm bored!" is the echo of nearly everyone else's deepest feeling. For Pauline's hard-bought calm leaves her terrified of boredom and she is "painfully oppressed by an hour of unexpected leisure" (p. 134); Dexter fights a sense of "stealing boredom" (p. 66); and everyone in the novel leads the kind of overscheduled life the Welland family in *The Age of Innocence* leads in the attempt to stave off the terror of the empty moment. The incessant activity and the multitude of escapes that mute the unpleasant and stifle pain do not prevent life from being rather dull. Unfortunately, as Lita says, "You can't take out an insurance against boredom" (p. 230).

It is Lita who is most frank and open about what is actually happening in her world, and although she is totally self-absorbed and utterly without values, her honest hedonism has a certain appeal. It is this quality that entrances Dexter Manford, for Lita "was the one person in his group to whom its catchwords meant absolutely nothing. The others, whatever their private omissions or indulgences, dressed up their selfish cravings in the same wordy altruism," but "one could never fix her attention on any subject beyond her own immediate satisfaction, and that animal sincerity seemed to Manford her greatest charm" (p. 190).

The plot of the novel concerns the Wyant-Manford clan's battle to keep Lita from her satisfactions and to keep her a virtuous wife. One of the greatest ironies of the story is that the leader of the campaign is Dexter Manford, the man who longs to be Lita's lover.

Hopelessly entangled in the lives of all the others is the second intruder in the novel, Pauline's daughter, Nona Manford. Nona, at age twenty, is, like Judith Wheater, the only adult among children. In this "easy rosy world" (p. 74), Nona is the only person who worries; she muses "I feel like the oldest person in the world, and yet with the longest life ahead of me" (p. 281). Ostensibly a flapper and a companion of Lita, Nona is perceived by her mother as "Poor Nona" because she has "no enthusiasms, no transports of faith" (p. 147). Nona's anxieties and her adult status make her an outsider in her own family, yet it is to Nona that everyone turns for understanding and guidance, for Nona is the only person who faces reality[16] and who genuinely cares about someone besides herself. Her role is a difficult one:

> There were moments when Nona felt oppressed by responsibilities not of her age, apprehensions that she could not shake off and yet had not enough experience of life to know how to meet. One or two of her girl friends — in the brief intervals between whirls and thrills — had confessed to the same vague disquietude. It was as if, in the beaming determination of the middle-aged, one and all of them, to ignore sorrow and evil, "think them away" as superannuated bogies . . . as if the demons the elder generation ignored, baulked of their natural prey, had cast their hungry shadow over the young. (Pp. 47-48)

Nona is the family's natural victim, and she knows it. "Somebody in every family had to remember now and then that such things as wickedness, suffering and death had not yet been banished from the earth . . . perhaps the children had to serve as vicarious sacrifices" (p. 48).

And the climax of the novel is, inevitably, the sacrifice of Nona. When Lita Wyant brings down the house of cards by engaging in an affair with Dexter, and when Arthur Wyant, in a drunken, misguided act of chivalry, rushes into their bedroom to defend his son's honor, Nona, running to the scene, is shot. The real climax of the novel is not, however, the slight wound that Nona receives, but, as Edmund Wilson notes, "the capacity of her [Wharton's] characters for continuing to evade the situation even when it has apparently brought the roof down on their heads."[17] For, instead of the discovery of the lovers leading to at least two divorces, multiple recriminations, and emotional scenes, life goes on — serenely. Everyone merely travels, for "when rich people's nerves are out of gear the pleasant remedy of travel is the first prescribed" (p. 362). Pauline and Dexter go to the Far East, Arthur to "a private inebriate asylum in Maine" (p. 361), and Lita and Jim to France, where Lita can amuse herself with "the Grand Prix, the new fashions and the new plays" (p. 361). Only Nona is left behind, in a hospital bed, the only piece of evidence that anything bad has happened, and thus someone to be avoided. Her final wish in the novel is an appropriate one: she cries that she wants only to go into "a convent where nobody believes in anything" (p. 373).

In a world in which "belief" has become a byword for evasion, in which one can "believe" in false spiritual guides or panaceas or can delude oneself into "believing" lies, to wish to find a place where no one "believes" in anything is an admirable ambition. Nona, the only character who "didn't always believe, like her elders, that one had only to be brisk, benevolent and fond to prevail against the powers of darkness" (p. 48), does not fit into the world of Twilight Sleep. Her final act, motivated by her love for her family, was the only act of genuine commitment in a world of true "believers." And the Manfords' reaction to it, their flight from Nona, represents their awareness that Nona is not like them, that she will not join them in the search for easy answers and instant solutions. Their flight from Nona reveals also the essential selfishness and cruelty of those who "believe" in the credos of this superficial world. Nona's action and her family's reaction to it contrast the shallow, cruel, self-centered attitudes of society in the twenties with one individual's search for a life of greater depth and meaning. As Geoffrey Walton says, Nona is "the real positive" in the novel: "a combination of free intelligence and human sympathy,"[18] and as such she must inevitably be an alien in society. For Nona is another in that series of women — Ellen Olenska, Sophy Viner, Judith Wheater — whose experience and intelligence enable them to see the real, and who therefore threaten the security of those around them.[19]

In *Twilight Sleep* the two intruders act in opposite ways: one, Lita, as the exaggeration of her society's flaws; the other, Nona, as a center of sanity in a mad world. In Wharton's companion novels, *Hudson River Bracketed* and *The Gods Arrive*, the intruder, Halo Tarrant, functions in another way — as a teacher. For the two novels are novels of education, books that trace the growth of Vance Weston as a writer and as a person.

Halo, in her roles of friend, muse, and mistress, is mainly responsible for Vance's growth.

Vance Weston, the protagonist of both novels, grew up in a Babbitt-like Midwestern atmosphere where "the real business of life was to keep going, to get there — and 'There' was where the money was, always and exclusively."[20] Vance's early life in such towns as Advance and Euphoria, besides being the vehicle for a considerable amount of satire by Wharton,[21] leaves Vance with a certain admiration for efficiency, but also with a feeling that "as a diet for his soul it was deficient in nourishment" (p. 17). His intellectual awakening begins when Vance, recovering from both a broken heart and a case of typhoid, spends a summer of convalescence in the Hudson River Valley. For the aspiring writer, the new environment is something of a shock.

> Paul's Landing was like a place that enterprise of every sort had passed by, as if all its inhabitants had slept through the whole period of industrial development which Vance Weston had been taught to regard as humanity's supreme achievement. If Euphoria values were the right ones — and he had no others to replace them with — then the people who did not strive for them were predestined down-and-outers, as repugnant to the religion of business as the thief and adulterer to the religion of Christianity. And here, in the very part of his immense country which represented all that Western wealth strove for and Western ambition dreamed of, Vance found himself in a community apparently unaware that such strivings and ambitions existed. (Pp. 43-44)

It is not long before Vance's Euphoria values, which center on the ideal of a radio, a car, electricity, and a telephone for every household, are supplanted by the values of the Hudson River environment. For Vance is soon taken to an old house, The Willows, of which his cousins are the caretakers. The very facade of the house suggests "vastness, fantasy and secrecy" (p. 57) to Vance. It represents the past, about which he is totally ignorant, and once inside the house he is fascinated. The portrait of Miss Lorburn, the woman who once owned the house, sets Vance to musing, "the peculiar dress, the sad face, resembled nothing Vance had ever seen; but instantly he felt their intimate relation to all that was peculiar and unfamiliar in the house. The past — they all belonged to the past, this woman and her house, to the same past, a past . . . remote from anything in Vance Weston's experience . . ." (p. 61). The Willows' library is full of books that Vance, familiar only with James Whitcomb Riley, Ella Wheeler Wilcox, and a little Longfellow and Whittier, has never heard of. As he digs into "Kubla Khan," a woman with a faint resemblance to the portrait of Miss Lorburn enters the room. She is Halo Spears, whose relatives own The Willows, and her appearance in the midst of Vance's ecstasy of discovery is to him the intrusion "of something alien, substantial, outside of his own mind, a part of the forgotten world of reality" (p. 64).

For a long time Halo remains a mixture of fantasy and reality to Vance. She becomes both muse and mother, teacher and comrade, for, startled by his enthusiasm and surprised by his meager literary background, Halo gives Vance books to read, takes him to a mountaintop to see the sunrise, criticizes his poetry, and listens sympathetically to his dreams. "Vance thought of her as goddess-like and remote, mistress of the keys of knowledge and experience; her notice had flushed him with pride, but it seemed a part of the mysterious unreality of everything in this new world" (p. 96). It is difficult for Vance to know how to "place" Halo; she is of an old family, she takes for granted a culture Vance has never heard of, yet she is free, frank, open. He "had never met anybody who made things so easy, yet was somehow so gaily aloof" (p. 100). Like so many other intruders, she is enormously receptive, both to life and to the individual, and she is particularly linked to nature: Vance feels her to be "the mysterious vehicle of all the new sensations pouring into his soul — as if she had been the element harmonizing the scene, or a being born of the sunrise and the forest" (p. 101).

The pair continues to meet at The Willows, and Halo provides Vance with the first practical contact of his career; she introduces him to the literary adviser of a small magazine, who publishes Vance's first short story. Halo's influence and teaching are temporarily interrupted, however, when both she and Vance marry unsuitable mates.

Vance, like so many other Wharton males, marries a conventional, limited young girl, his cousin Laura Lou Tracy. She is "so frail, immaterial almost, that she might vanish at a rash word or motion" (p. 205), and her uncritical adoration of Vance seems a refreshing contrast to Halo's high standards. For with Laura Lou, Vance will always be "older and stronger than she was," and will "know more than she did about everything" (p. 243).

Almost immediately, Vance begins to doubt the wisdom of his marriage. On his honeymoon the calendar over the bed bears the admonition, "Little Children, Love One Another" (p. 245), a suitable piece of advice for the marriage of two emotionally immature people. Even on their wedding night, as Vance watches Laura Lou sleep, he feels "a faint apprehension at what he had done, at his own inexperience as well as hers, and the uncertainty of the future." He realizes that he has "bound himself to this child, he, hardly more than a child himself in the knowledge of men and in the mysterious art of getting on" (p. 247). It is not long before Vance is fully aware of Laura Lou's "mental limits," and of the fact that his writing, his literary life, "the things which counted for him," will "never count for her" (p. 271). The expected comparison of his wife to Halo follows, for while Laura Lou can never enter "the world of his mind, with its consuming curiosities, its fervid joys," Vance and Halo, he knows, "might have walked those flaming ramparts [of new ideas] together" (p. 337).

Halo, meanwhile, has become equally trapped. Pressured by her family's financial needs, she has married Lewis Tarrant, the man who has been lending her family money and who has rescued her brother from various disgraceful situations. Halo at first convinces herself that Lewis is a generous, kind man, but before long she admits that she is imprisoned in "a world of suffocating dissimulations" (p. 184) and that "all Lewis's generosity . . . had proceeded not from the heart but from the head. He wanted her; she suited him; he had bought her" (p. 353). And, since Tarrant is supporting the entire Spear family, Halo envisions herself "chained to him for life" (p. 352).

The association between Vance and Halo is renewed when Vance is employed by Tarrant's new amusement, a literary magazine called *The New Hour*. Again Halo becomes Vance's muse. His first novel, *Instead*, is on the surface about old Miss Lorburn, but in another sense describes Halo. Its theme is to be "the mysterious substitution of one value for another in a soul which had somehow found peace" (pp. 337-38), and Vance perceives Halo as someone who "had to give up things too . . . a vision of life" (p. 358). While Vance works on the book, Halo becomes "that other consciousness which seemed an extension of his own, in which every inspiration, as it came, instantly rooted and flowered, and every mistake withered and dropped out of sight" (p. 359). Not only does Halo serve as inspiration/alter ego during this period, but she also introduces Vance to certain aspects of the New York literary life: to other writers and to new ideas. She holds little parties to introduce Vance to the "right" people and she protects Vance from her dilettante husband, who is jealous of Vance's talent.

Until almost the very end of *Hudson River Bracketed*, the union of Halo and Vance remains a marriage of minds. It is not until the final chapters of the book, when Laura Lou (rather conveniently) dies of tuberculosis and Halo is freed from Tarrant's grasp by a large inheritance, that the possibility of a true marriage for the couple develops. But the final words of the book are ambiguous. Even as Vance and Halo are freed, something remains to separate them. When Vance tells Halo of his wife's death, and when he comforts her in her shock, he feels "as if he were sitting down on the floor to comfort a child that had hurt itself . . . he wondered if at crucial moments the same veil of unreality would always fall between himself and the soul nearest him; if the creator of imaginary beings must always feel alone among the real ones" (p. 560).

The conflict that remains unresolved at the end of *Hudson River*

Bracketed is supposed to be one peculiar to the life of the artist: must the writer remain forever detached from reality, even from those he loves, simply because of the nature of his art? Must he be eternally the observer of life? The problem with this ending to the novel, and with the novel itself, is that, as Geoffrey Walton says, Vance "does not strike one as a personality or an artist of great distinction."[22] It is difficult to take him seriously as a writer. Vance has a habit of thinking in capitalized abstractions — the Past, the Mothers, the dark Unknown, Beauty — which strikes the reader not as profound but pretentious. And Vance's constant retreat from the problems of everyday living into his own world of imagination seems more like a naive but enormous self-absorption than a mark of genius. His secret inner self, "an irreducible core of selfness (he found no other word for it); a hidden cave in which he hoarded his secret treasures as a child hoards stony dead star-fish and dull shells of which he has once seen the sea-glitter, though he can make no one else believe in it" (p. 272), is reminiscent of Ralph Marvell's private retreat into his fantasy cave or Selden's exclusive "republic of the spirit." Because Vance can so easily withdraw into his "core of selfness," for example, he remains for a long time unaware of Laura Lou's sickness, and he aggravates her condition by taking her on midwinter excursions to the forest and seashore, oblivious to what such trips do to her.

Whether Vance Weston is a believable writer or not, it is through tracing his development as an artist that Edith Wharton has the chance to express various criticisms of the literary world. As her early chapters on the Midwest focus on the replacement of all values by the values of business, with "success" as "the only criterion of beauty" (p. 10), so her main concern in the literary world is for the commercialization of art, the transformation of the writer into a salable commodity. Thus Vance's publishers, Dreck and Saltzer, lock him into a three-year contract that allows him little freedom and almost no share of the profits, and when his first novel is a success, they want another, right away, just like it. Vance, under pressure to produce and to produce fast, learns about "this dreadful system of forcing talent, trying to squeeze every drop out of it before it was ripe; the principle of the quick turnover applied to brains as it was to real estate" (p. 311). He is exposed to literary parasites like Lewis Tarrant and Jet Pulsifer (of the famous Pulsifer Prize), who attempt to buy themselves an artist and to bask in the reflected glory. He learns of the system of favors, which requires him to praise a work by another author (whatever he thinks of it) in return for support of his own work. And when Vance begins to meet other young writers, Wharton has an opportunity to comment on certain modern writers and their work: "The brilliant verbal gymnastics — or the staccato enumeration of a series of physical aspects and sensations — they all left him with the sense of an emptiness underneath, just where, in his own vision of the world, the deep forces stirred and wove men's fate'' (p. 335).[23]

Outside of the literary marketplace, outside really of any group, is Halo Tarrant, who ''in a world of shifting standards, had always held fast to her own values'' (p. 183). Halo does not represent the past, nor is she allied with the trendy writers of the time. She does not exploit, flatter, or trap Vance Weston. Rather, she is the clear but critical intelligence that helps to form him into the writer he desires to be.

Hudson River Bracketed involves Halo Tarrant in the literary educa- tion of Vance Weston. In its sequel, *The Gods Arrive*, Halo plays the largest role in Vance's sentimental, or emotional, education.

The Gods Arrive begins happily. Halo has become Vance's mistress, and the pair travel to Europe, Halo contentedly wondering ''what happiness could equal that of a woman permitted to serve the genius while she adored the man.''[24] After a brief period of harmony, however, Halo's story becomes a chronicle of her losses: of loss of her own identity, of Vance the writer, and of Vance her lover.

Having taken one rebellious step in moving in with Vance before she has obtained a divorce from Tarrant, Halo faces complications she had never anticipated. ''She was beginning to realize that in throwing in her lot with Vance she had entered into an unknown country — as unknown to her as Spain was to him, and with far fewer landmarks to guide her'' (p. 41). Her greatest fear is that, having made a commitment to Vance that is not sanctioned by society and having staked everything on the relationship, she will lose him. Vance, more than ever the egotist of *Hudson River Bracketed*, begins to take Halo for granted; he expects her to handle all the details of daily life, to organize their wanderings, and to create an orderly home life from which he can withdraw at will.[25] Rather than assert herself, Halo, obsessed by ''the one vital point: would he weary of her or would she be able to hold him?'' (p. 83), becomes as sub- missive as the meekest wife. ''She had to love Vance more passionately, and to believe in his genius more fervently and continuously, because she had staked so much on her love and her faith'' (p. 84). The woman who had been a source of strength to Vance is transformed into a dependent, fearful child whose policy is to ''hold her breath and watch'' (p. 46), and who can now ask, ''What's loving but pretending?'' (p. 314).

Halo's self-effacement does not at first extend to the area of Vance's work, for she continues to dream of ''seeing his gift unfold under her care'' (p. 28). But her frank criticism begins to be unwelcome to Vance, who now prefers adulation and praise. Ignoring the advice of ''this girl who was his other brain, his soul and his flesh'' (p. 26), Vance turns to more spurious influences, to Alders, who calls himself ''The Scholar Gypsy'' (p. 45) and whose ''thin glaze of culture'' (p. 44) conceals his "unsatisfied social cravings" (p. 63). Alders persuades Vance to write another historical romance, *The Puritan in Spain*, which is a facile replay of his earlier success, *Instead*. Vance's reaction to the success of *The Puritan* and to Halo's dislike of it reveals the true reasons for his rejection of her influence. Vance himself is not pleased with the book; it "had come too easily; he knew it had not been fetched up out of the depths" (p. 71), and yet "one half of him was proud of the book, and believed all that his readers said in praise of it" (p. 72). Halo has come to represent Vance's true, best self, which he is now betraying; he would prefer to hear praise than to listen to his own inner voice, which Halo echoes: "he knew she did not care for it [the book]. Perhaps that was the real source of his dissatisfaction; he told himself irritably that he was still too subject to her judgments" (p. 72). Vance begins to avoid Halo's critical eye, for it shows him his own compromised standards.[26]

Vance's next book again shows a departure from his own best instincts. This novel, *Colossus*, is planned as "a sort of compendium of all that life had given him — and received from him" (p. 167), and Halo, who is not permitted to see the early chapters, rightly guesses it to be Vance's attempt to "do a masterpiece according to the new recipe" (p. 99). Vance, who has taken to associating with the Bohemian literary set of Paris and London, now tries to write to please his new friends, and Halo realizes that "he had rightly guessed that Halo would warn him against the danger of sacrificing his individuality to a fashion or school. . . . instinctively, he had anticipated her disapproval" (p. 99) and kept the book from her.

The influences surrounding Vance at this time are not only literary ones. Halo finds herself excluded from Vance's social world as well as from his artistic one. Halo is uncomfortable in Bohemian circles; she "felt herself an outsider in this world which was to set her free" (p. 82); "she would never be at home among these people whose way of living was not the result of passion but of the mere quest for novelty" (p. 91). While Halo finds no place among the avant garde, she is also excluded from traditional society. In an obvious criticism of the double standard,[27] Wharton shows Vance, a celebrity, welcomed into polite society, while the woman he lives with is "cut" by the same social groups. Vance's excursions into both "in" and "out" groups increase in number and length, while Halo remains behind, waiting, serenely welcoming Vance back whenever he decides to return.

When Vance becomes the vogue among the fashionable rich, Halo loses him as a lover. Vance reencounters Floss Delaney, formerly his sweetheart in Euphoria, now a millionairess and a "latter-day Undine Spragg,"[28] and everything he once valued — work, Halo, self-esteem — is obscured by his desire for Floss. Although Floss openly and repeatedly humiliates and rejects Vance, and although her own father tells Vance that "money's her god . . . it's the only thing that'll get her what she wants; and what she wants is the earth" (p. 228), Vance becomes obsessed with her. He pursues her over two continents, returning to Halo for comfort when Floss has particularly humiliated him.

Halo's self-effacement expands until she has almost ceased to exist, even for herself, but it is her critical intelligence that finally saves her. The quarrel that finally restores Halo to herself is not about Vance's infidelities, but about his work. When Vance finally reads the manuscript of *Colossus* to Halo, she cannot pretend to like it. Her comments on the novel are an astute evaluation not only of Vance's artistic problems but of his romantic ones:

> I have an idea you haven't found yourself — expressed your real self, I mean — in this book as you did in the others. You're not . . . quite as free from other influences . . . echoes. . . . I feel that you may have let yourself be too much guided, directed — drawn away from your own immediate vision. (P. 336)

Vance cannot bear Halo's criticism, and before long Halo decides to leave Vance, not only in order to allow him to be "free as air" (p. 312), but because she has decided not to continue to live as Vance's ignored best self, but as herself. Concealing the fact of her pregnancy from Vance, she returns to The Willows, her one desire now "to be alone; to go my own way, without depending on anybody. I want to be Halo Spear again — that's all" (p. 362).

It takes considerably longer for Vance to find his own way, and it is failure that finally forces him to face himself. *Colossus* fails, and Vance must acknowledge that "Halo had been right. . . . 'Colossus' was not his own book . . . but a kind of hybrid monster made out of his own imaginings with those imposed upon him by the literary fashions and influences of the day" (p. 386). Disappointment with his novel is coupled with disillusionment about Floss Delaney. Vance at last sees her for what she is, and her spell is broken. Confused and suffering, Vance returns to his family, and there his grandmother's dying words puzzle him: "Maybe we haven't made enough of pain — been too afraid of it. Don't be afraid of it" (p. 402).

In the northern woods, where Vance retreats to "work out some sort of plan from the dark muddle of things" (p. 404), his grandmother's message becomes clear. In his solitude Vance reads *The Confessions of St. Augustine*, and one passage, in which the saint describes the voice of God calling to him, haunts Vance: "I heard Thy voice crying to me: 'I am the Food of the full-grown. Become a man and thou shalt feed on

Me' " (p. 411). To Vance, this is "the message of experience to the soul," and "the key to his grandmother's last words" (p. 411). He realizes that "it was time to eat that food; time to grow up; time to fly from his sheltered solitude and go down again" (p. 414) to life, however painful it might be. His future, Vance decides, "was to be ruled by realities, not illusions" (p. 417).

It is fitting that a novel that has involved so much movement, tracing Vance's restless journeys from himself, should end where Vance's adult life began, at the Hudson River. Here a repentant Vance finds Halo, and tells her, "I'm not fit for you, yet, Halo; I'm only just learning how to talk. . . ." It is Halo's laugh that ends the novel, as, revealing her pregnancy to Vance and opening her arms to him, she says, "But then I shall have two children to take care of instead of one!" (p. 432).

The roles of the lovers have again been reversed; Vance is now the dependent child and Halo the maternal, protective figure she was at the beginning of the relationship. The scene is not, however, an endorsement of a life of "voluntary abnegation dedicated to the service of others," as Elizabeth Ammons sees it,[29] but rather an emblem of Halo's rediscovered strength and maturity. Before Vance can come back to Halo, his deepest and best self,[30] she must travel back to her own selfhood, must become a person again. At the end of the novel Halo is not the woman who lived for Vance and through Vance; she has learned "to follow her own way, neither defiantly nor apologetically, but as if it were of more concern to herself than it could possibly be to others" (p. 423). Having learned to reconstruct her own life alone, Halo is now strong enough to help Vance to rebuild his.

As in *Hudson River Bracketed*, the tale of the artist precipitates considerable criticism of literary movements and literary parasites, but much more of the criticism of this novel develops from society's treatment of Halo, or from her relation to society. The hypocrisy of the double standard is stressed, and those who accept Halo when she is an outcast are generally the more admirable characters. The picture of the idle rich at play, similar to certain scenes in *The Children*, is contrasted to the simplicity of Halo's life. Halo is not linked to the modern rebels, for her taste of such life only makes her aware "how deeply rooted in her were the old instincts of order and continuity" (p. 306). Neither is Halo a symbol of tradition, however.[31] Although her own experiences make her increasingly aware of the stabilizing qualities of marriage, she prefers to free Vance and bear a child alone rather than to marry without Vance's love. Halo is a blend of both convention and nonconformity, as the last scenes in the novel make clear. For she is living at The Willows, symbol of the past and continuity, but she is living there alone, about to give birth to an illegitimate child. Among all the influences, movements, and social sets of *The Gods Arrive*, only Halo, finally, develops the courage to be alone, to be free.

Edith Wharton's novellas are not without equally solitary intruders. In Wharton's first published novella, *The Touchstone* (1900), the intruder is a dead woman, Margaret Aubyn. Although she is dead before the action of the story begins, her inescapable presence, her memory, forces the hero, Stephen Glennard, to reevaluate his actions and attitudes.

Margaret Aubyn, a famous novelist, had had an affair with Glennard. Glennard had never loved Mrs. Aubyn, and when her brutish husband died, leaving her free to marry, Glennard rejected the woman. Even after Mrs. Aubyn dies, Glennard remembers the whole affair with a certain distaste for his own part in it:

> he chafed at his own inadequacy, his stupid inability to rise to the height of her passion. His egotism was not of a kind to mirror its complacency in the adventure. To have been loved by the most brilliant woman of her day, and to have been incapable of loving her, seemed to him, in looking back, derisive evidence of his limitations; and his remorseful tenderness for her memory was complicated with a sense of irritation against her for having given him once for all the measure of his emotional capacity.[32]

One of the reasons for Glennard's rejection of Mrs. Aubyn was her very brilliance, for "it was not that she bored him; she did what was infinitely worse — she made him feel his inferiority" (p. 18). And Margaret Aubyn's "mental ascendancy" (p. 18) was not tempered by the traditional femininity that would have appealed to Glennard; he found her lacking in beauty, and incapable of using what prettiness she had to her best advantage. Her genius would have been forgiven her if she had been stylish and more attractive, but, Glennard reflects, "Genius is of small use to a woman who does not know how to do her hair" (p. 19).

After Mrs. Aubyn's death Glennard falls in love with a much more conventional type, Alexa Trent.[33] Glennard cannot marry Alexa, however, because he lacks the money he needs to support her. He solves this problem by selling, privately, Margaret Aubyn's love letters to him. The published letters (their recipient unidentified) are a best seller, and Glennard gets the money and marries Alexa. But he is now, more than ever, haunted by Margaret Aubyn.

When he hears his friends discuss the letters, Glennard begins to recognize what his action in selling them has made him. As one person comments, the letters reveal "the woman's soul, absolutely torn up by the roots — her whole self laid bare; and to a man who evidently didn't care; who couldn't have cared" (p. 67). Not only does Glennard now fear discovery of his connection to the letters, but he also shrinks from the "garb of dishonor" (p. 91) in which his action has clothed him.[34]

Paradoxically, Glennard now begins to fall in love with Mrs. Aubyn. When he sees her photograph in a magazine, "all that was feminine in her, the quality he had always missed, stole toward him from her unreproachful gaze; and now that it was too late, life had developed in him the subtler perceptions which could detect it in even this poor semblance of herself" (p. 115). Mrs. Aubyn, dead, exerts more of an influence on Glennard than she ever did alive; but her effect on Glennard is not merely to humiliate him. By revealing Glennard to himself, Mrs. Aubyn helps him to purge himself of his baseness; her role is to transform, to reform Glennard. Gazing at her photograph, Glennard "felt himself laid bare to the inmost fold of consciousness. The shame was deep, but it was a renovating anguish: he felt like a man whom intolerable pain has roused from the creeping lethargy of death" (p. 115).

When Glennard confesses everything to his wife, Alexa is perceptive enough to see the positive aspects of his suffering. She advises her husband to make something valuable of it all, to "put good spirits in the house of evil" (p. 155), for, she explains, Mrs. Aubyn has "given you to yourself. . . . Don't you see . . . that that's the gift you can't escape from, the debt you've been pledged to acquit? Don't you see that you've never before been what she thought you, and that now, so wonderfully, she's made you into the man she loved?" (p. 156).

The pattern that was to be used in so many different ways in other, longer, Wharton works, is here in miniature in the first novella: the unconventional yet superior woman, through her relationship with a man, changes him, challenges him, and, in a sense, frees him. The one difference in *The Touchstone* is that the influence of the intruder is exerted here after her death.

The emphasis is on the intruder as challenger of society's hypocrisies in one of Wharton's last novellas, *New Year's Day* (1924), one of four works published under the general title *Old New York*. The setting is the setting of *The Age of Innocence*, with many of the same peripheral characters — Mr. van der Luyden, Sillerton Jackson — and a narrator who is, like Newland Archer, a young man raised in New York society. The narrator's rather dull childhood has been enlivened by one memorable event: the fire at the Fifth Avenue Hotel on New Year's day. At age twelve the boy had watched the hotel burn, and he had seen, running from the building, Mrs. Lizzie Hazeldean and her lover, Henry Prest.

The incident, which destroyed Lizzie's reputation, caused the young boy to fall in love with her.

Was she beautiful — or was she only someone apart? I felt the shock of a small pale oval, dark eyebrows curved with one sure stroke, lips made for warmth, and now drawn up in a grimace of terror; and it seemed as if the mysterious something, rich, secret and insistent, that brooks and murmurs behind a boy's conscious thought, had suddenly peered out at me.[35]

Years later, as a young man, the narrator befriends Lizzie Hazeldean and learns her story.

Lizzie, like Lily Bart, was born into an extravagant and somewhat disgraced family. Penniless, she was taken in by a wealthy woman who expected her to be a docile companion and who soon resented Lizzie's prettiness and popularity. When Mrs. Mant unjustly accuses Lizzie of stealing, Lizzie, with nowhere to go, marries the woman's favorite nephew, Charlie Hazeldean. What followed was, surprisingly, a truly harmonious marriage filled with love. It is only when Charlie develops serious heart problems that Lizzie again experiences unhappiness. For the couple's money begins to run out, and Charlie, desiring nothing for himself, worries about providing his wife with all the luxury she is used to. The worry is destroying Charlie's health, and Lizzie takes action, using the only resources she has.

Lizzie, like previous Wharton heroines, is the adult among innocents, and she knows it. She "had long since come to regard most women of her age as children in the art of life. Some savage instinct of self-defence, fostered by experience, had always made her more alert and perceiving than the charming creatures who passed from the nursery to marriage as if lifted from one rose-lined cradle into another" (p. 49). As a woman, Lizzie "knew her business" (p. 52); she knows how to be feminine and appealing, how to flirt, to "turn and twist the talk as though she had her victim on a leash, spinning him after her down winding paths of sentimentality, irony, caprice . . . and leaving him, with beating heart and dazzled eyes, to visions of an all-promising morrow" (p. 72). The knowledge of how to handle and manipulate the male is Lizzie's one asset, her only skill, and, totally faithful to her husband, she has never used it to any extent. Now, desperate to alleviate her husband's worries, she uses that skill — for her husband.

Lizzie initiates the affair with the rather fatuous Henry Prest for the money he gives her. The money, whose source is unknown to Charlie, lightens his last days and he dies with his love for his wife intact, oblivious to the scandal that the hotel fire created. After Charlie's death, Prest, who imagined Lizzie to be madly in love with him, offers to marry her. Lizzie destroys Prest's picture of her as adoring woman by her rejection of his offer: "You thought I was a lovelorn mistress; and I was only an expensive prostitute" (p. 114).

Her words do more than wound Henry's pride; they offend his taste. "Mistress! Prostitute! Such words were banned. No one reproved coarseness of language in women more than Henry Prest; one of Mrs. Hazeldean's greatest charms . . . had been her way of remaining, 'through it all,' so ineffably 'the lady' " (pp. 114-15).

It is simply too much for Prest to believe; neither his ego nor his conventions will allow him to believe that Lizzie was "that kind of woman" (p. 121) and that he was duped into buying her services. When Prest attempts to excuse Lizzie's coarseness on the grounds that she is feeling remorse, she strikes that illusion down also; "I'd do it all over again tomorrow — for the same object! I got what I wanted — I gave him that last year, that last good year. It was the relief from anxiety that kept him alive, that kept him happy" (p. 124).

Prest's final appeal to Lizzie threatens her with total exclusion from New York society; his sense of honor forces him, he says, to save the woman he has compromised, to rehabilitate her. But at this "glimpse of the old hackneyed axioms on which he actually believed that his conduct was based," Lizzie again feels her essential difference from Prest and his world, "her remoteness from the life he would have drawn her back to" (p. 127). She simply does not care, now that her husband is dead, about her reputation. "If all New York wants to ostracize me, let it! I've had my day. . . . No woman has more than one. Why shouldn't I have to pay for it? I'm ready" (p. 128).

And Lizzie does pay. New York, unable to permit any open rebel to live in its midst, pushes her out. Eventually, as the years pass, Lizzie's punishment is somewhat lightened; although she is still "not a lady on whom other ladies called" (p. 137), she begins to form her own little circle, composed primarily of younger people and a few daring spirits. She eventually moves just within the social pale, but is still regarded as a somewhat scarlet woman. Ironically, those inside her circle, including the narrator, characterize it as a place of "great dignity and decency" (p. 137), and Lizzie, having once been unfaithful to her living husband, keeps her life "emotionally, sentimentally" (p. 150) empty from the day of his death. The narrator, her only confidante, sums Lizzie up in this way: "She had done one great — or abominable — thing; rank it as you please, it had been done heroically" (p. 150).

What is ironic, of course, is the fact that Lizzie's action, her infidelity itself, is not what makes her either a heroine or an outcast. It is her refusal to disguise her act, her insistence on seeing it for what it is, that challenges New York and that makes Lizzie both heroine and pariah. The essential difference between Lizzie and New York is implicit in the distinction the narrator makes between the two atmospheres; for old New York is "a warm pink nursery," a place of evasion and illusion, but Lizzie's world is "a place of darkness, peril," but also of the "enchantments" (pp. 133-34) of the real.

And so the list of intruders grows: a prostitute, a flapper, a nurse guilty of euthanasia, a heartbroken writer. The setting changes, the characterizations vary, but the woman is a constant presence, injecting reality and certain unchangeable standards into whatever world she enters.

NOTES

1. Only Undine Spragg and, as will be discussed, Lita Wyant of *Twilight Sleep* do not function in exactly this way. Rather than propose an alternative to the societies they invade, they disrupt them by enacting a socially accepted role to the point of absurdity or evil. However, even in the case of Undine or Lita, their exaggerated role-playing makes them seem different from the more muted characters around them.

2. "Viewing the Custom of Her Country: Edith Wharton's Feminism," pp. 529-30.

3. *The Fruit of the Tree* (1907; reprint ed. New York: Charles Scribner's Sons, 1914), p. 54. Citations in the text are to this edition.

4. Nathaniel Hawthorne, *The Blithedale Romance*, Norton Critical Edition, ed. Seymour Gross and Rosalie Murphy (New York: W. W. Norton and Co., 1978), p. 224.

5. *The Novel and Society, A Critical Study of the Modern Novel*, p. 118.

6. Geoffrey Walton comments that Amherst, an "intense individualist . . . has little real feeling for other individuals and, though extremely self-centered, . . . does not really know himself." He "lacks ordinary human understanding of almost every situation apart from the public and industrial." *Edith Wharton: A Critical Interpretation*, p. 94.

7. *Edith Wharton: A Study of Her Fiction*, p. 116. Louis Auchincloss says that "Amherst lacks the basic guts to stand behind his second wife . . . when she is in trouble over a thoroughly justified mercy killing." *Edith Wharton: A Woman in Her Time*, p. 66. Similarly, R. W. B. Lewis (*Edith Wharton*, p. 181) comments that Amherst's lack of understanding of Justine's act reveals "a stubborn moral obtuseness." Margaret McDowell ("Viewing the Custom of Her Country: Edith Wharton's Feminims," p. 532) also stresses Amherst's bondage to convention.

8. *Edith Wharton's Heroines: Studies in Aspiration and Compliance*, p. 32.

9. "Viewing the Custom of Her Country: Edith Wharton's Feminism," p. 532.

10. Q. D. Leavis ("Henry James's Heiress: The Importance of Edith Wharton," p. 83) says that in *The Fruit of the Tree* Wharton "revealed the split between the capitalist ruling class and the oppressed mill-hands, the worthlessness of the lives of the one and the misery of the lives of the other."

11. If one judges the charitable nature of the characters by this criterion, even Bessy, who has "the penetration of the heart" (p. 88), seems somehow more genuine than Amherst.

12. *Twilight Sleep* (New York: D. Appleton and Co., 1927), p. 306. Citations in the text are to this edition.

13. *Edith Wharton's Heroines: Studies in Aspiration and Compliance*, pp. 164-65.

14. This is noted by Cynthia Griffin Wolff, *A Feast of Words*, p. 374.

15. Blake Nevius remarks that, since Wyant "is a contemporary of Ralph Marvell, his fate may be construed as a revelation of what was in store for the latter had he lived." *Edith Wharton: A Study of Her Fiction*, p. 210.

16. Margaret McDowell (*Edith Wharton*, p. 117) mentions that only Nona courageously confronts the real.

17. "Twilight Sleep," *New Republic* 51, no. 653 (June 8, 1927):78. Of this ending, Margaret McDowell remarks that it shows that "insensitivity so completely encloses the modern rich that they cannot even recognize the scathing fire through which they walk." *Edith Wharton*, p. 117.

18. *Edith Wharton: A Critical Interpretation*, pp. 147, 151.

19. *Twilight Sleep* is one of Wharton's later novels that have come under attack, mainly because it is seen as another of her diatribes against the new generation. In addition, Cynthia Griffin Wolff (*A Feast of Words*, p. 376) cites the chaotic plot and the "sloppy management of the social criticism," and Gary Lindberg (*Edith Wharton and the Novel of Manners*, p. 11) says it is simply not a good book. On the other hand, Geoffrey Walton (*Edith Wharton: A Critical Interpretation*, p. 141) explains the loose construction of plot as a deliberate deployment of "a group of people in circumstances that are bound to expose their weaknesses," and calls the novel "a remarkably consistent piece of satire" (p. 150). Edmund Wilson, in his review of the book in *The New Republic* ("Twilight Sleep," p. 78) praises the novel, and Q. D. Leavis ("Henry James's Heiress: The Importance of Edith Wharton," P. 81) says it "compares favorably with Huxley's and other novels treating of the same kind of life." It is difficult to see the novel as a blanket attack on the new generation if Nona is its heroine. Similarly, an interpretation of the novel that focuses on intruders Lita and Nona discloses a certain unifying element in the book.

20. *Hudson River Bracketed* (New York: D. Appleton and Co., 1929), p. 15. Citations in the text are to this edition.

21. Blake Nevius says that Wharton creates "a caricature of Midwestern life so gross that we can take it only as a literary expression of the aversion toward America which came out in the intimate conversation of her later years." *Edith Wharton: A Study of Her Fiction*, p. 75.

22. *Edith Wharton: A Critical Interpretation*, p. 170. Cynthia Griffin Wolff (*A Feast of Words*, p. 394) says that *Wharton* "fails to explain why Vance Weston wants so desperately to write; she fails as well to demonstrate a convincing link between his life and his work."

23. Blake Nevius says that Vance is a vehicle for some of Wharton's most cherished conventions about art. *Edith Wharton: A Study of Her Fiction*, p. 224. R. W. B. Lewis (Edith Wharton, p. 492) says that she is "unrestrainedly satiric about the popular literary modes of the moment," partly out of defensiveness and partly out of a sense of hurt at being herself underrated in favor of younger writers.

24. *The Gods Arrive* (New York: D. Appleton and Co., 1932), p. 29. Citations in the text are to this edition.

25. Louis Auchincloss calls Halo an "irritatingly efficient heroine." *Edith Wharton*, p. 40. Blake Nevius says that Halo, in *The Gods Arrive*, "withdraws voluntarily into the background, content like the heroine of a sentimental novel to suffer nobly and uncomplainingly." *Edith Wharton: A Study of Her Fiction*, p. 233.

26. Margaret McDowell, highly critical of Halo's behavior, says that "because Halo insists on loving the artist as well as the man, her love becomes finally a repressive influence upon the man she is ironically straining to serve." *Edith Wharton*, p. 135. Blake Nevius, however, cites Vance's falseness to his ideals: "In *The God Arrive* the Vance who in the earlier novel had been permitted to voice some of Mrs. Wharton's maturest reflections on art and life is at times clearly a poseur, whose conversation bristles with most of the cant phrases of his profession." *Edith Wharton: A Study of Her Fiction*, p. 230.

27. Blake Nevius makes this point. *Edith Wharton: A Study of Her Fiction*, p. 233.

28. Geoffrey Walton, *Edith Wharton: A Critical Interpretation*, p. 171.

29. *Edith Wharton's Heroines: Studies in Aspiration and Compliance*, p. 180.

30. Blake Nevius makes an interesting analysis of the three women in Vance's life. Laura Lou "represents an ideal of womanhood easily satisfied by the standards of Euphoria," and her influence on Vance is regressive; the attraction exerted by Floss Delaney is wholly irrational, and for that reason powerful and dangerous; Halo "calls forth the most permanent and reliable, if not the deepest impulses of his creative imagination." *Edith Wharton: A Study of Her Fiction*, pp. 233-34.

31. E. K. Brown ("Edith Wharton," *Etudes Anglaises*, p. 19) describes the union of Vance and Halo as the linking of the energies of the West and the traditions of the East.

32. *The Touchstone* (1900; reprint ed. New York: AMS Press, 1969), p. 4. Citations in the text are to this edition.

33. Elizabeth Ammons (*Edith Wharton's Heroines: Studies in Aspiration and Compliance*, p. 4) calls Alexa a "girl": "dependent, reticent, unintellectual, and domestic."

34. Elizabeth Ammons says that Glennard is forced to admit the egotism that caused him to reject Margaret Aubyn's love in the first place. *Edith Wharton's Heroines: Studies in Aspiration and Compliance*, p. 3.

35. *New Year's Day* (New York: D. Appleton and Co., 1924) pp. 14-15. Citations in the text are to this edition.

6

Future Alliances: *The Buccaneers*

So far, the story of the intruder has been the story of exclusions; the outsider, invading society and disrupting it, is repeatedly cast out of a world that cannot tolerate her. Lily Bart is left to die alone, Ellen Olenska is ceremoniously shipped out of New York, and Sophy Viner loses Givré. Loneliness is the common fate. Even if the intruder remains in society, she remains as a prisoner, like Mattie Silver or Nona Manford, forever an alien, severed from all meaningful human associations.[1] In Edith Wharton's last, unfinished novel, *The Buccaneers* (published posthumously in 1938), the story of the intruder becomes not a tale of loneliness and isolation, of the severance of human ties, but one of alliances, connections, links. *The Buccaneers* is a novel of union — of marriages, love affairs, friendships, of the alliance of women, all in some sense intruders, who help one another to achieve their goal. Its theme deals with another union, the·merging of the best of the traditional and of the modern, united to create a brighter future and a better world.

The time period of *The Buccaneers* is that of *The Age of Innocence*, but the setting is not socially exclusive New York but rather Saratoga, where the new Wall Street millionaires amuse themselves at the races while their wives gossip on hotel verandahs and their daughters do as they please. It is the daughters of the parvenus, Annabel and Virginia St. George, Lizzie and Mabel Elmsworth, and Conchita Closson, who are the focus of the novel. As fresh and pure as May Welland, but much less mannered and much more eager for life, the five girls fill the novel, as they fill Saratoga, with natural charm. Blake Nevius says that Wharton is "frankly and in a thoroughly Jamesian sense delighted"[2] with her American girls, and early descriptions of them convey her delight:

> Ah ... the girls! ... The fancy had taken them to come in late and to arrive all together; and how, arm-in-arm, a blushing bevy, they swayed across the threshold of the dining-room like a branch hung with blossoms ... happy girls, with two new dancers for the weekend, they had celebrated the unwonted windfall by extra touches of adornment: a red rose in the fold of a fichu, a loose curl on a white shoulder, a pair of new satin slippers, a fresh moiré ribbon. ... To those two foreigners [the new dancing-partners] they embodied "the American girl," the world's highest achievement.[3]

151

It is difficult to associate these girls, so vital yet uncalculating, with that other daughter of new money, Undine Spragg, but in one way they are like her. For they belong nowhere, they have no membership in any society; their lives are a series of movements — disordered, undisciplined — from hotel to hotel. Rich American beauties, they have no place, no status. Their fathers are too busy with money and sport, their mothers too bewildered by their sudden wealth, to provide much direction. Yet both the girls and their mothers are ambitious; they want to conquer the social world, and the first step in that conquest must be education, training in how "to behave like ladies" (p. 51). So a teacher, a social guide, another outsider, Laura Testvalley, enters the group.

Miss Testvalley comes highly recommended, for she has spent long years in the houses of the British aristocracy, but her past is the typically colorful one of the Wharton intruder. She is the granddaughter of an Italian patriot, "Genarro Testavaglia of Modena, fomentor of insur-rections, hero of the Risorgimento," and distant cousin of Dante Gabriel Rossetti.

> The Testavaglias, fleeing from the Australian inquisition, had come to England at the same time as the Rosettis, and contracting their impossible name to the scope of English lips, had intermarried with other exiled revolutionaries and anti-papists, producing sons who were artists and agnostics, and daughters who were evangelicals of the strictest pattern, and governesses in the highest families. (P. 40)

Although Laura has followed the female line in her choice of work, she has inherited the spirit of her male ancestors. " 'If I'd been a man,' she sometimes thought, 'Dante Gabriel might not have been the only cross in the family' " (p. 41). Correct, well-bred, Laura has already defied convention by engaging in a discreet affair with Lord Richard Marable, son of one of her employers. Eventually, motivated by the need to earn more money for herself and the relatives she assists, Laura risks every-thing to seek her fortune in America. Her first governess job in New York is with the socially prominent Parmores, but the life is dull and stuffy, and Laura suspects that "the real America was elsewhere" (p. 41). She finds it with the Saratoga belles.

Her first glimpse of her new charges comes when the St. George girls and their friends meet her at the Saratoga station: "out of the hack poured a spring torrent of muslins, sash-ends, and bright cheeks under swaying hat-brims. Miss Testvalley found herself in a circle of nymphs shaken by hysterical laughter" (p. 42). Not at all awed by the woman who is supposed to mold their characters, the girls greet her with a game: the "enchanted circle" breaks, and the girls line up, for Laura is to guess just whose governess she is to be. The answer, in truth, is: all of them. For, although hired by Mrs. St. George for her daughters, Laura becomes governess, mother, sister, and friend to them all.

The first alliance of the novel is formed, the union of the European outsider with the American buccaneers. Laura is the girls' first and most important teacher. But, unlike so many intruders, other symbolic teachers, Laura does not force her pupils to face what is wrong with society; she does not show them that they must withdraw from the world in order to preserve their identity. This teacher is a positive force, drawing her changes into the social world, preparing them for conquest. She brings their freedom and individuality to the old, traditional environment; she blends their strength with the best of the past. She merges the good from both worlds to form a new and better one.[4] When the snobbish Mrs. Parmore criticizes Laura's new charges on the grounds that "among the people you're with now there are no social traditions," Laura is tempted to rejoin, "None except those they are making for themselves" (p. 65), and this imagined reply reflects the appeal the parvenus have for Laura. They are the new, the free, the future, and Laura, through them, will help to form the future. She teaches them to behave "like ladies" in the truest sense; her definition of the term is based not on class distinctions or snobbery, but on natural goodness and the poise that comes from accepting oneself. Her own innate gentility is the example the young girls will follow.

Laura helps to engineer the first marriage of the group, that of Conchita Closson, the wildest of the girls, to Laura's own former lover, Richard Marable. The marriage is not an evil, manipulated affair, and Laura's part in it is not at all that of a Madame Merle, for Laura has no remnant of attachment for Lord Richard and no bitterness or illusions about her own association with him. Conchita wants Richard, a kind of wild younger son himself, and Laura helps her to get him. After bringing Richard into the fold, Laura then uses her influence with him to get the other girls, Lizzie Elmsworth and Virginia St. George, into New York society. The scene is a particularly funny comment on New York snobbery, for Richard can get the girls invitations to the Assembly Ball only by pretending they are his aristocratic sisters, Lady Ulrica and Honoria. Once the girls get inside the bastion of old New York, Fifth Avenue pronounces them accomplished and dazzling, and the girls score their first, if deceitful, victory. Ironically, the outsider, the eternal servant, has managed to bring the girls inside.

While Laura has thus allied herself with all five young ladies, her deepest sympathies extend to only one of them, the youngest, who soon emerges as the center of the novel. She is Annabel (Nan) St. George, at sixteen still too young for society, and the most sensitive and vulnerable of the lot. Laura can see herself in the child, and, on the night of the Assembly Ball, when Nan is left behind with her governess, Laura observes

> at Nan St. George's age, Miss Testvalley, though already burdened with the care and responsibilities of middle life, had longed with all Nan's longing to wear white tulle and be invited to a ball. She had never been invited to a ball, had never worn white tulle; and now, at nearly forty, and scarred by hardships and disappointments, she still felt that early pang. (P. 79)

Nan will go to balls; Laura will see to it. With Nan, Laura is most open, loving, and maternal. As she watches the lonely girl asleep on her bed, Laura muses, "She might have been my own daughter" (p. 90).

Having successfully maneuvered the girls into New York, Laura decides to take them where the real triumphs — and the titles — are: to London. Her advice to her comrades on the new field of battle reflects Laura's belief in their essential quality; for they are not to become chameleons, like Undine, eager to cast off their own style. Instead, Laura tells them, "Try and feel that you're as good as any of these people you're going about with . . . act in your own way . . . that will amuse them much more than if you try to copy them" (p. 122).

Faced with a world unlike any they have seen before, the five girls are drawn closer than ever. As Conchita acknowledges, they must present a united front in the face of the enemy: "We've each got our own line," she says, "and if we only back each other up we'll beat all the other women hands down. . . . If we stick to the rules of the game, and don't play any low-down tricks on each other . . . we'll have London in our pocket next year" (p. 158). The alliance is much more than a mutual defense pact, however; it is a connection forged out of the innate decency and generosity of the girls.[5] The true strength and goodness of the connection is revealed in one of the most memorable scenes in the novel, the poker game at Runnymede.[6]

The young ladies have rented a summer cottage at Runnymede, and already the young Englishmen are flocking to them, attracted by this "group of fearless and talkative girls, who said new things in a new language, who were ignorant of tradition and unimpressed by distinctions of rank" (p. 158). Although early success gratifies the buccaneers, their happiness is marred by the growing rivalry between Virginia St. George and Lizzie Elmsworth, both of whom are in love with Lord Seadown. Seadown is fascinated by both girls, but has declared himself to neither. He is afraid of the wrath of his rapacious mistress, Lady Churt, from whom the Runnymede cottage has been rented. His fear of Lady Churt has not prevented Seadown from frequenting Runnymede, however, and it is to the cottage that an angry Lady Churt comes in search of her lover. Conchita and some of the Englishmen are playing poker, and Lady Churt is drawn into the game, which soon becomes less an innocent amusement than a battle for Seadown. When Lady Churt loses the game, she cries, "I'm completely ruined — down and out . . . . I'm afraid you're all too clever for me, and one of the young ladies had better take my place." Conchita advises her not to lose heart, and Lady Churt's reply again refers more to her love affair than to the game: "I assure you I've never minded parting with that organ. It's losing the shillings and pence that I can't afford" (p. 204).

When Virginia and Lizzie are asked to join the game the battle really begins, for they decline, because "girls don't play cards for money in America." "No," counters the enraged mistress, "I understand the game you young ladies play has fewer risks and requires only two players" (p. 204). Her remark is directed at Virginia, whom she takes to be her strongest competition for Seadown, and who submits to this abuse in silent bewilderment.

Having lost at cards, Lady Churt proceeds to lose at love. Again casting her challenge at Virginia, she commands Lord Seadown to leave with her. "The fact is," she tells him, her eye on Virginia, "it's time your hostesses found out that you don't go with the house; at least not when I'm not living in it" (p. 206).

Lizzie Elmsworth, herself in love with Seadown, sacrifices her own happiness in a daring defense of her friend: "Virginia! What are you waiting for? Don't you see that Lord Seadown has no right to speak 'till you do? Why don't you tell him at once that he has your permission to announce your engagement?" (p. 207). Thus is another victory for the American side gained, and thus are two marriages achieved. For not only does Seadown find his choice made for him, but Lizzie is rewarded for her action as well. Hector Robinson, a young and wealthy member of Parliament who has watched this scene with an increasing and amazed admiration for Lizzie, makes her his wife.

As Laura Testvalley watches her girls make their matches and win their battles, she worries about Nan, for "she felt that Belgravia and Mayfair, shooting-parties in great country-houses, and the rest of the fashionable routine to which Virginia and the Elmsworth girls had taken so promptly, would leave Nan bewildered and unsatisfied" (p. 220). But Nan is forming her own attachments, of a different kind. She is falling in love with history, with the past. While the others go to the great country houses to meet the right people, Nan discovers in them something more important to her, a sense of culture and continuity she has never known. At Seadown's family home, "her soul opened slowly and timidly to her kind, but her imagination rushed out to the beauties of the visible world;

and the decaying majesty of Allfriars moved her strangely. Splendour neither frightened her, nor made her self-assertive as it did Virginia; she never felt herself matched against things greater than herself, but safely merged in them'' (pp. 133-34).

Nan's love of the past links her to the two men who are to figure most importantly in her life, Guy Thwarte, the hero of the novel, and the Duke of Tintagel, who will marry Nan. Geoffrey Walton calls Guy Thwarte ''an unqualified value from the first; he combines devotion to tradition and 'point to point' riding with personal charm and adaptability to the present and future.''[7] Wharton makes him ''tall and lean, and full of the balanced energy of the hard rider and the quick thinker'' (p. 107). His energy and practicality distinguish Guy Thwarte from the typical Wharton hero. For although he is poor and although he loves the past, Thwarte does not languish in ineffectual dreams of it. He is devoted to the ancestral home, Honourslove, and determined not only to keep it but to improve it. Trained for the aristocratic position of a diplomat, Thwarte gives it up and goes for a more lucrative career, enduring years of ''hard drudgery with an eminent firm of civil engineers'' (p. 109). Realistic and strong, yet capable of loving and preserving the best of the past, Guy Thwarte would seem to be the ideal mate for Nan.

But it is his house and not him that Nan first adores. Unlike the shabby Allfriars, Honourslove is a house that is cared for and properly maintained. Like another young American girl, Isabel Archer, Nan finds that ''the stones of the house, the bricks of the walls, the very flags of the terrace'' are ''full of captured sunshine. Nan, though too ignorant to single out the details of all this beauty, found herself suddenly at ease with the soft mellow place, as though some secret thread of destiny attached her to it'' (p. 136).

It is to an entirely different kind of man, however, that Nan attaches herself. He is the Duke of Tintagel, a timid young man dominated by his mother and oppressed by his position, a man whose ''real tastes were for small matters, for the minutiae of a retired and leisurely existence.'' When he was a child the Duke's secret dream was to be a man who sold clocks, who ''sat among them in his little shop, watching them, doctoring them, taking their temperature . . . listening to their chimes, oiling, setting and regulating them'' (pp. 171-72). Tintagel, whose first name is, appropriately, Ushant, needs a bride, but he is tired of title seekers and fortune hunters. ''I shall never form an attachment,'' he tells his mother, ''until I meet a girl who doesn't know what a Duke is!'' (p. 170).

Nan is, of course, just that girl, but, significantly, when she meets him in the ruins of an old family castle and does not recognize him as a duke, Ushant's vanity is wounded. Yet he is also fascinated. ''He had never before met a young lady alone in a ruined castle, and his mind, nurtured on precedents, had no rule to guide it. But nature cried aloud in him that he must somehow see her again'' (p. 184). He eventually decides he wants her for his wife, and he consults, not with Nan's parents, but with Laura Testvalley, about this marriage. What the Duke admires in Nan, he explains, is ''her childish innocence, her indifference to money and honours and — er — that kind of thing.'' But Laura warns him, ''you can hardly regard her as a rare piece for your collection. . . . Nan is one thing now, but may be another, quite different, thing in a year or two. Sensitive natures alter strangely after their first contact with life.'' Ushant's answer is ominous: ''Oh, but I should make it my business to shield her from every contact with life'' (p. 227).

An egotist, and ''dimly conscious that he was dull himself,'' Ushant craves a brilliant wife, but ''feared a dull wife less than a brilliant one, for with the latter how could he maintain his superiority?'' (p. 175). Nan St. George seems to be the answer to the Duke's prayers, for he is charmed by her childlike openness, and he mistakes her ignorance of tradition for a malleable innocence that he can control. To Ushant, Nan seems ''too young and timid to have any opinions on any subject whatsoever'' (p. 245), and she is therefore no threat to a man who is timid himself.

Why Nan accepts the Duke is another matter entirely, since her first reaction to him is to pronounce him ''one of the stupidest young men I ever met'' (p. 186). It is not the status of a duchess nor Ushant's wealth that attracts Nan. Rather, the Duke and Tintagel Castle represent that fascinating world of the past with which Nan has just become acquainted. As Geoffrey Walton comments, Nan marries the Duke not for a title, but for history.[8]

Three years after Nan's marriage, the intruders have achieved a brilliant social success: ''A blast of outer air had freshened the stagnant atmosphere of Belgravian drawing rooms, and while some sections of London still shuddered (or affected to shudder) at 'the Americans,' others, and the uppermost among them, openly applauded and imitated them.'' But social standing, no matter how lofty, has not brought with it the expected happiness. The novel now narrows its focus to Nan, and although her marriage has been the biggest coup of them all, it has made her more of an outsider than ever, for in all social circles, Nan remains ''a figure apart'' (p. 243).

If Nan is alienated from her new environment, she also feels trapped within it, ''isolated in her new world, no longer able to reach back to her past, and not having yet learned how to communicate with her present'' (p. 262). Even the other free and individualistic American girls have been changed by their assimilation into the old world.[9] Troubled and confused, Nan worries not only about her own situation but about the others.

What relation . . . did the Conchita Closson who had once seemed so ethereal
and elusive, bear to Lady Dick Marable, beautiful still . . . but who had lost
her lovely indolence and detachment, and was perpetually preoccupied about
money, and immersed in domestic difficulties and clandestine consolations; or
to Virginia, her own sister Virginia, who had seemed to Annabel so secure,
so aloof, but who, as Lady Seadown, was enslaved to that dull half-asleep
Seadown, absorbed in questions of rank and precedence. (P. 261)

Nan's sister and friend find conventional channels for their energy and
discontent: the discreet affair, the acceptable snobbery. Only Nan refuses
to fight unfairly or to become what is expected of her. She becomes a
disruptive, disturbing force within her own family; to her husband "her
presence in his house seemed only to increase his daily problems and
bothers" (p. 258), and to his mother Nan is equally a problem: "It's not
that she's *stupid* . . . but she puts one out, asking the reason of things
that have nothing to do with reasons" (p. 248). Such comments as "I
think I'm tired of trying to be English" (p. 293), and "I don't think I
want to be a mother of Dukes" (p. 294) turn the Tintagel household
upside down.

Yet dissatisfaction becomes a kind of education for Nan; within the
stuffy and repressive atmosphere of Tintagel Castle she begins to find
certain values that had been missing in America. During a particularly
fierce quarrel with her mother-in-law, Nan hears the luncheon gong
sound, and the Dowager Duchess immediately composes her angry
features and descends to her guests, who must not be kept waiting. There
is something admirable about this, Nan perceives. "A year ago Annabel
would have laughed at these rules and observances; now, though they
chafed her no less, she was beginning to see the use of having one's
whims and one's rages submitted to some kind of control" (p. 296). Nan
remembers her own home, "the noisy quarrels about nothing, the paltry
preoccupations, her mother's feverish interest in the fashions and follies of
a society which had always ignored her," and England seems so much
better, for here there is a background, "of history, poetry, old traditional
observances, beautiful houses" (p. 305). Unhappy in her marriage,
alienated from all around her, Nan seeks for a substitute life, and her
growing love of the past seems to provide it. "Would it not be possible, in
some mysterious way, to create for one's self a life out of this richness, a
life which would somehow make up for the poverty of one's personal
lot?" (p. 305).

Edith Wharton does not allow her heroine to become a kind of
Newland Archer, however, locked into a conventional life, escaping only
into culture and consoling himself that there was good in the old ways
after all. In *The Buccaneers* Nan is to free herself, to take radical steps to

hold on to the best of the old and yet to move on to the new. The past is not enough; it cannot substitute for life. The Duchess must not look to tradition for fulfillment; she must form her own future.

Nan's release from convention begins with the renewal of two friend-ships, with Laura Testvalley and with Guy Thwarte. Nan turns to Laura in an attempt to rescue "the old Annabel" (p. 262), and Laura helps her both to do this and to become a new person. Laura, who "had remained her firm sharp-edged self" (p. 262), has also remained an outsider, poor, alone, on the fringes of society, once again governess to the British aristo-cracy. She reenters Nan's life in a new role, as friend and confidante, and she encourages Nan to resume her friendship, with Guy Thwarte.

Guy Thwarte, like Nan, has changed. He still loves the past that his family home represents for him, but he is now incapable of assuming his expected role in society. Four years of hard but financially rewarding work in South America and marriage to a Brazilian who subsequently died have made Thwarte something of a stranger in his former surround-ings. "Guy, knowing so acutely what was expected of him, was vainly struggling to become again the young man who had left England four years earlier; but strive as he would he could not yet fit himself into his place in the old scheme of things. The truth was, he was no longer the Guy Thwarte of four years ago, and would probably never recover that lost self" (p. 266). Sir Helmsley Thwarte, his father, stands at the head of those who expect him to resume the life he was trained for; he hopes that Guy will soon marry a typical English girl, someone "safe and unexciting" (p. 348). But Guy Thwarte does not choose safety; instead he chooses the Duchess of Tintagel.

The relationship of the two begins as friendship, and Nan is grateful that in "this great lonely desert of life stretching out before her she had a friend . . . who understood not only all she said, but everything she could not say" (p. 314)[10] It is to Guy Thwarte that Nan describes her life as "a match between one's self and one's gaolers" (p. 346), and to whom she reveals her dream "to try again . . . somewhere where I could be myself" (p. 287). Although the unfinished novel breaks off with neither Nan nor Guy having openly declared their love for one another, it becomes increasingly apparent that this love exists. Such passages as Nan's musing that "it must be less wicked to love the wrong person than not to love anybody at all" (p. 311) indicate that the American girl has found her proper mate. And Wharton's outline for the novel makes it clear that the union of the two rebels, aided by Laura Testvalley, was to have been the climax of the book.

Sir Helmsley Thwarte, the widowed father of Guy, a clever, broken-down and bitter old worldling, is captivated by Miss Testvalley, and wants to marry her; but meanwhile the young Duchess of Tintagel has suddenly decided to leave her husband and go off with Guy and . . . Laura Testvalley, moved by the youth and passion of the lovers, and disgusted by the mediocre Duke of Tintagel, has secretly lent a hand in the planning of the elopement, the scandal of which is to ring through England for years.

Sir Helmsley Thwarte discovers what is going on, and is so furious at his only son's being involved in such an adventure that, suspecting Miss Testvalley's complicity, he breaks with her, and the great old adventures, seeing love, deep and abiding love, triumph for the first time in her career, helps Nan to join her lover . . . and then goes back alone to old age and poverty. (pp. 358-59)

Nan is to be given her chance to try again, with a man who will allow her to be herself. The novel would end, then, with two great alliances: the scandalous and highly romantic union of the lovers, and the extraordinary friendship of Laura Testvalley for Nan, characterized by Laura's selflessness and courage.

The projected alliance of Nan and Guy Thwarte is more than a melodramatic conclusion to a period piece. Geoffrey Walton comments:

In theme, if not as history, *The Buccaneers* begins where her novels of the 1920s, *Twilight Sleep* and *The Children*, leave off — in social anarchy. And, by involving the anarchic spirits in all their free vitality with a social system which is at once very old and very stable, it gradually works toward a vision of social reintegration with moral and intellectual concomitants, a concept of balance between ancient order and dignity and new, sincere, and unconventional individualism. This theme is presented in terms of the career of the heroine, beginning as Nan St. George, becoming the Duchess of Tintagel, and expected to end as Mrs. Guy Thwarte.[11]

The planned ending is a hopeful one, and the hope, Margaret McDowell says, seems "to lie less in the influence of Americans on the English than in that of a new kind of young people in both nations who value tradition and art at the same time that they seek change in social patterns."[12] This new generation, Cynthia Griffin Wolff comments, will redeem the insufficiencies of the old.[13]

Since *The Buccaneers* is a novel of connections, this final union is a bright and appropriate ending to a book filled with a rich glow, a warmth. Critical appraisal of *The Buccaneers* is positive; Blake Nevius, for example, calls it "a novel which, had she finished it, would probably have taken its palce among her half-dozen best."[14] The excellence of the novel creates a certain problem, of course, for those who dismiss all Edith Wharton's later work as inferior.

While the novel is undoubtedly better than certain other late works, it is, in pattern and theme, not so different from them. As noted earlier, Walton links it to *Twilight Sleep* and *The Children*, and both he and Blake Nevius note resemblances between Nan St. George and Nona Manford.[15] But *The Buccaneers* resembles other of Wharton's later work, and much of her earlier work as well, in one important way: in this novel it is the intruder who is the moral center, who carries the positive values. In *The Buccaneers*, as in *The Children* or *The House of Mirth*, it is according to how society meets the intruder's standards that it is measured.

It is difficult to determine exactly *who* the central intruder is in *The Buccaneers* — Gaillard Lapsley feels that Laura Testvalley dominates the book;[16] Geoffrey Walton opts for Nan St. George.[17] It is reasonable to view them as sharing the center of the book, because in all essentials they are so much the same: Nan St. George is what the young Laura might have been had she been rich; Laura, what Nan might become after a meager and disappointing life. Walton calls Laura ''one of Edith Wharton's great creations,'' a ''free intelligence . . . an independent woman of the world in a wholly complimentary sense, without fixed class associations and able to establish herself anywhere on her own terms.''[18] The character haunted even her creator, for in *A Backward Glance* Edith Wharton explained how this character appeared in her mind, already possessing a name:

> Laura Testvalley. How I should like to change that name! But it has been attached for some time now to a strongly outlined material form, the form of a character figuring largely in an adventure I know all about, and have long wanted to relate. Several times I have tried to give Miss Testvalley another name, since the one she bears, should it appear ever in print, will be even more troublesome to my readers than to me. But she is strong-willed, and even obstinate, and turns sulky and unmanageable whenever I hint at the advantage of a change; and I foresee that she will eventually force her way into my tale burdened with her impossible patronymic.[19]

As Cynthia Griffin Wolff suggests, it is not difficult to guess the source of Laura's name. Testvalley is very similar to Valley of Decision, the title of Wharton's first novel, and Laura has an Italian background and revolutionary forebears that call to mind the setting of that novel.[20] In fact, *The Buccaneers* as a whole most resembles that early Wharton novel, *The Valley of Decision*. Both are set in a time of enormous changes, in which the old order is threatened. *The Valley of Decision* contains a heroine who is capable of dealing with change, who has anticipated and planned for it and is strong and brave. *The Buccaneers*, in essence, splits the character of Fulvia Vivaldi into two heroines, Laura Testvalley and Nan St. George. Laura possesses Fulvia's intellectual and social background, and thinks as Fulvia thinks, but Nan St. George acts as

Fulvia acts. In the outline for *The Buccaneers*, Wharton writes that Nan "is, or thinks she is, as ambitious as the others [the other girls of the novel], but it is for more interesting reasons; intellectual, political, and artistic" (p. 358). Laura has, of course, been the biggest influence in forming Nan, intellectually, politically, culturally, and Laura begins to live through Nan, to sacrifice her own chance for marriage when she sees the "deep and abiding love" (p. 359) of Nan and Guy Thwarte. Laura Testvalley's life is too limited, too lacking in opportunities, for her revolutionary spirit to exercise itself. Instead, Nan St. George must act as Fulvia did, unconventionally, openly violating the rules of sexual conduct of her day. Nan must disrupt the ordered aristocratic society with her questions, as Fulvia disturbed Odo Valsecca's life.

All three woman — Fulvia, Laura, Nan — embrace the future and even help to form it. Each of the three may be described in the terms Wharton's outline used for Nan; "the girl who had understood the real values of life and when she saw herself in danger of losing what she had come to reckon the greatest of them was ready to sacrifice everything rather than that" (p. 367). The women value love highly and sacrifice various parts of themselves for it: Fulvia, her independence and her reputation; Laura, her own hopes for a comfortable marriage; Nan, her place in society. All three also believe in other values: individual freedom, honesty, tolerance, and compassion for others. The women share the clarity of vision that enables them to see their worlds for what they are, and the energy to improve them.

It is the fates of the early and late heroines that create the significant differences between the novels. For Fulvia, in her search for a better life and for positive change, allies herself with a man who is weak and who fails her. The intruder is destroyed; the future, struggled against and evaded, becomes the horrible chaotic present with which *The Valley of Decision* ends. The fates of Nan and Laura are to be different. Laura, it is true, must be sacrificed, but her personal loss will help to produce the one truly happy ending in a Wharton novel. Nan, the last of the intruders, will find her mate — the man strong enough and brave enough to face the future with her, to join her outside.

NOTES

1. Even Undine is excluded from the one position she really wants, from diplomatic circles.

2. *Edith Wharton: A Study of Her Fiction*, p. 238.

3. *The Buccaneers*. Essay appended by Gaillard Lapsley (New York: D. Appleton-Century Co., 1933), pp. 34-35. Citations in the text are to this edition.

4. Margaret McDowell (*Edith Wharton*, p. 138) calls Laura the link between the young girls and the conservative older generation in both America and England.

5. It is worth noting that the open generosity of the invaders can be contrasted to the jealous exclusiveness of the more socially prominent Parmore girls of New York.

6. Gaillard Lapsley, in his afterword to *The Buccaneers*, particularly admires the poker scene, commenting that in it "the invaders have secured themselves and the reader understands that they have done so not merely by beauty, unconventionality and high spirits. The handling of the situation by two unsophisticated girls had released moral forces simple perhaps and not of a very high order, but hitherto unsuspected by themselves and the reader." "A Note on *The Buccaneers*," p. 362.

7. *Edith Wharton: A Critical Interpretation*, p. 185.

8. Ibid., p. 191.

9. Margaret McDowell says that "the men and the society which the buccaneers conquer are, after all, not really worthy of their beauty, intelligence, and courageous spirits." *Edith Wharton*, p. 138.

10. Guy Thwarte's understanding of Nan contrasts with Ushant's obtuseness. Nan's most frequent remark to her husband is "You don't understand."

11. *Edith Wharton: A Critical Interpretation*, p. 177.

12. *Edith Wharton*, p. 141.

13. *A Feast of Words*, p. 405.

14. *Edith Wharton: A Study of Her Fiction*, p. 237. Similar evaluations have been made by Cynthia Griffin Wolff (*A Feast of Words*, p. 398), R. W. B. Lewis (*Edith Wharton: A Biography*, p. 528), Margaret McDowell (*Edith Wharton*, p. 139), Geoffrey Walton (*Edith Wharton: A Critical Interpretation*, p. 176), and by Wharton's literary executor, Gaillard Lapsley, who published the unfinished work because it was "too good to hold back." (As quoted in R. W. B. Lewis, *Edith Wharton: A Biography*, p. 528).

15. *Edith Wharton: A Study of Her Fiction*, p. 177.

16. "A Note on *The Buccaneers*," p. 367.

17. *Edith Wharton: A Critical Interpretation*, p. 176.

18. Ibid., p. 181.

19. *A Backward Glance*, pp. 202-3

20. Wolff, however, continues to say that the first novel denounced revolution and warned of the destructive nature of all human passion; this last novel is thus a contrast. *A Feast of Words*, p. 401.

Conclusion

An analysis of Edith Wharton's novels that concentrates on the pattern of the intruder indicates that Wharton herself defies the long-accepted stereotype of her as a fossilized old New Yorker, relic of an irrelevant past. Wharton the writer is no spokesman for the values and conventions of a lost aristocratic society, and she advocates no return to the proprieties and order of her youth. But while Wharton is not true to that accepted stereotype, she is true to her *own* type. Her work reveals a consistency of attitudes, a cluster of values previously overlooked or slighted.

The key to the "type" of writer that Wharton is lies in an admiring comment she once made about the French. "Sooner than any other race the French have got rid of bogies, have 'cleared the mind of shams,' and gone up to the Medusa and the Sphinx with a cool eye and a penetrating question,"[1] she observed, and this statement really describes her own conduct as a writer. If Wharton's fiction has any central function, it is to clear the world of its sacred shams, and Edith Wharton approaches the established verities of whatever period she writes about with that cool analytical eye she so much admires. Wharton's novels may be seen as a series of penetrating questions, questions about "the reason of things that have nothing to do with reasons,"[2] questions that disturb the complacency of society and that often provoke uneasy and defensive responses.

Wharton's greatest talent was the ability to recognize the secret gods of American society and to approach them with an air of irreverence, an attitude nearly sacrilegious, to expose them as the empty idols they are. She understood that what America worshiped more than anything else was wealth. She knew that her mother's dictum, "Never talk about money, and think about it as little as possible,"[3] reflected not a disdain for wealth but an attempt to hide an obsession. She watched (and chronicled) the rise of the Beauforts, the Rosedales, and the Abner Spraggs of the world to the position of national heroes, and she showed the results of this overwhelming materialism. Novel after novel depicts the consequences of regarding the world as a marketplace, describes the dehumanization of those frozen in materialism, especially of the women who become commodities. In old New York the most salable woman, Wharton perceived, was the virginal child bride, May Welland; later a taste developed for the more sophisticated but equally ornamental type of Lily Bart; in the twenties a more corrupted but equally decorative type, the flapper, Lita Wyant, prevailed. But each was the commodity demanded by a materialistic world — a woman without soul, without self, distorted and twisted from her true nature into a marketable product, one whose nightmare form was Undine Spragg.

Wharton knew it was not only women who suffered from this worship of wealth. If women lost their souls to become pretty things, men sold their souls — Ralph Marvell to attain his fantasy of egotistic escape, Selden and John Amherst to maintain secure positions in worlds they pretended to disdain. And the business of acquiring, protecting and increasing one's wealth, Wharton saw, kept one from the business of living. Again she contrasted the attitudes of Americans with the values of the French, and again the French proved superior. "For the immense majority of the French," Wharton explained, moneymaking "is a far more modest ambition, and consists simply in the effort to earn one's living and put by enough for sickness, old age, and a good start in life for the children.' This conception of business "has the immense superiority of leaving time for living, time for men and women both."[4] It was time denied the more mercenary America, where men spent their real lives on Wall Street, frantically trying to make money, and women were deprived of even that life and were pacified instead with enormous powers of consumption, endless chances to gratify their whims and thus to stifle their discontent.

Such unhappiness was only one kind of misery in a money-worshiping world, and Wharton did not forget this. For every matron who languished in a drawing room and every magnate who sweated at the stock exchange, there was a far more desperate case, a person at the bottom of the social ladder to whom money, very little of it, meant the difference between starvation and survival. Wharton, the supposed society novelist, draws numerous pictures of the other side of the social tapestry, of the lives of those sacrificed to create a luxurious world for May Welland and Anna Leath. Sometimes she gives us a complete portrait of such victims, a detailed and compassionate view of what it is like to be poor in a world where only wealth counts. The story of Newland Archer is not the only story Wharton can tell; she cares equally (and writes as effectively) about the downfall of Lily Bart, the barren poverty of Mattie Silver and Ethan Frome, and the humiliation of the social lackey, Sophy Viner or Laura Testvalley. Wharton can (and does) describe the horror of a New England cotton mill as well as the boredom of a New York ball.

Money, that supreme American god, was Wharton's first target. This obsessive materialism degraded and destroyed many, and its power ruled in every period of American life that Wharton observed. But Wharton saw another American deity as almost equally dangerous, for she understood the consequences of the country's veneration of another false god — the idol of pleasure.

Pleasure is perhaps too strong a word to describe the secret god of old New York, for there the hidden idol was the milder goal of peace of mind, freedom from unpleasantness. Wharton knew that everyone seeks this peace, but she also perceived that what made old New York evil was its desire to achieve this peace at any cost. Human lives must be sacrificed to keep unpleasantness from Fifth Avenue and Washington Square; Ellen Olenska must be driven back to the prison of a miserable marriage, Newland Archer must be denied any real life, all to keep the frown from Mrs. Manson Mingott's face. And as old New York evolved into the wealthier, looser society of the postwar world, Wharton chronicled the evolution of the god of pleasantness into the god of pleasure; the desire for a mildly amusing life became transformed into the search for a wildly entertaining one. Genteel archery contests at Newport blossomed into extravagant yachts and Ritz hotels; the sedate tours and travels of the old rich became the nomadic existence of the Cliffe Wheaters and the Dexter Manfords. But both worlds, as Wharton understood, with their desperate evasion of reality and horror of pain, were populated by people in an arrested state of development, hiding from life behind their infantile pleasures.

Conflict, tragedy, and pain were terrifying to Americans, and Wharton saw that their way of dealing with them was through belief in another god — the easy answer. Wharton knew that what America expected of life was "a tragedy with a happy ending":

> "A tragedy with a happy ending" is exactly what the child wants before he goes to sleep: the reassurance that "all's well with the world" as he lies in his cosy nursery. It is a good thing that the child should receive this reassurance; but as long as he needs it he remains a child, and the world he lives in is a nursery-world. Things are not always and everywhere well with the world, and each man has to find it out as he grows up. It is the finding out that makes him grow, and until he has faced the fact and digested the lesson he is not grown up — he is still in the nursery.[5]

America did not want to believe that "things are not always and everywhere well with the world," and preferred to retreat to the formula, to the answer that avoided conflict and required no thought. In Newland Archer's world the easy answer was the resort to the dictates of good form; for every problem there was an immediate and accessible rule to follow. When these rules fell apart, revealed as the empty conventions they were, Wharton identified a new set of panaceas that came to be worshiped in the twenties. These were the gurus, masseurs, rejuvenators, and spiritual advisers of the time, the people who sustain Pauline Manford's existence in "an atmosphere of universal simplification," who feed her need to believe that "America really seemed to have an immediate answer for everything, from the treatment of the mentally deficient to the elucidation of the profoundest mysteries."[6] Whether the time was 1870 or 1920, Wharton satirized the folly of this retreat from the complexity of life's conflicts.

Just as Wharton saw that obsessive materialism was particularly destructive of women, who did not make money and thus counted for little, so she saw that a society filled with infantile evasion particularly diminished women's already limited existence. For again it was women, relegated to the limited life of leisure and denied access to man's world of financial dealing that at least had *some* conflict in it, who became most childish. From the perpetually virginal May Welland and her mother, whose only permitted interests were clothes, food, children, and gossip about women who had other interests, to Judy Trenor and Bertha Dorset, whose lives followed the same basic schedule with a little more travel and infidelity thrown in, to the clubwoman Pauline Manford, women were kept in their place — a nursery world full of other children like them. Not only did Wharton understand the particularly pathetic nature of the "innocence" valued in the 1870s; she realized that the superficially freer life of the matron of the twenties was equally limited. She perceived that the world of the "new woman" of the postwar world, "with her 'boards' and clubs and sororities, her public investigation of everything under the heavens from 'the social evil' to baking powder, and from 'physical culture' to the new esoteric religion" was "exactly like the most improved and advanced and scientifically equipped Montessori-method baby-school."[7] It was still a nursery world because it was still a place set apart from the real and vital world of men, a place where women, denied any real power, were allowed to play at life and thus to trivialize the issues of a world they never really saw. And, paradoxically, Wharton saw that this segregation of women, this stunting of their emotional growth, helped only to keep a whole society childish. Linked for life to child wives, men were denied authentic adult relationships and were stunted themselves. "No nation can have grown up ideas till it has a ruling caste of grown-up men and women," Wharton said, "and it is possible to have a ruling caste of grown-up men and women only in a civilisation where the power of each sex is balanced by that of the other."[8] Without such a balance of power, America remained the Valley of Childish Things.

Unlike the men and women she observed and satirized, Edith Wharton had "grown-up ideas," for she refused to live in the women's nursery world and she preferred the risk of conflict and pain to the stultifying life of evasion. Like her own intruders, Edith Wharton continually challenged the sanctities of the sheltered life, for she knew that such a life "must either have a violent and tragic awakening — or never wake up at all."[9] Her fiction, full of these challenges of the national gods, is a continuing attempt to awaken her society from its complacent slumber.

Wharton herself knew that to truly live meant to risk life in the open. A rich woman, she denied herself the sanctuary of her established class and role to become a writer. And, as a writer, she again refused to conform: she was a little too scandalous, with her tales of mistresses and illicit love, for the New York of her youth, and far too stuffy, in her criticism of the shallow twenties, for the America of her old age. Again, she would not be typed. And again, she remained true to her own type. Continually searching, seeking, exploring society in her novels, Wharton continued to grow, so that at age seventy-five she was writing what would, completed, have been one of her best works. By taking risks, by refusing the shelter of imposed roles, Wharton embraced all of life, and thus as an old woman was able to exult, "I am born happy every morning."[10] Wharton the writer, like her intruder heroines, survives because at her core she was life-affirming, filled with a fearless curiosity that enabled her, over and over again, to face the Sphinx with a penetrating eye.

NOTES

1. *French Ways and Their Meaning*, pp. ix-x. It must be noted that Wharton was never wholly uncritical of France. Her portraits of the imprisoning aspects of the De Chelles chateau (*The Custom of the Country*) and of the mother-in-law of Anna Leath, the Francophile Marquise de Chantelle (*The Reef*), obsessed with the empty traditions she has married into, as well as her descriptions of the unscrupulous Malrives family of *Madame de Treymes*, show the less admirable side of French life. But certain qualities that Wharton found in France made, for her, an effective contrast to the flaws she perceived in America.

2. *The Buccaneers*, p. 248.

3. *A Backward Glance*, p. 57.

4. *French Ways and Their Meaning*, p. 108.

5. Ibid., p. 65. In using the phrase *a tragedy with a happy ending*, Wharton is quoting William Dean Howells, who used the term to describe the demands of the American theater audience.

6. *Twilight Sleep*, p. 226.

7. *French Ways and Their Meaning*, p. 101.

8. Ibid., p. 113.

9. Ibid., p. 65.

10. *A Backward Glance*, p. 372.

Selected Bibliography

Ammons, Elizabeth. "The Business of Marriage in Edith Wharton's *The Custom of the Country.*" *Criticism* 16 (1974):326-38.

_____. *Edith Wharton's Heroines: Studies in Aspiration and Compliance.* Dissertation; Univ. of Illinois at Urbana-Champaign, 1974.

Anderson, Hilton. "Edith Wharton as Fictional Heroine." *South Atlantic Quarterly* 69 (1970):118-23.

Auchincloss, Louis. *Edith Wharton.* Minneapolis: Univ. of Minnesota Press, 1961.

_____. *Edith Wharton: A Woman in Her Time.* New York: Viking, 1971.

Beach, Joseph Warren. *The Twentieth-Century Novel.* New York: Appleton-Century-Crofts, 1932.

Bell, Millicent. *Edith Wharton and Henry James: The Story of Their Friendship.* New York: George Braziller, 1965.

Boynton, Percy. "Edith Wharton." *Some Contemporary Americans.* Chicago: Univ. of Chicago Press, 1924. Pp. 89-107.

Bristol, Marie. "Life Amogn the Ungentle Genteel: Edith Wharton's *The House of Mirth Revisited.*" *Western Humanities Review* 16 (1962):371-74.

Brown, E. K. "Edith Wharton." *Etudes Anglaises* 2 (1938):16-26.

Canby, Henry Seidel. "Fiction Sums Up a Century." *Literary History of the United States.* Edited by Robert Spiller et al. New York: Macmillan, 1963, Pp. 1208-12.

Carlson, Constance Hedin. *Heroines in Certain American Novels.* Diss., Brown Univ., Providence, R.I., 1971.

Chopin, Kate. *The Awakening.* Norton Critical Edition. Edited by Margaret Culley. New York: W. W. Norton, 1976.

Coxe, Louis O. "What Edith Wharton Saw in Innocence." *New Republic* (27 June 1955), pp. 16-18.

Doyle, Charles C. "Emblems of Innocence: Imagery Patterns in Wharton's The Age of Innocence." *Xavier University Studies* 10 (1971):19-25.

Grant, Robert. *Unleavened Bread.* New York: Scribner's, 1900.

Harvey, John. "Contrasting Worlds: A Study in the Novels of Edith Wharton." *Etudes Anglaises* 7 (1954):190-98.

Hawthorne, Nathaniel. *The Blithedale Romance*. Norton Critical Edition. Edited by Seymour Gross and Rosalie Murphy. New York: W. W. Norton, 1978.

_____. *The Scarlet Letter*. Norton Critical Edition. Edited by Sculley Bradley, Richard Croom Beatty, and E. Hudson Long. New York: W. W. Norton, 1961.

Howe, Irving. "Introduction: The Achievement of Edith Wharton." In *Edith Wharton: A Collection of Critical Essays*, Edited Irving Howe. Englewood Cliffs, N. J.: Prentice-Hall, 1962. Pp. 1-18.

_____. "A Reading of *The House of Mirth*." Introduction to *The House of Mirth* by Edith Wharton. New York: Holt, Rinehart and Winston, 1962. Reprinted in *Edith Wharton: A Collection of Critical Essays*, edited by Irving Howe. Englewood Cliffs, N. J.: Prentice-Hall, 1962. Pp. 119-29.

Jacobson, Irving. "Perception, Communication and Growth as Correlative Themes in Edith Wharton's *The Age of Innocence*." *Agora* 2, no. 2 (1973):68-82.

Jessup, Josephine Lurie. *The Faith of Our Feminists*. New York: Richard R. Smith, 1950.

Johnson, Samuel. *Rasselas*, in *The Norton Anthology of English Literature*, vol. I. Ed. by M. H. Abrams. New York: W. W. Norton, 1968. Pp. 1815-40.

Kazin, Alfred. "Two Educations: Edith Wharton and Theodore Dreiser." *On Native Grounds: An Interpretation of Modern American Prose Literature*. New York: Reynal and Hitchcock, 1942. Pp. 73-90.

Kellogg, Grace. *The Two Lives of Edith Wharton: The Woman and Her Work*. New York: Appleton-Century, 1965.

Lawson, Richard H. *Edith Wharton*. New York: Frederick Ungar, 1977.

Leavis, Q. D. "Henry James's Heiress: The Importance of Edith Wharton." *Scrutiny* (December 1938). Reprinted in Irving Howe, ed. *Edith Wharton: A Collection of Critical Essays*. Englewood Cliffs, N. J.: Prentice-Hall, 1962. Pp. 73-88.

Lewis, R. W. B. *The American Adam: Innocence, Tragedy and Tradition in the Nineteenth Century*. Chicago: Univ. of Chicago Press, 1955.

_____. *Edith Wharton: A Biography*. New York: Harper and Row, 1975.

_____. "Introduction." *The Age of Innocence*, by Edith Wharton. 1968; reprinted. New York: Scribner's, 1970.

Lindberg, Gary. *Edith Wharton and the Novel of Manners*. Charlottesville: Univ. of Virginia Press, 1975.

Lovett, Robert Morss. *Edith Wharton*. New York: Robert M. McBride, 1925.

Lyde, Marilyn Jones. *Edith Wharton: Convention and Morality in the Work of a Novelist*. Norman: Univ. of Oklahoma Press, 1959.

Lynskey, Winifred. "The 'Heroes' of Edith Wharton." *University of Toronto Quarterly* 23 (1954):354-61.

McDowell, Margaret B. *Edith Wharton*. Boston: Twayne, 1976.

———. "Viewing the Custom of Her Country: Edith Wharton's Feminism." *Contemporary Literature* 15 (1974):521-38.

McIlvaine, Robert. "Edith Wharton's American Beauty Rose." *American Studies* 7 (1974):183-85.

Monroe, Nellie Elizabeth. *The Novel and Society: A Critical Study of the Modern Novel.* Chapel Hill: Univ. of North Carolina Press, 1941. Pp. 114-33.

Montgomery, Judith H. "The American Galatea." *College English* 32 (1971): 890-99.

Nevius, Blake. *Edith Wharton: A Study of Her Fiction.* 1953; reprinted. Berkeley: Univ. of California Press, 1961.

Niall, Brenda. "Prufrock in Brownstone: Edith Wharton's *The Age of Innocence.*" *Southern Review: An Australian Journal of Literary Studies* 4 (1971):203-14.

Parrington, Vernon L. "Our Literary Aristocrat." *The Pacific Review* (June 1921). Reprinted in Irving Howe, ed., *Edith Wharton: A Collection of Critical Essays*. Englewood Cliffs, N. J.: Prentice-Hall, 1962. Pp. 151-54.

Persons, Stow. *The Decline of American Gentility*. New York: Columbia Univ. Press, 1973.

Plante, Patricia R. "Edith Wharton: A Prophet without Due Honor." *Midwest Review* (1962), pp. 16-22.

Randall, John H. "Romeo and Juliet in the New World: A Study in James, Wharton and Fitzgerald 'Fay ce que voudras.'" *Costerus* 8 (1973):109-76.

Robinson, James A. "Psychological Determinism in *The Age of Innocence.*" *Markham Review* 5 (1975):1-5.

Russell, Frances Theresa. "Melodramatic Mrs. Wharton." *Sewanee Review* 40 (1932):425-37.

Trilling, Diana. "*The House of Mirth* Revisited." *The American Scholar* (Winter 1962-63). Reprinted in Irving Howe, ed., *Edith Wharton: A Collection of Critical Essays*. Englewood Cliffs, N. J.: Prentice-Hall, 1962. 103-18.

Trilling, Lionel. "The Morality of Inertia." In *Great Moral Dilemmas*, edited by Robert MacIver. New York: Harper and Bros., 1956. Reprinted in Irving Howe, ed., *Edith Wharton: A Collection of Critical Essays*. Englewood Cliffs, N. J.: Prentice-Hall, 1962. Pp. 137-46.

Tuttleton, James W. "Leisure, Wealth and Luxury: Edith Wharton's Old New York." *Midwest Quarterly* 7, no. 4 (1965):337-52.

Veblen, Thorstein. *The Theory of the Leisure Class: An Economic Study of Institutions*. 1899; reprinted. New York: Modern Library, 1934.

Walton, Geoffrey. *Edith Wharton: A Critical Interpretation*. Rutherford, N. J.: Fairleigh Dickinson Univ. Press, 1970.

Wegelin, Christof. "Edith Wharton and the Twilight of the International

Novel." *Southern Review* 5 (1969):398-418.

Wharton, Edith. *The Age of Innocence*. Introduction by R. W. B. Lewis. 1920; reprinted New York: Scribner's, 1970.

_____. *A Backward Glance*. 1934; reprint ed. New York: Appleton-Century, 1936.

_____. *The Best Short Stories of Edith Wharton*. Edited with Intro. by Wayne C. Andrews. New York: Scribner's, 1958.

_____. *The Buccaneers*. Essay appended by Gaillard Lapsley. New York: Appleton-Century, 1938.

_____. *The Collected Short Stories of Edith Wharton*. 2 vols. Edited with an Intro. by R. W. B. Lewis. New York: Scribner's, 1968.

_____. *The Custom of the Country*. 1913; reprint ed. New York: Scribner's, 1941.

_____. *Ethan Frome*. 1911; reprint ed. New York: Scribner's, 1970.

_____. *French Ways and Their Meaning*. New York: Appleton, 1919.

_____. *The Fruit of the Tree*. 1907; reprint ed. New York: Scribner's, 1914.

_____. *The Gods Arrive*. New York: Appleton, 1932.

_____. *The House of Mirth*. 1905; reprint ed. New York: Scribner's, 1933.

_____. *Hudson River Bracketed*. New York: Appleton, 1929.

_____. *Madame de Treymes*. New York: Scribner's, 1907.

_____. *The Marne*. New York: Appleton, 1918.

_____. *New Year's Day*. New York: Appleton, 1924.

_____. *The Reef*. New York: Appleton, 1912.

_____. *A Son at the Front*. New York: Scribner's, 1923.

_____. *Summer*. New York: Appleton, 1917.

_____. *The Touchstone*. 1900; reprint ed. New York: AMS Press, 1969.

_____. *Twilight Sleep*. New York: Appleton, 1927.

_____. *The Valley of Decision*. 2 vols. New York: Scribner's, 1902.

Wilson, Edmund. "Justice to Edith Wharton." *The Wound and the Bow*. New York: Oxford Univ. Press, 1947. Reprinted in Irving Howe, ed., *Edith Wharton: A Collection of Critical Essays*. Englewood Cliffs, N. J.: Prentice-Hall, 1962. Pp. 19-31.

_____. "Twilight Sleep." *New Republic* 51, no. 653 (8 June 1927): p. 78.

Wolff, Cynthia Griffin. *A Feast of Words*. New York: Oxford Univ. Press, 1977.

_____. "Lily Bart and the Beautiful Death." *American Literature* 46 (1974): 16-40.

Index